DIVINE RAGE

DIVINE RAGE

Malcolm X's Challenge to Christians

MARJORIE CORBMAN

ORBIS BOOKS
Maryknoll, New York 10545

ORBIS BOOKS
Maryknoll, New York 10545

Fathers and Brothers
MARYKNOLL™

Founded in 1970, Orbis Books endeavors to publish works that enlighten the mind, nourish the spirit, and challenge the conscience. The publishing arm of the Maryknoll Fathers and Brothers, Orbis seeks to explore the global dimensions of the Christian faith and mission, to invite dialogue with diverse cultures and religious traditions, and to serve the cause of reconciliation and peace. The books published reflect the views of their authors and do not represent the official position of the Maryknoll Society. To learn more about Maryknoll and Orbis Books, please visit our website at www.orbisbooks.com.

Manufactured in the United States of America

Names: Corbman, Marjorie, author.
Title: Divine rage : Malcolm X's challenge to white Christians / Marjorie Corbman.
Description: Maryknoll, New York : Orbis Books, [2023] | Includes bibliographical references and index. | Summary: "Malcolm X asked: Does Christianity have nothing more to offer than spiritual "novocaine," enabling Black Americans to suffer peacefully?"—Provided by publisher.

Identifiers: LCCN 2022041738 (print) | LCCN 2022041739 (ebook) | ISBN 9781626985087 (print) | ISBN 9781608339709 (ebook)
Subjects: LCSH: X, Malcolm, 1925-1965—Influence. | Black theology. | Suffering—Religious aspects—Christianity. | Race relations—Religious aspects—Christianity.
Classification: LCC BT82.7 C69 2023 (print) | LCC BT82.7 (ebook) | DDC 230.089/96073—dc23/eng/20221110
LC record available at https://lccn.loc.gov/2022041738
LC ebook record available at https://lccn.loc.gov/2022041739

This book is dedicated
with gratitude
to all those
"of whom we are not worthy" (Hebrews 11:38)
who have given or risked their lives
in the Black struggle for freedom in America

Contents

Introduction

"We Cannot Let Violence Overcome Nonviolence"

She had not known—Diane Nash recalled, three months after the fact—she had not known in the church that night just how in danger she was.[1] On May 21, 1961, a mob of enraged local white residents surrounded the First Baptist Church of Montgomery, Alabama. Inside the church, a service was being held in support of visiting civil rights activists, including Reverend Martin Luther King Jr. and the Freedom Riders, an interracial group traveling together to challenge segregation in interstate bus travel. Among the Freedom Riders was the twenty-one-year-old John Lewis, his head covered with a bandage after being attacked by another mob at the Montgomery bus station a day earlier.[2] The around-one-thousand people in the church could hear the gathering mob outside, and they soon realized they had been surrounded. With no protection from the local police, those inside were forced to stay the night, praying they would survive.[3] The church's pastor, Reverend Solomon Seay, led the gathering in singing freedom songs, as King retreated into the minister's office and spoke on the phone with the United States attorney general, Robert F. Kennedy, for hours, pleading with him to convince his brother, President John F. Kennedy, to send in federal troops.[4] Nash, despite her self-consciousness about her weak singing voice, sang along with the congregation as they prayed for their lives and for their freedom.[5] "In the dire danger in which we were that night," she said later, "no one expressed anything except concern for freedom and the thought that someday we'll be free. We stayed there until

1

dawn and everyone was naturally tired, but no one said so ... I don't think I've ever seen a group of people band together as the crowd in the church did that night."[6]

The twenty-three-year-old Nash was, in large part, responsible for the Freedom Rides that had put the gathering in so much danger. The original Freedom Rides, organized by the Congress of Racial Equality (CORE), had come to a dramatic and violent halt after a mob brutally attacked the Freedom Riders and firebombed the Greyhound bus in which they had been traveling, causing them to abandon the rest of their trip through the Jim Crow South. Lewis and Nash were insistent about the need to make an excruciating decision: the Freedom Rides could not be ended by violence. Nash, the leader of the Nashville branch of the Student Non-violent Coordinating Committee (SNCC), led the charge in organizing Nashville-based volunteers to continue the Freedom Rides.[7] Neither she nor those she organized were naïve about the dangers facing them. In the 2010 PBS documentary *Freedom Riders*, John Seigenthaler, who had served as assistant to the attorney general, recalled making a phone call to Nash, attempting to convince her to call off the Freedom Rides by warning her of the violence those involved would face. As he raised his voice, asking her if she realized that someone could get killed, she replied calmly: "Sir, you should know, we all signed our last wills and testaments last night before they left. We know someone will be killed. But we cannot let violence overcome nonviolence."[8]

Nash and Lewis were both fierce proponents of the Christian Gandhian philosophy of nonviolent direct action that gave shape to the civil rights movement in the 1950s and 1960s. Their teacher, Reverend James Lawson—the teacher of all of the Nashville-based student leaders—had first been introduced to Mohandas Karamchand Gandhi's philosophy through the Fellowship of Reconciliation (FOR), whose executive secretary,

A. J. Muste, was a Presbyterian minister, labor activist, and a staunch pacifist.[9] Lawson, inspired by the tenets of Christian nonviolence, had served a year in prison as a draft resister and conscientious objector to the war in Korea. He then spent three years in Nagpur, India, with Methodist missionaries, with the primary objective of learning more about Gandhi and the movement he had initiated on the ground.[10] Gandhi's teaching of *satyagraha* or soul-force (his word for "nonviolence"), he felt, was the very embodiment of what he most admired in the life of Jesus Christ.[11] For Gandhi himself, *satyagraha* was the necessary political counterpart of the "single-minded devotion (*abhyasa*) [to the Truth, i.e., God] and indifference to all other interests in life (*vairagya*)" lauded by Krishna in the *Bhagavad Gita*.[12] It was a political commitment rooted in spiritual discipline:

> In the application of Satyagraha I discovered in the earliest stages that pursuit of truth did not admit of violence being inflicted on one's opponent but that he must be weaned from error by patience and sympathy ... So the doctrine came to mean vindication of truth not by infliction of suffering on the opponent but on one's self.
>
> But on the political field the struggle on behalf of the people mostly consists in opposing error in the shape of unjust laws. When you have failed to bring the error home to the lawgiver by way of petitions and the like, the only remedy open to you, if you do not wish to submit to error, is to compel him by physical force to yield to you or by suffering in your own person by inviting the penalty for the breach of law ... There come occasions, generally rare, when [the civil resister] considers certain laws to be so unjust as to render obedience to them a dishonour. He then openly and civilly breaks them and quietly suffers the penalty for their breach.[13]

Lawson, like others in the Fellowship of Reconciliation, saw in this originally Hindu philosophy a perfect explanation of the "soul-force" of Jesus in his life, death, and resurrection.

Lawson left India firmly convinced of the capacity of a nonviolent mass movement of civil disobedience to produce not only revolutionary political change, but, more profoundly, an entire way of being grounded in love and the recognition of each person's divine dignity: *the beloved community*.[14] Lawson, along with other veterans of the Fellowship of Reconciliation, especially Bayard Rustin and Glenn Smiley, were instrumental in converting the most visible leader of the civil rights movement, Martin Luther King Jr., into a committed disciple of Gandhi. Rustin, too, had spent time in India, and saw in Gandhian nonviolence a model of an "anticolonial" and "confrontational" popular movement that had the potential to attack racial injustice at its root in the United States.[15] When Rustin first met King, then a twenty-eight-year-old minister and recent PhD who had been selected as the spokesperson for the Montgomery bus boycott, King had, Rustin said later, "very limited notions about how a nonviolent protest should be carried out."[16] It was in engaging in the struggle itself, Rustin said, in actually living out the commitment demanded by campaigns of nonviolent direct action that King came to an understanding of Gandhi's philosophy.[17]

The same was true for Nash, who, despite the intense violence, incarceration, and danger she and other SNCC activists faced, assented to the core concepts of Christian Gandhian nonviolence wholeheartedly and uncompromisingly: "We have decided that if there is to be suffering in this revolution (which is really what the movement is—a revolution), we will take the suffering upon ourselves and never inflict it upon our fellow man, because we respect him and recognize the God within him."[18] For her and for the other Nashville-based students of

Lawson, nonviolence was more than a successful tactic; it was divine revelation. SNCC's statement of purpose proclaimed this core belief: "We affirm the philosophical or religious idea of nonviolence as the foundation of our purpose, the presupposition of our faith, and the manner of our action. Nonviolence as it grows from Judaic-Christian traditions seeks a social order of justice permeated by love. Integration of human endeavor represents the crucial first step towards such a society."[19] The profound courage demonstrated by the Freedom Riders testifies to the radical nature of this creed, as does the extraordinary success of campaigns of sustained nonviolent direct action to end legal segregation in the South. While the civil rights movement of the 1960s is often portrayed as a "moderate" or "reformist" movement, it was in fact, as Clayborne Carson has argued, a profoundly radical and truly mass movement unlike anything that had been seen in the United States for decades.[20] Dorothy Zellner, a white staff member of SNCC, summarized succinctly the revolutionary character of the movement: "I tell people that we probably, for those brief years, are the only Americans who ever experienced racial equality ... Not because we weren't racial, because everybody knew and was conscious of that, but because the context was, if you're going to be with us you're going to take a bullet."[21]

Black against Babylon:
The Rise of Black Power

By the mid-1960s, however, the mood of many in the movement had changed. The tactics espoused by civil rights activists had proved remarkably effective in inspiring the racial sympathies of northerners for Black people in the South, and had facilitated a number of significant legal victories, most notably the Civil Rights Act of 1964 and the Voting Rights Act of 1965. Measurable change for the lives of Black people living in the northern ghettos, however, was absent. Efforts for desegregation both in the South and the North (e.g., school desegregation) continued to face adamant white resistance and violence. The sympathy of northern whites for the desegregating protestors of the South often did not carry over into a desire to dismantle the barriers to social and economic well-being of Black people in their own cities, and police brutality continued unabated. A number of assassinations of and attacks on Black leaders exacerbated a feeling of despair and frustration. Participants in the movement had become uncertain of its founding principles as suspicions grew that calls to universal love and reconciliation masked the power relations that perpetuated racism, or, worse, actually undercut recognition of Black humanity. In 1964, the Black Baptist minister and scholar Joseph R. Washington Jr. criticized the civil rights movement's philosophy of nonviolence in its insistence that protestors act not in a human, but in a "superhuman" manner in response to violence: "When a pregnant woman is kicked in the streets of Birmingham, dignity [according to the philosophy of nonviolence] demands that neither she nor anyone else protect either her or the unborn innocent child. At this point nonviolence loses any claim to being human and takes on superhuman qualities."[22] These critiques became gradually more mainstream and more strident. Calls to remain nonviolent, argued Stokely Carmichael and Charles V. Hamilton in *Black Power: The Politics of Liberation in America* (1967), had "misled some into believing that a black minority could bow its head and get whipped into a meaningful position of power … From our viewpoint, rampaging white mobs and white nightriders must be made to understand that their days of free headwhipping are over. Black people should and must fight back."[23]

Figures like Lewis and Nash had become, by the mid-'60s, a "minority" within SNCC,[24] something made eminently clear when Lewis was replaced as chairman of SNCC by Stokely Carmichael, who represented both the more militant and the more northern (Carmichael was born in Trinidad and raised in New York) shift in emphasis for the movement.[25] Unlike Lewis and Nash, Carmichael's initial "allegiance to nonviolence rested more on practical than on moral considerations."[26] It would be a mistake, however, to characterize Carmichael's approach as secular and pragmatic as opposed to the spiritual vision of activists like Lewis, Nash, Lawson, King, and Rustin. Carmichael's increasing valorization of armed self-defense and Black separatism was not a *rejection* of the spiritual grounding of the earlier civil rights movement. It was, instead, an embrace of an alternative spiritual vision.

"How is this beautiful race of people, black people, gonna survive Babylon?" Carmichael asked his audience in February 1968, at a Black Panther Party (BPP) rally, following SNCC's merger with the BPP.[27] Babylon, the empire that invaded, conquered, and held captive the population of the Kingdom of Judah in the sixth century BCE, was the preferred name of Black nationalists for America.[28] For Elijah Muhammad, the leader of the Black nationalist religious group the Nation of Islam, the ancient destruction of Babylon, which, according to the Bible, fell due to its wealth, pride, and corruption,[29] was an event that could only be fully witnessed in the imminent fall of the modern-day Babylon, America.[30] Elijah Muhammad's language, and especially the language of his most famous protégé, Malcolm X, now animated the imagination of the movement in the way that the words of Gandhi and King had done for the proponents of Christian nonviolence. "That nation that is doomed to be judged by God is America," Malcolm X had proclaimed in a 1961 sermon at the New York Church of God.

It's Uncle Sam who today is guilty for the crime that he has committed against these twenty million black people.

If God condemned Pharaoh for enslaving those people, and God condemned Nebuchadnezzar for enslaving those people in Babylon, and a man here today more vicious than Nebuchadnezzar ever was, more vicious than Pharaoh ever was, has enslaved our people and brutalized our people in this house of bondage for longer than four hundred years. And if you think that God judged Pharaoh for what he did, and that God judged Nebuchadnezzar for what he did, and God is going to forgive the [pounds fist on the podium] American white man who has brutalized you worse than anybody ever has, I say you got the wrong understanding.[31]

Carmichael, a few years later, spoke with the same fire and the same religious references. "When Moses crossed the Red Sea he left some people behind," he preached in 1966. "We are going to leave some Uncle Toms behind."[32]

Behind these words of Muhammad, Malcolm, and Carmichael is the legacy of what is sometimes called Black messianic-nationalism.[33] From Marcus Garvey's African Orthodox Church, to the Moorish Science Temple of America, to Black Hebrew Israelites, to the Shrine of the Black Madonna, to (most prominently of all) the Nation of Islam, these religious groups—always marginal to the Black American experience, but also highly influential on Black political thought—reject "'Negro' identity as an oppressive white creation" and advocate instead for "the substitution of a new ethnic identity predicated on a belief in the unique spiritual importance of Black people."[34] The social scientists who coined the term, Hans A. Baer and Merrill Singer, listed the "core features" of messianic-nationalism as:

(1) belief in a glorious Black past and subsequent "fall" from grace;

(2) vocal opposition to and criticism of American society and whites in general;

(3) anticipation of divine retribution against the white oppressors;

(4) assertion of Black sovereignty through the development of various rituals and symbols, such as national flags, anthems, and dress, and a separatist economic base as well as, plus at least in some cases, an interest in territorial separation or emigrationism; and

(5) chiliastic and messianic expectations of a new golden age for Black people.[35]

These groups, throughout the twentieth century and into the twenty-first, proclaimed God's rage against white America and foretold that God would manifest the mental and spiritual "resurrection" of their people.[36]

Malcolm X, drawing on this long tradition, offered an alternative vision to that of the beloved community shared by Nash and other believers in a nonviolent revolution. Malcolm instead saw in the global, armed anticolonial resistance of non-white peoples a manifestation of God's righteous wrath: "It is the rise of the dark world that is causing the fall of the white world," he asserted in a 1963 speech.

> As the white man loses his power to oppress and exploit the dark world, the white man's own wealth (power or "world") decreases. His world is on its way down; it is on its way out ... and it is the will and power of God himself that is bringing an end to the white world ... Judgment day is the final hour when God himself sits in the seat of justice and judges these white nations (or the white world) according to the deeds they committed and the seeds they sowed when they themselves sat in the seat of power.[37]

Even after departing the Nation of Islam in 1964, Malcolm X retained the apocalyptic worldview of his earlier speeches. "I believe that there will ultimately be a clash between the oppressed and those that do the oppressing," he told an interviewer in January 1965, soon before his assassination the following month. "I believe that there will be a clash between those who want freedom, justice, and equality for everyone and those who want to continue the systems of exploitation."[38] As South African theologian Willa Boesak has argued, it is impossible to understand the political demands made by Malcolm X without taking into account his theological worldview: for Malcolm, "resolving God's wrath requires a thorough redress of the wrongs blacks have had to suffer."[39] The delay of this justice had, for Malcolm, an expiration date: the overdue bill would be collected if it were not paid. He continued to describe, as he had for years, though previously in more explicitly religious terms, the Black struggle as part of "a global rebellion of the oppressed against the oppressor, the exploited against the exploiter."[40] Soon, people would have to choose what side they were on.

For many who had witnessed the horrors of white violence in the Jim Crow South or the degradation and injustices faced by Black urban communities in the North, Malcolm's words gave voice to what they barely dared say, or hope. As the 1960s went on, more and more longed for the fall of Babylon he and Muhammad before him had preached. The message would ignite a period of revolutionary fervor in American politics that no one could ignore—echoes of which can still be heard today.

Martin versus Malcolm: A Theological Debate

What would it mean to see Martin Luther King Jr. and Mohandas Gandhi, on one hand, and Malcolm X and the Nation of Islam, on the other, as providing competing religious frameworks for

Americans engaged in the struggle for justice? It would, at the very least, challenge the way in which the civil rights and Black Power movements are usually portrayed. As Kerry Pimblott has recently argued, the standard narrative about Black organizing in the second half of the twentieth century contrasts the "centrality" of Black churches for the movement from 1955 to 1965 with a "secularizing" and especially non-Christian turn in the rise of Black Power from 1966 onward. Pimblott demonstrates to the contrary both that the role of Black churches was more ambivalent than typically understood for the earlier civil rights movement, and that Christian institutions continued to engage in different ways with the later Black Power movement.[41] The portrayal of the Black Power movement as largely secular or even anti-religious also does not take into account how, in the words of Jeffrey O. G. Ogbar, the Nation of Islam "dominat[ed]" the discourse on Black nationalism that gave birth to Black Power.[42] The fact that most Black Power advocates were not Muslim made no more difference than that most civil rights era Gandhians were not Hindu. Malcolm X, by adapting the Nation of Islam's Black nationalist mythology into a theology of anti-colonial struggle undertaken by the non-white world majority, offered a new and galvanizing spiritual worldview for many disillusioned with the Gandhianism espoused by earlier movement leaders. While some activists would follow Malcolm X out of Christianity to Islam, others would adapt Malcolm X's theology to different religious and cultural contexts. The emergence of Black liberation theology during this time is only one among many examples of religious figures and communities grappling with the challenge posed by Malcolm X, and it is not the only example of Christians doing so.

The importance of viewing the differences between Martin Luther King Jr. and Malcolm X as religious, however, goes beyond reframing our understanding of political movements in the 1960s and 1970s. Malcolm X and Martin Luther King Jr.—and their respective advocates—inspired one of the most important theological debates of the twentieth century, over the relationship between religion and violence. While the religious thought of Martin Luther King Jr. has frequently been treated seriously and analyzed, this has not always been true for Malcolm X. Historically, scholars have underemphasized the religious character of Malcolm X's life and thought, as Louis A. DeCaro Jr. has argued, preferring to interpret Malcolm X "primarily from a political perspective."[43] More recently, scholars of religion and especially African American Islam have devoted attention to Malcolm X as a religious thinker and even as a theologian.[44]

In this book, I aim to trace the transformative role of Malcolm X on American politics and religion, including his influence on Christian theology and communities. The chapters that follow will explore the remarkably wide-reaching impact of his theology on activists, scholars, artists, and others of all backgrounds. Beginning with his mysterious encounter with a non-white God beside his bed in his prison cell during the earliest days of his conversion, his ministry in Harlem, and his embrace of Sunni Islam, the book then turns to his spiritual influence after his death on the Black Arts Movement, the Black Power movement, Black liberation theology, and other revolutionary struggles. It tells the stories of Malcolm himself and of those who have been shaped and challenged and transformed by his religious thought. In the pages to come, my hope is that the voices of these figures—sometimes thrilled, sometimes horrified, sometimes prophetic, sometimes enamored, sometimes heartbroken—come through in all of their distinctness, charged with the power and pain of the movements they represent.

1

The Final Disaster

Divine Justice and the Nation of Islam

Storm on the Horizon: Malcolm X in Prison

On August 9, 1949, the twenty-four-year-old Malcolm Little wrote his brother Philbert about an incident that occurred on a recent evening at Norfolk Prison Colony. He had been staring out the window into the courtyard where a group of other men, despite the storm clouds rapidly accumulating above them, had gathered. Malcolm listened to the approaching thunder as it drew nearer, wondering why no one was paying attention, why no one was bothering to get up and go inside. When the clouds finally burst, the men started running, but by the time they made it inside, they were already drenched. "Now, that started me thinking, and wondering," Malcolm told Philbert. "Allah always warns before there is a change." He asked himself if it would be like that "in the End." Then, too, people would see and hear "the signs of the inevitable all around them," but would not notice until it was too late, until they had been "caught in the Final Disaster."[1]

At the time he wrote this letter, Malcolm, completely to his own surprise, was enthralled: with God, with the prophets, with the coming day of divine justice. "Night after night I beg

Allah to let me be His humble Servant," he wrote, "to let His Light Shine within me so all will know WHOM I SERVE."[2] His letters from this time express excitement, gratitude, rapture, a striking contrast to the content of the letters penned prior to his conversion. The year before, Malcolm had written Philbert in clear frustration. It had hurt him, he said, that Philbert had said that "we are happy to own you as a brother." This was condescending, Malcolm explained. "That sounds like tolerance, which is: allowing something that cannot be helped or whoely [*sic*] improved." He similarly pleaded with him to avoid what he then viewed as artificial language about religion: "Under no circumstances don't preach to me. I mean the way enclosed in your letters. That sounds phony. All people who talk like that sound phony to me because I know that is all it is; just talk."[3] Philbert, Malcolm explained in his autobiography, "was forever joining something," and his convert's enthusiasm, at the time, had bothered him. When Philbert had first written about joining a "holiness" church, and later the Nation of Islam, Malcolm admitted that he had responded in ways he was ashamed to think of later.[4]

Now, Malcolm was aglow with the same convert's ardor. He pleaded with Philbert to write to him more often, and especially to send him religious literature and to speak about the Bible. When Philbert neglected to send him material he had promised, Malcolm wrote that he was breaking his heart.[5] He was studying as much as he could—feverishly, wholeheartedly—but he worried whether his interpretations were correct. Still, he concluded: "If I'm right it is He; if I'm wrong it is me."[6] The intensity of his pursuit, combined with the loneliness and pain of prolonged incarceration, seemed at times to overwhelm him. In March 1951, a year before his release from prison, he wrote Philbert's wife, Henrietta, that he needed to take a break from serious thought for a few months and recover from his "long sojourn in space."[7]

As exhausting as Malcolm's search could be for him, it filled him with joy. He followed Elijah Muhammad's instructions to "read your Bible and Holy Qur-an,"[8] but did not have access to a translation of the Qur'an until 1950, when another man in the prison was able to obtain a copy that Malcolm borrowed.[9] Mostly, he "read the bible continuously," striving to uncover its hidden meaning for his people as they waited in hope for God's coming justice.[10] "Joshua is even now making the walls of Jericho rock," he wrote to Henrietta,

> and they cannot stand the pressure that His Shouters of Truth are creating [Joshua 6]. Sister, when those Walls fall, woe be unto the inhabitants who are not in the *House of Rahab* [Joshua 2] … The devil is roaring, because he knows he has but a short time to go. Who can withstand the Wrath of Allah. The tears of Joy roll down my cheeks, as I see the Black Man throughout the world coming together in True Brotherhood, for the first time in many years, to throw the white man out of their land, and drive him into the sea.[11]

That roaring devil was the "collective white man," who, Malcolm now realized, "had acted like a devil in virtually every contact he had with the world's collective non-white man."[12] But the devil's time, Elijah Muhammad taught, had already expired. And the day was coming "when ALLAH, in HIS own good time," would take "the devil off our Planet."[13]

A Nighttime Visit from a Non-White God: Malcolm's Conversion

Malcolm later recalled that when his brother first told him that the white man was the devil, his entire life up till then had flashed before his eyes.[14]

You let this caged-up black man start thinking, the same way I did when I first heard Elijah Muhammad's teachings; let him start thinking how, with better breaks when he was young and ambitious he might have been a lawyer, a doctor, a scientist, anything. You let this caged-up black man start realizing, as I did, how from the first landing of the first slave ship, the millions of black men in America have been like sheep in a den of wolves. That's why black prisoners become Muslims so fast when Elijah Muhammad's teachings filter into their cages by way of other Muslim convicts. "The white man is the devil" is a perfect echo of that black convict's lifelong experience.[15]

Malcolm, of course, was speaking about his own life. As a child growing up outside of Lansing, Michigan, white supremacists had burned his family home to the ground,[16] and later, Malcolm always believed, had murdered his father, who was found dead—his skull crushed in, his body nearly torn in half by a streetcar—on the road when Malcolm was six years old.[17] A few years later, Malcolm was removed from his home and put into foster care by white welfare workers, and his mother was consigned to a mental hospital by a court order.[18] After finishing eighth grade, Malcolm moved to Boston to live with his older half-sister, Ella. In order to provide extra income that his series of menial jobs in both Boston and New York could not supply, Malcolm began to sell marijuana and engage in forms of petty theft. He developed an addiction to cocaine and gradually escalated his criminal activity, eventually forming a burglary gang with two of his friends and three white women. Most of the gang was arrested, and Malcolm and his friend Shorty Jarvis were sentenced to four six- to eight-year concurrent sentences.[19] According to Malcolm, the court made it clear that this unduly harsh sentence for first-time offenders was in reality a punishment for sleeping with white women.[20]

In prison, after being introduced to the teachings of Elijah Muhammad by his visiting siblings, Malcolm underwent a dramatic conversion experience. After reflecting seriously on the Nation of Islam's beliefs about the "white devil" and the divine origin of Black humanity, Malcolm was "struck numb" by their truth; he compared his experience to that of the apostle Paul on the road to Damascus.[21] In response, he began to pray, though it took him, he said, a week to bring himself to bend his knees in prayer. "Picking a lock to rob someone's house was the only way my knees had ever been bent before."[22] Malcolm began to devour the books of the prison library, searching for confirmation of Muhammad's doctrines.

Then, he met God. One night, lying in his bed in the midst of personal turmoil, he realized that someone else was with him in his prison cell.

> He had on a dark suit. I remember. I could see him as plainly as I see anyone I look at. He wasn't black, and he wasn't white. He was light-brown-skinned, an Asiatic cast of countenance, and he had oily black hair.
>
> I looked right into his face.
>
> I didn't get frightened. I knew I wasn't dreaming. I couldn't move, I didn't speak, and he didn't. I couldn't place him racially—other than that I knew he was a non-European. I had no idea whatsoever who he was. He just sat there. Then, suddenly as he had come, he was gone.[23]

He would come to identify the man in his prison cell as W. D. Fard, the enigmatic founder of the Nation of Islam, who was believed by its members to be Allah in person.[24]

Malcolm's autobiography relates this event without explanation—as one of Malcolm's biographers, Louis DeCaro Jr., has noted—despite the fact that Malcolm revised many other sections in that chapter and other chapters after leaving the Nation

of Islam.[25] It is very unlikely that Malcolm continued to believe
after his departure from the Nation that this nighttime visitor had been Fard; when asked by another former member of
the Nation if he had seen Fard during his pilgrimage to Mecca,
Malcolm answered that it was time to face "reality" and move
beyond these "old notions."[26] DeCaro concludes that Malcolm
must have experienced something genuine that night which he
could not entirely disown, even after he could no longer understand the event in the same way.[27]

The visit of this mysterious "non-European" man to his cell
represented something important to Malcolm in his search for
God in the world. He was constantly on alert, convinced that he
could use his own intuition to decipher signs of divine action
in nature, in historical events, in biblical symbols. "Things are
jumping out there [in the world], I know," he wrote Philbert. "It
can be 'felt' in the atmosphere. I'm unaware of what is actually
occurring, but I know it is being directed by the Hand of Allah
and will rid the planet of these wretched devils."[28] He believed
that he could sense a coming disaster: "I intuitively feel something is about to happen. When I feel like this, something usually does."[29] And, with the same intuition, he believed that he
could sense God's presence: "The atmosphere itself," he wrote,
"is comprised and controlled by the vibrations of our words, the
vibrations of our thoughts, and the vibrations of our feelings ...
All being of the Same Essence and comprising that Holy Spirit
that moves the Universe ... All are One ... All in All ... Allah!"[30]

Malcolm X was for many years a faithful servant of Elijah
Muhammad, but his loyalty to the Nation and its prophet was
always complicated by his desire to see God, and to see God's
actions in the world, for himself. Malcolm's longing to identify
a divine hand at work in current events would later serve as one
of the main factors in his break with the Nation of Islam. But at
the time of his imprisonment, Elijah Muhammad's teachings—

about the coming judgment of the devil and the reign of the Black man on earth—were in perfect harmony with his spiritual experiences. He was learning to see God present in his people, and in their struggle to be free.

"He Would Come in the Last Day": Elijah Muhammad and W. D. Fard

"Their captivity was ending, because God was black"—so James Baldwin summarized the central message of the Nation of Islam.[31] The Nation's belief in a "judgment [that] will take place as God revealed, in America,"[32] was inseparable from its belief in the divinity of a non-white man: W. D. Fard. Malcolm X, as his thought and spirituality developed, would come to see in this teaching a call for the collective non-white peoples of the world to enact revolutionary justice on earth. The basic building blocks of Malcolm's later thinking were already present in the message Baldwin paraphrased: the Black God was here, now, ready to judge the world. This idea changed Malcolm X's life; it also changed Elijah Muhammad's.

Elijah Poole (later Muhammad) was born in 1897 in Sandersville, Georgia, the sixth child of William Poole, a Baptist preacher, sharecropper, and mill worker, and Marie Hall, who worked as a domestic servant.[33] Elijah dropped out of school in the fourth or fifth grade in order to provide additional income for the family, and from then until 1923 worked at farms, mills, and with a railroad company.[34] In the early 1920s, he, his wife, Clara, and his children moved to Detroit. As part of the Great Migration, during which millions of Black Americans fled the horrors of lynching, harassment, and labor exploitation in the South for northern cities, Muhammad witnessed the cruelty of white racial power in both the North and the South. He had witnessed multiple lynchings, and himself had experienced the degradation of Black workers in the South; at one farm, the white owner held workers at gunpoint while his wife whipped them.[35] After moving to Detroit, the violence did not stop: "I moved to Detroit because I thought the life might be better, but even there the first year I saw my people shot down right on the street without any justice whatsoever. I had seen there two of our people killed on the street by the police without any justice whatsoever and without any effort on our people's part to do anything or to help."[36] By 1931, when Elijah Muhammad met W. D. Fard, he was out of a job and considering taking up preaching—work toward which he had always felt called, but also considered impossible due to his lifelong aversion to Christianity.[37]

Muhammad said that he had heard of Fard through a friend of his father, Abdul Muhammad.[38] Abdul Muhammad had previously been a member of Noble Drew Ali's Moorish Science Temple, an earlier movement of Black Americans that identified with Islam. The Nation of Islam and the Moorish Science Temple were both examples of the diverse religious movements that emerged during the Great Migration.[39] Mainstream, established Black churches in the North were often unable and at times unwilling to meet the needs of the incoming migrants, and, as a result, argue Hans Baer and Merrill Singer, a "common strategy adopted by the migrants to deal with this situation was to establish storefront and house churches," which took on sometimes unconventional forms, including a number of self-identified Jewish and Islamic sects.[40]

As Sherman Jackson has argued, part of the attraction to adopting a Muslim identity was Islam's independence from white control, its perceived connection with Africa (including awareness that many enslaved people brought to America from Africa had been Muslims), and its reputation for armed political resistance against European powers.[41] The versions of Islam preached by these movements bore little resemblance to mainstream, global Islam, but the desire to identify as Muslims was essentially grounded in the belief that Islam stood, as W. D. Fard, Elijah Muhammad, and Malcolm X would all proclaim, for "freedom, justice, and equality."[42]

Elijah Muhammad was ready for this message. He went to hear Fard speak but was prevented by the crowdedness of the venue from meeting him personally.

> I waited after the second meeting so I might have a turn to meet him, so we lined up to go by and shake hands with him because he was shaking hands with us all. And when I got to him I shaked my hands with him and told him that I recognized who he is and he held his head down close to my face and he said to me, "Yes, Brother." I said to him: "You are that one we read in the Bible that he would come in the last day under the name Jesus." I said, "You are that one?" Here he looked at me very serious when I said that to him, and finally he said; "Yes, I am the one that you have been looking for in the last two thousand years; I am the one. But you go ahead now brother, that is good."[43]

An early member of the Nation of Islam, Sister Carrie Muhammad, also recalled Fard alluding to a secret identity. According to her, Fard stated during one of his earliest speeches: "I came from the Holy City of Mecca. More about myself I will not tell you yet, for the time has not yet come. I am your brother. You have not yet seen me in my royal robe."[44]

Fard's claim to a hidden, perhaps divine identity was supported by his mysterious origin, which is still disputed today. He was identified by law enforcement (despite Elijah Muhammad's fervent denial) as Wallace Dodd Ford, a man who was arrested on two occasions, first for possession of alcohol—during Prohibition—and second, for allegedly selling drugs.[45] Stories of Ford's origins abound; he has been described as being of "Polynesian … Jamaican, Palestinian, Syrian, Indian, Turko-Persian, or Afghani" descent.[46] Whether or not Ford and Fard were identical figures, his followers have always understood Fard as having had one white and one non-white parent. For the Nation of Islam, which highly discouraged interracial relationships, this backstory required an explanation, which Elijah Muhammad explained that Fard had given him.

> He said that His father knew he could not be successful in coming to a solid white country, and he being a solid Black man. So, He taught me that His Father said, "I will go and make me a Son. And I will send my Son among them, looking like them." Think over that! "My Son, they will think He is one of them, and He will find our lost people." … So, He said, His Father went up into the hills and there he found him a wife, a white wife.[47]

Sister Denke Majied, who was interviewed by Erdmann Doane Benyon in 1938, said that Fard began his ministry in Detroit by selling raincoats and silks door to door in Black communities, claiming that "the silks he carried were the same kind that our people used in their home country and that he had come from there." When his customers asked him to tell them more about their home country, he agreed to begin speaking to groups of people about their original Muslim identity and revealed himself as a prophet.[48]

Muhammad was electrified by Fard's teachings on the nature of white and Black humanity. For Muhammad, Fard's message provided a way "to get [his] people out of the grip of this white man," a resolution that he said was first firmly fixed in him after hearing his grandmother tell him personal stories of the "sufferings of slavery."[49] He was not the only one almost instantly transformed after meeting Fard. As an example, Brother Challar Sharrieff, one of Fard's first followers, described his conversion dramatically: "After I heard that sermon from [Fard], I was turned around completely. When I went home and heard that dinner was ready, I said: 'I don't want to eat dinner. I just want to go back to the meetings.'"[50] During Fard's brief (less than four years) period of leadership of the Nation of Islam, he amassed a following of between five and eight thousand followers.[51] Before his final disappearance in 1934, he was asked to leave Detroit by the police, who held the Nation of Islam responsible for an apparent ritual murder committed by one of Fard's followers, Robert Harris.[52] The police also may have wanted to suppress the organization for promoting anti-American, pro-Japanese sentiments.[53]

While Muhammad claimed to have been appointed by Fard as a successor and as his prophet, this was challenged by other followers of Fard. Muhammad was forced to flee Detroit out of fear for his safety, moving from "city to city and from place to place within the same city," preaching under different names.[54] In 1942, Muhammad was arrested, like many other members of the movement, for refusing to register for the draft.[55] It was during his four years in prison that Muhammad developed a plan for what would become a major source of the Nation of Islam's influence: its establishment of a network of farms and businesses with the goal of achieving Black economic independence.[56]

At the time Muhammad was released from prison, the Nation of Islam had dwindled down to around four hundred members. But his establishment of an "economic empire" of businesses and the energetic evangelism of his most dedicated followers revitalized the organization.[57] It was only in the mid-1950s and early 1960s, however, after Malcolm X finished his prison sentence and became the Nation of Islam's most effective and influential minister, that the group would reach its highest level of visibility and membership numbers.[58] It was largely through Malcolm X that the Nation's warning of an imminent divine reckoning for white America reached the world.

The Destruction of the Devil

The first section of the "Lost-Found Muslim Lesson No. 1" of the Nation of Islam begins with the declaration: "The Earth belongs to the original Black man … The Colored man or Caucasian is the Devil."[59] The term "devil" had a very specific meaning, which is to say, that one "has lost the knowledge of himself and … is living a beast life."[60]

The devil had not initially come into being as a "weak and wicked" beast.[61] Rather, he was made into one. His gradual loss of self-knowledge was the result of deliberate violence, summed up in the story of Yacub, the maker of the devil, a story recounted in detail in Lesson No. 2. Yacub, one of the original people, "was born with a determined idea to make a people to rule the earth for a term of six thousand years."[62] Yacub set out on an aggressive, centuries-long experiment in eugenics. Darker-skinned children were killed, while lighter-skinned children were cared for and then bred with other lighter-skinned people, eventually producing the abnormality of white skin and a type of human being whose "mental and physical power is much weaker than the original man."[63] According to this story, the manufacturing of the devil required immense cruelty:

The Nurse's law was to kill the Black babies at birth by sticking a needle in the brain of the babies or feed it to some wild beast; and tell the mother that her baby was an angel baby and that it was only taken to heaven, and some day when the mother dies, her baby would have secured her a home in heaven. But save all the brown ones and tell their mother that she was lucky that her baby was a holy baby; and she should take good care of her baby, educate it, and that some day it would be a great man. All nurses, doctors and ministers—Yacub put them under a death penalty who fail to carry out the law as it was given to them. Also the Cremator, who would burn the Black babies when the nurse brought it to him. Also death for them if they reveal the Secret.[64]

According to this origin myth, to be white is to be the end result of centuries of violence. Malcolm X expanded upon this in a speech in 1962, using the story of Yacub to explain the origin of white brutality:

> The Book says concerning the devil: "He was conceived in iniquity and born in sin." What does this mean? At the outset the nurses had to kill the little black babies, but after a while it got so that the mother, having been brainwashed, hated that black one so much she killed it herself … In order for the white one to come into existence, the darker one was always murdered, murdered, MURDERED! This went right into the nature of the child that was being born. The mother wanted a light baby when the child was being conceived. This went right into the baby. The mother hated black when the child was being conceived. This went right into the baby. So that at the end of the six hundred years, after planting the seed of iniquity right into the brain, right into the mind, right into the heart, right into the nature of these people, by the time they got the white man, they had someone who by nature hated everything that was darker than he was … And right to this very day the white man by nature wants to murder off the black, brown, and yellow. You don't have to teach him to kill the black man. He does it for sport. He does it for kicks. He does it because it's his nature to do it. Do you understand that?[65]

For Malcolm, as a member of the Nation of Islam, the story of Yacub provided a key to understanding "the collective white man" and his actions.

The Nation of Islam's lessons convey some uncertainty as to whether or not the process of brutalization that created the devil could potentially be reversed. "All the prophets have tried to reform him (devil), but were unable. So they have agreed that it cannot be done unless we graft him back to the original man which takes six hundred years. So instead of losing time grafting him back, they have decided to take him off the planet—who numbers only one to every eleven original people."[66] On the other hand, Lesson No. 1 explains that an individual devil, after studying for thirty-five to fifty years and "clean[ing] himself up," would be permitted to "call himself a Muslim son" and to wear the flag of Islam (which displayed letters standing for Islam, Freedom, Justice, and Equality on it)—though only on the condition that he never reveal the secrets of Islam.[67]

The cryptic language of the Nation of Islam's lessons was not always taken literally by the majority of the organization's members. This was especially true of the statement that "all Muslims will murder the devil because they know he is a snake and, also, if he be allowed to live, he would sting someone else … Each Muslim is required to bring four devils."[68] This statement, if taken literally, would emphatically contradict the policy of the Nation of Islam under Elijah Muhammad, who ascribed the destruction of the devil solely to God in the Day of Judgment, and forbade Muslims even to own and carry weapons.[69] Sonsyrea Tate, in her memoir of her childhood in the Nation of Islam, described her fear upon hearing the militant language of the Nation's lessons before understanding their symbolic meaning:

I didn't know that at eleven and twelve years old, my uncles already were beginning to understand that Elijah Muhammad wasn't talking about physically going out and killing four white people. Their teachers had explained to them that Elijah Muhammad was a prophet and that prophets don't always mean exactly what they say because prophets tend to speak in parables—symbolisms. He might have meant for his followers to go out and kill four people's devilish ways.[70]

For many in the Nation of Islam, its "parables" gave thrilling new meaning to the most familiar religious language. Terms such as "God," "Satan," "heaven," "hell," "resurrection," and "judgment" were all radically reinterpreted. God was no longer, as in traditional theology, invisible, bodiless, infinite, utterly transcendent—in the words of Lesson No. 2, "a spook [that] cannot be seen by the physical eye"[71]—God was "the Son of man, the supreme being, the (black man) of Asia."[72] God existed *only* as a human being: a Black man of the "original" people.[73] Muhammad explained: "You look forward to seeing God or the coming of the 'Son of man' (a man from a man) and not the coming of a 'spirit.'"[74] God was only hiding until the appointed hour, when he would "return the lost back to their own and to punish and destroy the wicked for their destruction of the righteous."[75] Muhammad saw the otherworldly, spiritual God of traditional Christian belief as a distraction from the very earthly salvation he preached: "There is no God in the sky stronger than we on the earth."[76] Heaven and hell, too, existed only in life on earth; there was no such thing as an afterlife or the physical raising of human beings from the dead. The only life of the world to come was the spiritual and mental resurrection of the "lost-found" Black nation.[77]

To be God meant to be Black; to be Black meant, in a sense, to be God. In a series of 1972 lectures, Muhammad declared that God was "Self-Created from an Atom of life," taking "flesh, bone and blood from the earth that He was created on."[78] God's

Divine Rage

self-creation was identical with the creation of Black people. "There was no such thing as God saying 'let us make a black-man,' because no man knows when the first blackman was made ... There's no such thing as a beginning to the Blackman, nor is there such a thing of proving truthfully that there's an end of Him."[79] As Lesson No. 1 had proclaimed: "The original man is the Asiatic Black man; the Maker; the Owner; the Cream of the planet Earth—Father of Civilization, God of the Universe."[80] Reflecting on this lesson, Sonsyrea Tate wrote of her childhood self: "I was glad to be born a black person and extra glad that I was one of the special black people chosen to be in the Nation of Islam."[81]

The power of the devil was at an end, and soon, Black people would take up their ancient birthright and rule the earth. The end of the six-thousand-year rule of the devil, according to the Nation, had occurred in 1914, and it only appeared to continue as a gesture of God's patience, giving time for Black people to return to Islam before the judgment.[82] The reigning white power was already obsolete, and the justice of God would soon be revealed. "These are the days," wrote Elijah Muhammad, "of God's or Christ's presence to destroy this evil world with all the deceptions that the people should again labor under a wicked and merciless ruler, the devil."[83] Before leaving the Nation of Islam, Malcolm X reveled in this hope. In a speech in 1963, the very last speech he would give as an official representative of Elijah Muhammad, he declared that "we are living in the time of 'prophecy fulfillment,' the time predicted by the ancient prophets of God, when this one God would use his one religion to establish one world here on earth—the world of Islam, or Muslim world ... which only means: a world of universal brotherhood that will be based upon the principles of truth, freedom, justice, equality, righteousness, and peace."[84]

Malcolm X and the Nation's Message

Malcolm X, by the time he was forced out of the Nation of Islam, still passionately believed in the world of freedom, justice, and equality that was just on the other side of divine judgment. This was the original insight for Malcolm Little, the teaching that had cast a bright light over the Scriptures for him, revealing under cover of symbols and stories the truth about himself and the world. He shared the belief of many Nation of Islam members that W. D. Fard's advent in this final period of history was the key to understanding the true meaning of both Christian and Muslim sacred texts. Malcolm summoned the immense powers of his creativity and intellect to search the Scriptures for this wisdom. "If anyone ever honed Black Muslim biblical application to a fine art, it was Malcolm X," wrote DeCaro.[85]

"The things that have come to light in my eyesight now, make me wonder how I could be so blind in the past," Malcolm wrote from prison in 1948.[86] But even in the glow of his recent conversion, Malcolm was adamant about reading the Bible on his own terms. "What I read from the Bible I try to do with my own mind," he told Philbert in June 1949. He knew this might lead to mistakes in interpretation, but he would rather make his own errors, he explained, than "wait for someone else to make the mistake and cause [him] to suffer any way for blindly following a blind leader."[87]

He had, he admitted, come to "many interesting conclusions" that were "violently contrary to popular belief."[88] He saw now that "the messiah" or Christ "doesn't have to mean *one person*, but could mean [a] 'select' group," one that had "been so wildly scattered by the forces of Satan" that they required divine gathering.[89] Black people, Malcolm mused, contained the fullness of the biblical story in themselves: they were all Jesus, they were all the tribe of Judah, they were all Judas, they were all

Simon (Peter).[90] Teaching himself to see his fellow Black people as bearers of divine meaning, as the main characters in God's story, profoundly transformed Malcolm's inner world. All Black people, even those who had set themselves against his message, had become awe-inspiring bearers of God's presence. He wrote to Philbert about a fellow Black prisoner who had opposed him, longing for him to be set free from his sufferings, which, he now knew, were the sufferings of Christ: "His True Brothers would soon extract the Nails from his hands, stop the Flow of Blood from his Bleeding Heart, and lift the wretched Crown of Thorns from his weary head ... and the Dark Corner of the Temple would soon be made Light, the Master Architect having completed His Creation ... and the Graves are even now giving up their dead."[91]

Black people had become holy for Malcolm, and so had their whole history. This was true for him even when it meant pushing the boundaries of the Nation of Islam's official teachings on the history of Black people in America. "Is Africa not the Holy Land?" he asked in 1949. "Is the Nile the river Jordan?"[92] This was Malcolm's way of thinking, not Elijah Muhammad's—the Nation of Islam, like the Moorish Science Temple before it, categorized Black people as "Asiatics," whose true home was the holy city of Mecca, not Africa. As Edward Curtis has shown, however, members of the Nation of Islam imagined their origins in diverse ways, drawing upon different lineages and symbols.[93] Malcolm was no exception. He was likely, on some level, remembering his parents as he wrote about the Holy Land of Africa: both Earl and Louise Little had been organizers with Marcus Garvey's Universal Negro Improvement Association, whose slogan was "Africa for the Africans."[94] The history of Black people in America, too, he concluded, must be sacred. Again diverging from the Nation's rhetoric, which portrayed Black Christianity in an almost entirely negative light, Malcolm described the spirituals as sacred: "The color is the 'root,' the root is the 'life,' the life is the Spirit, and the *Spirit is the Truth* ... God is Spirit, and it is a fact that His Songs, the Spirituals, can only be sung by those who possess His Spirit."[95] Following his release from prison in 1952, in a radio address for the Nation of Islam, Malcolm would refer to the spirituals again, illustrating their connection with the songs of lamentation sung by the exiled Jews in Babylon.[96]

Malcolm cherished what he had learned from the Nation of Islam: if he wanted to find God, he'd need to look at his own people. But just as his commitment to this central tenet brought him into conflict with the Nation of Islam's view of history, it also sparked tension with the organization's position on political action in the present. The Nation's official policy of political non-involvement was clear. During the time in which Malcolm X had become a Muslim, the Nation espoused what Muhammad's biographer, Claude Andrew Clegg III, has called "passive separatism," focusing on community empowerment and discouraging engagement with non-Muslim social movements.[97] However, this was at odds with the more radical orientation of its early years, when members had been inspired by the organization's radical rhetoric to acts of draft resistance, or courtroom riots after members were arrested.[98] It was Muhammad's four years in prison, Clegg speculates, that put an end to the Nation's "activist tendencies."[99] Following Muhammad's release from prison, he was determined to avoid the devastating effects of government suppression and incarceration on the movement and its members. He vehemently insisted on the Nation's peacefulness and unthreatening character to the US government even as he continued to preach the imminent destruction of white America.

Malcolm X continually strained to stay within the bounds of this official policy, when it seemed so obvious to him that the struggles of non-white people to overthrow their oppressors were God's work. At a rally in Harlem in 1960, Malcolm X declared that "the whole Dark World" agreed "that there can be no peace without freedom from colonialism, foreign domination, oppression and exploitation."[100] The unwillingness of the white world to come to terms with this truth was leading it, he proclaimed, to its "inevitable doom."[101] He compared contemporary oppressors to the ancient city of Nineveh in the biblical Book of Jonah—an oppressive, imperial city that was spared when it repented. "God will spare our slavemaster today too if he will repent," Malcolm said.[102] But he was not optimistic. If, as seemed to be the case, the white world continued in its stubborn refusal of God's demands for justice, then, "like the biblical houses of Egypt and Babylon (slave empires of the Bible), God will erase the American government and the entire race that it favors and represents, from this planet ... and God will then give the whole earth back to the Original Owners, The Black Man!"[103] This future reversal of power roles was inevitable, as "the masses are ready to burst the shackles of slavery whether the 'moderates' will stand up or not."[104] The call to action was clear. As Malcolm declared in a television interview on *The Open Mind* in October 1961: "All dark people today should get together and toss aside the shackles of a common oppressor and that common oppressor is that man who has been sitting up there in Europe."[105]

In 1962, the disagreement between Malcolm X and the Nation came to a head when the Los Angeles police killed a Nation member, Ronald Stokes, and raided the city's mosque. Elijah Muhammad forbade any kind of retribution. Malcolm, as recounted by Peniel Joseph, "exploded."[106] He reluctantly complied with Muhammad's orders, but, in his speeches and in his eulogy for Stokes, Malcolm gave voice to a different vision. He spoke, as he had on numerous occasions before, of the "dark world" rising up against its oppressors. "The death of Ronald

Stokes," wrote Joseph, "had pushed him to his breaking point with the Nation of Islam's policy of nonengagement in political activism and in his personal relationship with Elijah Muhammad. His departure from the group began in earnest as he eulogized Stokes in language more befitting a political leader than a Muslim minister."[107]

The break between Malcolm X and the Nation was, in many ways, political—but its roots were theological. Malcolm could no longer pretend he did not see what he so clearly saw: God was mounting the barricades. It was time his people followed.

2

God's Judgment of White America

Malcolm X's Challenge

Malcolm's Hunger

Many of Benjamin Karim's fondest memories of Malcolm X were of meals they shared together: "that man could eat!"[1] How he ate, though, was a lesson in itself to Karim, who was then one of Malcolm's assistant ministers at Temple No. 7 in Harlem: "Malcolm ate slowly, in silence, as if he were contemplating the flavor of every bite. His posture erect, his napkin in his lap, he always took the food to his mouth and never slurped, fumbled, gobbled, or blew to it."[2] He had "style, grace" in his manner of eating, but, Karim added, he "would light into a plate of braised lamb like a bear going for honey."[3] He had a "weakness" for banana splits, too, so much so that the minute he walked into one of his favorite restaurants, the waitress would immediately begin scooping vanilla ice cream into a bowl.[4]

Malcolm never forgot the hunger he had known intimately since his Depression-era childhood.[5] "There were times when there wasn't even a nickel and we would be so hungry we were dizzy," he remembered.[6] The hardest times came after his father's death. When Earl Little was still alive, the family had been "much better off than most town Negroes" because they raised a large portion of their own food.[7] Louise Little, his mother, would care for the baby chicks his father bought, and the whole family worked in their large vegetable garden. Malcolm recalled with gratitude that his mother had given him his own plot of the garden to tend.[8] He loved it. He loved the hard work of growing his own food, but also the sheer joy of working closely with the earth. "I loved especially to grow peas," he remembered. "I was proud when we had them on our table … And sometimes when I had everything straight and clean for my things to grow, I would lie down on my back between two rows, and I would gaze up in the blue sky at the clouds moving and think all kinds of things."[9] It was only after his father's death that the family—and his mother's mental health—began to go "swiftly downhill."[10] "Our family was so poor that we would eat the hole out of a doughnut."[11]

Hunger, he insisted to Karim, was the "strongest human urge," the most fundamental drive: the need for nourishment.[12] When his friends uneasily witnessed him hand fifty cents to a "winehead" who said he was hungry, Malcolm dismissed their concerns. He knew, he told them, that the man might not use the money for the hot meal he so needed. Still, he could not refuse a man who claimed to be hungry.[13]

Then Malcolm started talking about charity. The female ant, he told us, will regurgitate her food to feed another ant. Nature sends flying insects into the air to provide nourishment of birds on the wing, he said. Rain falls upon the earth, and in the soil its water brings minerals to the roots of plants. Out of one grain of corn grows a stalk that will bear an exceptionally generous seven full ears. Nature everywhere evidences God's bountiful charity, Malcolm showed us … Charity is taking advantage of the opportunity to feed [your brother], an opportunity, he said, that he himself would never miss.[14]

This was Malcolm X as Benjamin Karim knew him: insatiably curious about the mysterious workings of the universe, unfailingly generous, stalwart in his integrity. Malcolm, Karim asserted in an interview for the 1994 documentary *Malcolm X: Make It Plain*, was "honest and he was truthful and he was dedicated to the uplifting of black people ... He was deeply religious and he had a very strong, unwavering belief in God."[15] This, he added, was what made him a threat to Elijah Muhammad.[16] To view the theological, institutional, and personal rift that grew between Malcolm X and Elijah Muhammad in the first few years of the 1960s through the eyes of Benjamin Karim is to see how much of Malcolm's shifting position in this period emerged from the needs of his community, from people like Karim, who loved him—and who hungered for what he represented. When Malcolm X proclaimed, at the end of 1963, that a divine hand was at work in America's self-destruction, leading to his expulsion from the organization to which he had dedicated over a decade of his life, he was not only speaking on his own behalf.

One night in 1962, soon after Ronald Stokes was killed and Muhammad ordered his followers not to antagonize the Los Angeles police, Karim—then known as Benjamin 2X—walked with Malcolm and another assistant minister, Louis 2X,[17] from Harlem's Temple No. 7 Restaurant to the place where Malcolm had parked his Oldsmobile.[18] Temple No. 7 Restaurant at 116th Street and Lenox Avenue was, in Karim's words, "like an oasis or ... like the crossroads back there in ancient Timbuktu," a gathering place for "people from different walks of life" who wanted to meet with Malcolm. "If we weren't having meetings, if Minister Malcolm was in town ... he was there, and it's where we would sit around the table and ... drink coffee and eat bean pie."[19] Malcolm thought that the restaurant's cook, Sister Lana, "braised lamb shanks better than anyone in the Muslim world."[20] Temple restaurants, as the journalist Louis Lomax explained, were, along with the temple (or mosque) itself, the "nerve centers of work and worship" in the Nation of Islam.[21] Food was crucial to the identity of Nation members, as scholars such as Edward Curtis and Mary Potorti have since described; Elijah Muhammad's distinctive food laws set them apart.[22] The temple restaurant in Harlem, then, as Karim put it, was the center of the social life of New York's Nation of Islam community.[23]

That night, as Karim remembered it, on the way back to his car, Malcolm stopped suddenly and looked at his friends. "You know," he told them, "we talk about people being bitten by [police] dogs and mowed down by fire hoses, we talk about our people being brutalized in the civil rights movement, and we haven't done anything to help them." If either of Malcolm's friends said anything in response—either to defend Muhammad's order, or to agree with Malcolm—Karim did not record it in his memoir. They started walking again, but after only a few more steps, Malcolm stopped a second time. "We spout our militant, revolutionary rhetoric," he told them, "and we preach Armageddon, but when our own brothers are brutalized or killed, we do nothing."[24] He got into his car and started to drive home, leaving Karim and Louis 2X—who would come to be known as Louis Farrakhan—on the sidewalk.

Karim shared Malcolm's concerns. Muhammad's reluctance to join the fight against police violence puzzled him, especially after a member of the Nation had been killed. "Any number of Muslim brothers from any mosque anywhere in America," he wrote later, "would have been prepared at a moment's notice and at the cost of his own life, if necessary, to fly out to California in the cause of Islamic justice."[25] After all, he noted, the Nation preached over and over again that—unlike the civil rights leaders who espoused nonviolence as an expression of Christian love—Islam recognized the right to self-defense. Malcolm "felt sort of let down," Karim recalled, "and a lot of us did … because

we were people who said, 'Never be the aggressor, but if someone attacks you, we do not teach you to turn the other cheek.'"[26]
It was as hard for him as it was for Malcolm to understand how
to square the Nation's message with its political neutrality. It
was all the more difficult for him because it had in fact been an
earlier instance of police brutality, and Malcolm X's courageous
response to it, that had brought Karim to the Nation in the first
place.

Prior to becoming a Muslim, Karim—then Benjamin Goodman—was a United States Air Force veteran from rural Virginia who had moved to New York City and was working in
the shipping room of a record label company. Karim had ended
his time in the military full of disgust and anger toward white
Americans; his final break with white America occurred when
his commanding officer refused to allow him to fly home from
Korea in order to attend his mother's funeral. On the same
night, the officer allowed a white airman to leave the base and
fly to see his newborn child.[27] The incident brought to Karim's
mind a host of other humiliations, insults, and outrages he and
his family had undergone. As I heard him loading the magazine of his gun, "Round by round I remembered sneers, insults,
gibes, threats; too long I had tolerated, as every black man had,
the injustices of white supremacists, civilians and military men
alike."[28] He remembered his beloved, departed mother. In his
memories, Mary Goodman was young (she died at the age of
thirty-four, only sixteen years older than himself), affectionate
and friendly, a strong, determined woman with an "easy smile"
and a "free spirit."[29] She had always called him "Dickie-boy."[30]
He remembered the way so many white men, from employers
to catcallers, had diminished and abused her. He remembered
that she had called these men "worse than the devil," and had
promised that "for their wickedness God will pay them back."[31]
Picking up his gun, he started walking to his commanding offi-

cer's tent—but ran into a friend, who convinced him not to follow through with his plans of retaliation.

For all Karim's resentment of white power and violence, his
conviction that white Americans, his own "countrymen," were
now "strangers" to him,[32] he was hesitant when his co-worker,
Leo, began talking with him about the message of the Honorable Elijah Muhammad. The notion that Black Americans
should recover their glorious origins and embrace their equally
glorious destiny struck him as absurd; he imagined his ancestors "as half-naked savages stalking through tropical jungle,"
just the way Africans had always been portrayed to him in popular media and in school textbooks.[33]

Karim's attitude to the Nation of Islam changed abruptly in
April 1957, after the police beating of Hinton Johnson. A member of the Nation of Islam, Johnson had happened upon a group
of police officers beating another Black man as they put him
under arrest. Johnson and two friends tried to stop the police; he
told them, "You're not in Alabama—this is New York."[34] When
he and his friends refused to disperse, Patrolman Mike Dolan
beat Johnson with his nightstick, resulting in a brain hemor-
rhage and internal bleeding.[35] The police took Johnson and the
others into custody. When news got back to the Nation of Islam's
community in Harlem, and to its minister, Malcolm X, Malcolm
set in motion a chain of telephone calls, assembling a crowd of
Muslims to go with him to the precinct and demand to see Johnson.[36] At first, the police denied that Johnson was in custody, but
as a larger and larger group of people surrounded the station, the
police agreed to allow Malcolm in. After witnessing the condition Johnson was in and hearing from him about his injuries,
Malcolm demanded that Johnson be sent to a hospital to receive
medical care. Evidently concerned that the vigil outside the precinct would turn into a riot, the police agreed. Following Malcolm's order, the gathering moved from the station to Harlem

Hospital, keeping watch as Johnson was examined. After being treated, Johnson—still seriously wounded and unable to walk—was returned to the custody of police and brought back to the precinct. Again, the crowd gathered around the station, and again, Malcolm demanded Johnson be returned to the hospital. The police refused, but agreed to a request from Malcolm's lawyer, Charles Beavers, that Johnson's topcoat be folded underneath his head to be used as a pillow. At this point, around 2:30 AM, Malcolm returned to the crowd, giving them the order to go home. Stunned police officers watched as the crowd disappeared "as if in thin air."[37] According to James L. Hicks, who reported on the incident in the Harlem newspaper *Amsterdam News*, a policeman watching the crowd disperse said out loud, "No one man should have that much power."[38] Everyone knew what he meant. What he meant, wrote Karim, "was, 'No one *black* man should have that much power.'"[39]

It was precisely this show of power that amazed and attracted the previously skeptical Benjamin Goodman. "Here was a man," he wrote, "who could walk boldly into the jaws of the lion, walk proud and tall into the territory of the enemy, the station house of the 28th Precinct, and force the enemy to capitulate. Here was a man who could help restore the heritage, the pride of race and pride of self, that had been carefully stripped from us over the four hundred years of our enslavement here in White America."[40] After Karim heard about Malcolm X's showdown with police over the beating of Hinton Johnson, he knew he had to hear Malcolm speak. And when he did, his life changed.[41] Benjamin Goodman became Benjamin 2X.

Karim was not the only person awed by Malcolm X's role in the incident, especially after Johnson, with the help of Nation of Islam attorneys, successfully sued the New York Police Department, receiving a payment of $70,000, the largest award that had ever been granted in a case of police brutality.[42] The story was picked up by news outlets across the country, giving Malcolm X his first opportunity to preach on a national stage. By July 1957, Malcolm X was writing a weekly column in the *Los Angeles Herald-Dispatch*, warning his readers: "You must bear witness that according to the Bible, destruction of the Slavemaster by Almighty God cannot be avoided nor longer delayed. And, oh how well the Slavemaster (modern Pharaoh) knows this. Yes, this government which was founded upon the slavery and suffering of God's 'chosen people,' is quite upset today because of the teachings of MESSENGER MUHAMMAD (the modern Moses) as was the Biblical Pharaoh."[43] In August and September and then the following month, in October 1957, he delivered a series of lectures in Detroit that brought in thousands of attendees.[44] Asked by reporters in Detroit about confrontations between the Nation of Islam and police, Malcolm answered, "Islam is the religion of peace. Our people must awaken and realize that these displays of brutal savagery by the police throughout the country are not directed against any particular group among the so-called Negroes. These inhuman attacks against our people follow a general pattern, and are directed against all elements of our people here in America."[45] During this time, Malcolm increasingly became the public face of the Nation of Islam, traveling all over the country helping to build new temples for the organization.[46] In 1959, when the journalists Mike Wallace and Louis Lomax produced a television special on the Nation, *The Hate That Hate Produced* (1959), their choice to feature Malcolm X prominently was a result of the national reputation that he had first gained in the wake of the police beating of Hinton Johnson.

But back in Harlem, for Benjamin Karim, Malcolm was not only a fiery preacher of a coming Armageddon or a champion against police brutality. He was, most importantly, a *minister*, a term which, Karim explained, derives from "the Latin word for servant: our counselor, healer, judge, and peacemaker."[47] For Karim, Malcolm X was always and most importantly "the teacher at the blackboard with a world in his mind and a piece of chalk in his hand."[48] When Karim visited Harlem's Temple No. 7 for the first time after the news had spread about Hinton Johnson, this was the version of Malcolm he had met. On that occasion, Malcolm lectured for two hours on the history of slavery in America,[49] and Karim left "feeling like a big ball of twine [was] unraveling" inside his head as he sifted through "all the new ideas, concepts and arguments that Malcolm had spoken."[50]

The portrait of Malcolm X painted by Karim is one of boundless curiosity and iron commitment to the pursuit of truth. Malcolm held his recruits to the Nation to high standards; he not only taught them but labored to give them the tools to teach themselves. They received "syllabuses, assignments, reports, book lists," and were required to bring to their studies "a notebook, a dictionary, a thesaurus, a book of synonyms and antonyms, an etymology text, a library card, and an open, willing mind."[51] Malcolm shared his passion especially for studying history and languages, with a focus on non-European civilizations: Babylonia, Persia, Egypt, India.[52] He held screenings of films from the National Geographic Society, introducing his Harlemite compatriots to the Himalayas, or the East African Rift, or the ocean floor. On other nights, he shared movies with historical themes, including his favorite film, *Lawrence of Arabia*.[53] "Malcolm wanted us not only to discover the wonder and variety of all the realms in nature but also to appreciate their oneness as God's creation," Karim explained.[54]

The delight Malcolm took in learning about the world's wonders, past and present, was especially on display when he taught children. Karim recalled with evident fondness Malcolm's trips to the Museum of Natural History with the temple children, how he would ignite the imaginations of his young listeners as he lectured to them in front of exhibits on dinosaurs or Alaska Native peoples. As he "would talk to the children in their own language" about what he knew and ask them questions, he would draw in the attention of other children visiting with their families, who would climb up on the shoulders of their parents to get a glimpse of Malcolm speaking.[55] "His teaching had universal appeal. He inspired these seven-, nine-, ten-, and twelve-year-olds to think for themselves, to explore, to ask questions, to read."[56]

Malcolm's intellectual honesty, however, set him unavoidably on a collision course with the Nation of Islam and Elijah Muhammad.

Malcolm's God

In Karim's account, Malcolm's questioning of some of the central tenets of the Nation of Islam began around 1962, the same year in which Ronald Stokes was killed, when Elijah Muhammad's son, Wallace Muhammad, began pulling Malcolm's coat about Islamic doctrine.[57] This was during the same period, according to Karim and to Malcolm himself in his autobiography, that Malcolm and Wallace Muhammad began discussing their concerns about the ongoing rumors that Elijah Muhammad had had sexual relationships with a number of his young secretaries—and, in multiple cases, had fathered children.[58] Wallace Muhammad, the presumptive heir of the Nation of Islam with whom Malcolm said he always shared "an exceptional closeness and trust," had begun questioning his father's claim to prophetic authority long ago.[59]

Publicly, Wallace Muhammad had begun to alienate some Nation of Islam insiders, according to Dawn-Marie Gibson, after introducing elements of Sunni Islam as minister of the Philadelphia temple in 1958.[60] But personally, his estrangement from the Nation of Islam's teachings had much earlier origins, with roots in childhood. Ironically, the most important factor in his later break with the Nation was the instruction in Arabic he had received at a young age at the Nation's University of Islam. His Arabic, science, and mathematics instructor, a Palestinian Sunni Muslim named Jamil Diab, was, in Wallace Muhammad's words, a "very sincere person, very sincere in his faith, a very sincere and firm believer, rational believer, in the teachings of the Holy Prophet [Muhammad]."[61] Diab was careful never to contradict explicitly Elijah Muhammad's interpretation of Islam, including the divinity of W. D. Fard and the Nation's mythology of racial origins, in front of his students, but, Wallace Muhammad said, Diab nevertheless "had a way of introducing some religion, though not much, through Arabic."[62] For Wallace Muhammad, learning Arabic was the "key" to the Qur'an, and, in a broader sense, to Islam as a global community.[63]

Once Wallace Muhammad began to speak with Malcolm X about Islam, Karim wrote, Malcolm stopped mentioning Fard in his speeches. His references to Elijah Muhammad, similarly, became less frequent. Karim remembered finding Malcolm in the Temple No. 7 restaurant one day with his head bowed and elbows on the table. "I heard something today that affected me so badly I thought my brain cells were bleeding," he told Karim, but did not say what it was. Only later did Karim realize he was referring to Elijah Muhammad's relationships with his young secretaries.[64] The combined pressures of Elijah Muhammad's response to the death of Ronald Stokes, Wallace Muhammad's concerns about misrepresentations of Islamic doctrine, and the devastating news of Elijah Muhammad's hypocrisy and exploitation of young women in the community worked to strain Malcolm's relationship with Muhammad and the Nation.

Malcolm's growing estrangement from his mentor and the organization he represented, however, was not merely a passive reaction to external events. Malcolm had also begun on his own actively to seek out relationships and knowledge outside the boundaries of the Nation of Islam, both religiously, starting up a dialogue with a Sudanese student at Dartmouth College, Ahmed Osman, who sent him literature from the Centre Islamique des Eaux-Vives in Geneva,[65] and politically, attending the August 1963 March on Washington despite Muhammad's orders to the contrary.[66]

What did Malcolm X believe about God and God's relationship to the Black struggle for liberation on the verge of his break from the Nation of Islam at the end of 1963? It is difficult to say. While Malcolm X would most famously portray in his letter from the hajj and in his autobiography his transition from the Nation to Sunni Islam as a sudden awakening to the true meaning of Islam as a religion of universal brotherhood, the reality was more complex. Edward Curtis has demonstrated how Malcolm, following his break with the Nation, carefully navigated between competing visions of Muslim and Black identity: the Pan-Islamist language of Islamic missionaries (a movement crucial to Saudi Arabia's foreign policy), the Pan-Africanist and revolutionary socialist aims embraced by Gamal Abdel-Nasser in Egypt, and the concerns of movements for Black liberation in the United States.[67]

In his attempts to build connections with global communities and the leaders in the struggle for Black liberation at home, Malcolm was aware of the contradictions involved, but also where his ultimate loyalties lay. The day before he was assassinated, he replied to the criticisms of Said Ramadan, the Islamist director of the Centre Islamique des Eaux-Vives, denying that his prioritization of Black liberation was un-Islamic. "As a Black American I do feel that my first responsibility is to my twenty-two million fellow Black Americans who suffer the same indignities because of their color as I do," he wrote. This was all the more so, he added, as, "much to my dismay, until now, the Muslim world has seemed to ignore the problem of the Black American."[68] In the same interview, he asserted that he regarded "Africa as my fatherland," and that he was "primarily interested in seeing [Africa] become completely free of outside political and economic influence that has dominated and exploited it."[69] He warned that if the Arab world neglected to put into practice the "brotherhood and unity" required by Islam, "Allah can easily" raise up young people to replace their leaders.[70]

In late 1963, Malcolm X had not yet entered into these debates publicly. He was, however, increasingly concerned about the isolating policies of Elijah Muhammad, and the ways in which these policies contradicted what had so sparked his own imagination in the Nation of Islam's teaching: God's championing of the "Dark World" of the colonized, oppressed, abused, and enslaved. Rather than a straightforward transition from the racial mythology (the Yacub myth, white devils, the coming Armageddon) of Elijah Muhammad to membership in the worldwide Sunni community, Malcolm X's exit from the Nation of Islam was a complex and at times a contradictory attempt to remain faithful to that first vision of God he had had in Norfolk Prison Colony, when a man appeared by his bed one night. "Allah has talked to me before," he had written Beatrice Clomax X in 1952, "and once He sat beside my bed."[71] And as late as March 21, 1964, after he had formally split with the Nation of Islam but was still proclaiming his allegiance to Elijah Muhammad, he asserted in a letter to Muhammad that he was "still a believer in Master W. F[ard]. Muhammad as our Saviour Allah."[72] At the same time, as Karim noted, he had seemed increasingly less willing to refer to Fard in public for some time before being forced out of the Nation. In 1963, it appears, Malcolm X was suspended between opposing beliefs, paths, and visions; he both believed and did not believe in Elijah Muhammad's prophetic message. Over time, though not completely, Malcolm would resolve these dilemmas, synthesizing the aspects of the Nation's doctrine that had so powerfully transformed his life with the more standard Sunni Muslim beliefs and practice. But in 1963, he had yet to achieve this synthesis. He could not deny that he had met God in the face of a non-white man; he found it harder and harder to believe that Elijah Muhammad was the representative of this God.

Malcolm's Exit

Malcolm X's departure from the Nation of Islam, as long as it had been building up, came abruptly in the wake of the death of President John F. Kennedy, when Elijah Muhammad publicly distanced himself from Malcolm's characterization of the assassination as America's "chickens coming home to roost."[73] Muhammad himself, it should be noted, was not shy about predicting America's downfall. In the year in which President Kennedy was killed, Muhammad made his opinions about the American government clear on multiple occasions. He wrote in February 1963: "America knows that under her flag we have received nothing but hell; beatings and killings without due process of law, day and night; not only in the past but the present."[74] In April, he described the American government as the "angry savage beast" whose destruction was prophesied in the Book of Daniel.[75] After the president's death, however, Muhammad publicly asserted the Nation of Islam's shared grief for "our president,"[76] including penning a front-page article for *Muhammad Speaks* with the headline, "Muhammad on President Kennedy: Nation Still Mourns Death."[77]

Claude Clegg III's assertion, discussed in the previous chapter, that Muhammad's political cautiousness was rooted in a deeply ingrained and justified fear of white reprisal is reinforced by contemporary accounts of Muhammad's reaction to the presidential assassination. On the day President Kennedy died, the Fruit of Islam (the Nation's defense organization) held a meeting that was infiltrated by the Federal Bureau of Investigation. The FBI file from this meeting records that the Supreme Captain of the Fruit of Islam, Raymond Sharrieff, gave an explanation of Muhammad's order not to speak publicly about Kennedy's death: "Don't talk to your friends or on your jobs about this assassination ... The Christians have deep feelings about what has happened and if you say the wrong thing, you can find yourselves in trouble. You might even be killed."[78] Muhammad knew how devastating white violence and government suppression could be; protective of the movement he had built, he shut down any public discussion of the assassination by Nation members.

As after the death of Ronald Stokes, Malcolm could not reconcile the contradictions in the Nation's approach, why the leadership held back from reaching the natural conclusions of its radical theology. God was Black; God was rising in righteous judgment against all racism, colonialism, and oppression. Muhammad himself had asserted, over and over, and in so many ways, that "we are now living in the judgment, or doom, of the white man's world."[79] Black people, claimed Muhammad, were even now being restored to their original dignity through Islam, were being transformed into a "nation of righteousness and justice to serve as a star for the nations of their own kind forever."[80] Malcolm X, carefully watching the world for signs of God's ongoing revelation, went further. He had begun to see the militant struggle for worldwide decolonization as itself God's judgment on earth.

The comments that led to Malcolm's expulsion from the Nation of Islam occurred after a speech Malcolm gave at the Manhattan Center on December 1, 1963, soon after President Kennedy's death. In "God's Judgment of White America"—the speech's title—Malcolm began by reminding his hearers of God's judgment of past imperial powers: just as slavery caused the fall of Egypt and Babylon, and colonialism had caused the fall of white European powers, "the enslavement of millions of black people in this country is now bringing White America to her hour of judgment, to her downfall as a respected nation."[81] Malcolm encouraged those resistant to his warning in the audience to "search the Christian Scriptures" and, in parallel, to "search even the histories" of former empires.[82] "If God's unchanging laws of justice caught up with every one of the slave empires of the past, how dare you think White America can escape the harvest of unjust seeds planted by her white forefathers against our black forefathers here in the land of slavery!"[83] Malcolm read divine judgment into historical instances of imperial collapse. Slavery and oppression constituted a "bill owed" to the enslaved and oppressed "that must be collected,"[84] and, if America proved unwilling to atone, would be collected by "divine will and divine power."[85]

Malcolm pivoted seamlessly in the speech from his assertion of divine judgment to a denunciation of the contemporary political situation in the United States. Support of the civil rights movement by white politicians, he argued, was merely an attempt to avoid facing the seriousness of this judgment and the heavy weight of its cost.[86] He decried what he viewed as white co-option of the movement, and lamented the compromises Black leaders had been willing to make for "token" victories.[87] What had the support of white liberals, including that of President Kennedy, Malcolm asked, gained the demonstrators?[88] "The black masses are still unemployed, still starving, and still living in the slums … and, I might add, getting angrier and more explosive every day."[89] The compromises and half-measures that the movement leaders had been willing to settle for, so far, he insisted, constituted a lack of understanding of the nature of the revolution that was occurring globally, "the struggle of the nonwhites of this earth against their white oppressors" which had "swept white supremacy out of Africa, out of Asia, and is getting ready to sweep it out of Latin America."[90] This revolutionary struggle was divine payment, recompense; nothing could prevent it or stem its tide. "Like the flood in Noah's day, revolution drowns all opposition, or like the fire in Lot's day, the black revolution burns everything that gets in its path."[91]

Was it possible for white America to evade this dreadful judgment? According to Elijah Muhammad, it was not. Muhammad did frequently insist that America atone by relinquishing its territory and resources to Black Americans, as in the words of the "Muslim Program": "If the white people are truthful about their professed friendship toward the so-called Negro, they can prove it by dividing up America with their slaves."[92] However, Muhammad was equally insistent that white Americans would never meet this demand. "Today America's doom is set like a die. She cannot escape; it is impossible ... They were not created in any such nature to be a true friend to anyone, not even to themselves."[93]

Malcolm, in his speech and elsewhere, was more ambivalent. On the one hand, he repeated Muhammad's line: no, white Americans cannot escape as "God himself is the judge."[94] But Malcolm qualified his statement immediately. "*If* America can't atone for the crimes she has committed against the twenty-two million 'Negroes,' *if* she can't undo the evils she has brutally and mercilessly heaped upon our people these past four hundred years, *then* America has signed her own doom" [emphasis mine].[95] Malcolm concluded with the assertion that "if the government of White America truly repents of its sins against our people, *and atones by giving us our true share, only then can America save herself!* But if America waits for Almighty

God himself to step in and force her into a just settlement, God will take this entire continent away from her."[96] Malcolm, much more forcefully than Muhammad ever did, expressed his faith in the power of the revolutionary action of non-white peoples to force a "just settlement" and even repentance from the white holders of power and wealth.

Malcolm, following Muhammad's order to the letter if not the spirit of the law, avoided explicit mention of President Kennedy's recent assassination in his speech. However, he did not hesitate to devote a lengthy portion of his talk to accusations against the "late President" and his role in the civil rights movement. He asserted that a truly spontaneous, grassroots national movement behind the 1963 March on Washington had been coopted and neutralized by white liberal supporters, most notably and importantly, by President Kennedy himself: "When the late President had learned that he couldn't stop the march, he not only joined it himself but he encouraged all of his political bedfellows to join it. This is the way the white liberals took over the March on Washington, weakened its impact, and changed its course; *by changing the participants and the contents, they were able to change the very nature of the march itself.*"[97]

Benjamin Karim noted that these accusations were not new: "Malcolm had never been quiet about Kennedy. For months he had been accusing President Kennedy of willful deception in his stand on civil rights issues."[98] Still, Karim went on, Malcolm had no intention of expressly disobeying Muhammad's command when he gave his speech. He faltered only afterward, when a woman in the audience asked him about the assassination. While Muhammad had urged his followers to answer any such question with the simple words, "no comment,"[99] Malcolm began on safe enough ground—noting that the press had been goading members of the Nation of Islam to make a "fanatic, inflexibly dogmatic statement" expressing joy over the president's death.[100] Hearing laughter at his response, Malcolm pressed on, decrying how Kennedy had been "twiddling his thumbs" while others—like the civil rights leader Medgar Evers, the four young Black girls who had been murdered in a Birmingham church, the Congolese prime minister Patrice Lumumba, the South Vietnamese President Ngo Dinh Diem and his brother, Ngo Dinh Nhu—had been murdered.[101] President Kennedy's death was a case of "chickens coming home to roost," Malcolm explained.[102]

As a child, Malcolm's mother had carefully tended to the baby chicks his father brought home for the family. His family was proud to live on its own land, to raise its own food. When Malcolm was six, his father died—perhaps murdered. His family went hungry; his family fell apart.

"Being an old farm boy myself," Malcolm concluded, "chickens coming home to roost never did make me sad; they always made me glad."[103]

Malcolm's Revolution

The day after Malcolm's speech, on December 2, the *New York Times* ran a story: "Malcolm X Scores U.S. and Kennedy: Likens Slaying to 'Chickens Coming Home to Roost.'"[104] On December 4, Elijah Muhammad sent word to temples across the country that Malcolm X was suspended from his ministry for ninety days. Karim was at Temple No. 7 when the Nation's leadership called. "We were told that if Malcolm came back to the temple after the suspension, we should give him a job washing dishes in the restaurant."[105] By the time Malcolm finally made the decision to separate from the Nation of Islam and announce the formation of first one and then two new organizations, the Muslim Mosque Incorporated (MMI) and the Organization of Afro-American Unity (OAAU), Karim had already chosen his side. He left the Nation of Islam after publicly confronting the leadership of Temple No. 7 about a story in the *Amsterdam News* about a Nation-organized plot to kill Malcolm X. Around a third of the mosque's membership, Karim wrote, also followed Malcolm out of the Nation.[106]

The Muslim Mosque Incorporated was patterned explicitly on the Nation of Islam. Malcolm labored to stress this in his March 1964 announcement of his separation from the Nation of Islam and formation of the MMI. He still firmly believed, he said, "that Mr. Muhammad's analysis of the problem is the most realistic, and that his solution is the best one,"[107] and, like Muhammad, he recognized the need to trust in "divine guidance, divine power, and in the fulfillment of divine prophecy."[108] Having been forced against his will out of the Nation, he intended to build upon Muhammad's work by organizing a New York City-based mosque with the "spiritual force" necessary to heal and empower Black Americans.[109] Like he had as Muhammad's devotee, he emphasized the urgent need to address the "vices that destroy the moral fiber" of his community, but, in a sharp departure from Muhammad's approach, Malcolm declared that the mosque would "be organized in such manner to provide for the active participation of all Negroes in our political, economic, and social programs, despite their religious or non-religious beliefs."[110] Malcolm's mosque would not wait for God to bring on Armageddon. "The time has come," he asserted, "for the American Negro to fight back in self-defense whenever and wherever he is being unjustly and unlawfully attacked."[111] He and those who joined him would fight for their lives, but also for power: "we must control the politics and the politicians of our community."[112]

By the time that he announced the formation of the Organization of Afro-American Unity in June 1964, this initial vision of "militant ... racial solidarity"[113] had expanded under the influence of contacts in the Muslim world, the African continent, and in the Black American freedom struggle. In his speech—a much longer and more detailed talk than his introduction of the MMI—Malcolm laid out a radical and ambitious platform grounded in a commitment to global solidarity of all peoples of African descent. Both the name of the organization (clearly meant to evoke the Organization for African Unity) and the words of Malcolm's speech offered African struggles for decolonization as the model for Black American liberation: "Just ten years ago on the African continent, our people were colonized. They were suffering all forms of colonization, oppression, exploitation, degradation, humiliation, discrimination, and every other kind of -ation. And in a short time, they have gained more independence, more recognition, more respect as human beings than you and I have."[114] Malcolm underscored this connection throughout his speech: "that's what you and I are," he reminded his Harlem audience, "Africans."[115] Like the survivors of European colonialism in Africa, "you bear the scars of the same kind of colonization and oppression not on your body, but in your brain, in your heart, in your soul, right now."[116]

Malcolm declared the days of nonviolent direct action were "over, they're gone, that's yesterday."[117] Instead, he proposed an alternative model of political struggle: solidarity with the African diaspora around the globe; armed self-defense against white racial terror; rent strikes; Black self-direction of Black children's education, or, in case this is not put into practice, school strikes; voter registration and education drives; community mobilization against organized crime and drug trafficking as alternatives to policing; investing in Black-owned businesses and initiatives; and a "cultural" revolution of Black artists and thinkers aimed at "unbrainwash[ing]" Black Americans, "recaptur[ing] our heritage and our identity if we are ever to liberate ourselves from the bonds of white supremacy."[118] In contrast with the tactics of the civil rights movement, which targeted local and national American institutions, Malcolm asserted the need to join with the non-white majority of the world in utilizing global institutions, especially the United Nations, to condemn American human rights violations.[119]

While Malcolm had famously reversed his beliefs on race on the hajj a few months previously, having seen in the global solidarity of pilgrims at Mecca a vision of a future in which "blue-eyed blonds" and "black-skinned Africans" could join in unity and brotherhood, he remained unsentimental about what he saw as the tendency of white American activists to dominate and co-opt Black political struggles.[120] White allies of the movement, he proclaimed, "can help in the white community, but they can't join" the OAAU.[121] As a Muslim, he believed in the brotherhood of all humanity, he explained on February 16, 1965, less than a week before he was assassinated, but "I have to be a realist and realize that here in America we're in a society that doesn't practice brotherhood."[122] White American allies were on the whole not ready for the radical demands of the coming revolution: "I don't go for any nonviolent white liberals," he explained in January 1965. "If you are for me and my problems—when I say me, I mean *us*, our people—then you have to be willing to do as old John Brown did."[123]

The ways that Malcolm expressed in 1964 and 1965 his vision of the global revolution against white supremacy departed, in one significant way, from his earlier rhetoric: the uncompromisingly biblical and religious framework of his earlier speeches gave way to a more universal message. Eager to appeal to as many Black Americans and global communities as possible, Malcolm repeatedly asserted that he was speaking to people of all religious backgrounds: "It's true we're Muslims and our religion is Islam, but we don't mix our religion with our politics and our economics and our social and civil activities—not anymore."[124]

At the same time, the content of his political critique remained the same: his description of God's righteous judgment working in "the struggle of the nonwhites of this earth against their white oppressors" in December 1963 clearly echoed in his ostensibly more secular later speeches and statements.[125]

Even in the last year of his life, the theology behind Malcolm's revolutionary vision would at times surface in his interviews. "Every power that has participated in slavery of any form on this earth, in history," he told Bernice Bass in December 1964, "has paid for it, except the United States ... The Bible, in the Book of Revelation, says that he that leads into captivity shall go into captivity ... This is justice. So I don't think that any power can enslave a people and not look forward to having that justice come back upon itself."[126] Malcolm continued to portray revolutionary justice as divine reckoning, as apocalyptic judgment. When asked in January 1965 whether he still believed in Elijah Muhammad's prediction of a coming Armageddon, he responded:

> I believe that there will ultimately be a clash between the oppressed and those that do the oppressing. I believe that there will be a clash between those who want freedom, justice, and equality for everyone and those who want to continue the systems of exploitation ... I don't think that it will be based upon the color of the skin, as Elijah Muhammad had taught it. However, I do think you'll find that the European powers, which are the former colonial powers, if they're not able to readjust their thinking of superiority toward the darker-skinned people ... then these lines can easily be drawn.[127]

Similarly, at a meeting in Paris sponsored by an African cultural organization in November 1964, he retold the story of Joseph "in the Bible and in the Koran" and reminded his hearers that Joseph was only able to forgive his brothers who had sold him into slavery because "he was in a position to forgive them." In contrast, "the country that bought him and enslaved him was destroyed." In order for white Americans to avoid the same destruction today, he concluded, they had to pay the debts their ancestors had accrued.[128]

Malcolm's belief in the coming reckoning between white oppressors and the non-white world was rooted, always, in spiritual encounter, in the inner transformation that had occurred in him when he turned to see a visitor beside his bed in his prison cell. But his adaptation of the language of divine judgment to that of global revolution galvanized many young Black Americans who, previously, had lingered on the threshold of the Nation of Islam. Black Panther Party founder Huey Newton, for instance, began attending Nation of Islam mosques in Oakland and San Francisco as a college student, inspired by Malcolm X's style and program, but "could not deal with [the Nation of Islam's] religion."[129] Similarly, the prominent Black activist Angela Davis described her first encounter with Malcolm X—before his departure from the Nation of Islam—as one of ambivalence: she was fascinated hearing Malcolm "addressing himself to white people, chastising them, informing them of their sins, warning them of the Armageddon to come," but was unable to "identify with his religious perspective."[130] The Nation's embrace of Black identity and Black power served as an inspiration for later Black movements—as Elaine Brown, the only female chairwoman of the Black Panther Party, explained, the party's "ten-point platform and program had been shaped by the Nation's doctrine."[131] At the same time, she wrote, "the party had always aligned itself specifically with Malcolm X."[132] Although he would not live to see it, the next chapter in the Black struggle for liberation belonged to his vision of worldwide solidarity, decolonization, and revolution.

Malcolm's End, Malcolm's Beginning

The man who would come to be seen as the embodiment of the Black Power movement was running out of time. Karim remembered walking once again with Malcolm to his car "not long before the end."[133] Malcolm had been turned down when he had tried to buy a life insurance policy, he told Karim, in light of the manifold threats to his life. "That tells you how much my life is worth."[134] Karim recalled the sound their feet made, trudging through the sleet on the sidewalk in their winter boots. "No, Brother Minister," he replied, "your life is invaluable to us."[135] Malcolm smiled.

Karim opened up the OAAU rally on the day that Malcolm X was murdered, February 21, 1965, in the Audubon Ballroom in Washington Heights. And after the room was cleared out, after his dear friend's and minister's body was removed, Karim remained. Stunned, looking around the empty room, he spied a ring on the floor of the stage. It was set with a black stone, engraved with a single word, in Arabic: *Allah*. It had been Malcolm's; it had been shot off his finger. Karim saved it to return to Malcolm's wife, Sister Betty Shabazz.[136]

On February 21, 1967, the second anniversary of Malcolm's death, Huey Newton and a cadre of armed members of the Black Panther Party for Self-Defense made their way through the San Francisco airport to the runway of an arriving plane, and then boarded it, guns in tow. They greeted the woman they had come to escort, and whom they had come to honor: Betty Shabazz.[137] "Malcolm's spirit is in us," Huey Newton wrote.[138] But not only in them: the age of the "angry children of Malcolm X" had arrived.[139]

3

The Religion of Black Power

Malcolm X and Black Revolutionary Spirituality

Becoming God: Malcolm's Heirs in the Black Revolution

The founder of the Black Panther Party, Huey Newton, was obsessed with death—or so Elaine Brown, who would become the chairwoman of the party from 1974 to 1977, wrote in her memoir, *A Taste of Power: A Black Woman's Story* (1992). In Newton—her comrade, sometimes lover, and the "other part of [her] soul"[1]—she found a mirror of her own "profound sorrow over life,"[2] someone who could understand the terrifying, periodic awareness she had experienced since childhood of alienation from the world, from meaning, from God: "It was a feeling that I was akin to ether, not made of flesh and bone, as though I had no body."[3] Newton, in Brown's narrative, is a tragic character: in possession of rare talents and inexhaustible energy, propelled by a fiery longing to eliminate "the alienation between human life on the planet and the rest of nature," to experience freedom, true spiritual freedom, for himself and for his people, a man who ultimately was destroyed by his all-consuming anger over his inability, like "any other black in America," to achieve what he so wholly desired.[4]

One night shared together in bed, in the borrowed apartment of a white civil rights attorney, Newton bared his heart to Brown. "A lot of what I am has to do with fear," he told her, a fear that he saw also in her. His toughness, his readiness to defend himself by any means necessary, he explained, was a shield against the threats he had faced growing up as a light-skinned, "pretty" outsider in his neighborhood. He recognized, he told her, this debilitating fear in a different form in his people; he saw how Black people's fear of "the Man" converted itself almost automatically into self-hatred. He longed to "tear off [the] mask" of the brutal system of racist violence under which they both lived, to "expose the whole face of the Man." But the party, he insisted, could not take down the system; that was a feat only possible for a god. His truer hope, his most sincere desire, he confided, was "to *realize* 'God,' which is not some dominating power sitting above us. God is all humanity in concert with nature. *We* are God, though we've yet to *become* God. But mostly," he concluded, "I want to be free to live on my terms and die on my terms."[5]

Newton, as Brown told it, never achieved this freedom. She narrated the descent of the party, which she had believed to be "the true vanguard of a new revolution in America," into nightmarish intragroup violence under Newton's leadership.[6] In the 1970s, the party buckled under the weight of sustained government and police repression, factional warring, and the "brutal abuses" of Newton's "absolute leadership."[7] Ultimately, she wrote, Newton's fear won out over his striving for freedom.[8] The memoir ends with Brown, her young daughter in tow, fleeing the Black Panther Party, her heart broken over the loss of the man she still loved and would "go on loving," and the party she had "sworn to die for" and into which she had invested all of her devotion for her people.[9] She lamented that the party might be defined by "its worst, not its best … our food and other programs that provided a concrete means for our people to survive and develop the will to make revolutionary change in America."[10] She mourned the dream she and Newton had shared, a dream that, so her narrative makes clear, was at heart a spiritual one: a longing to overcome the "fear and pain" of a world without meaning, to "repeal God's works, which were not good"[11]—as Brown remembered herself thinking as a child—to "*realize* God," to "*become* God,"[12] to create a new world of justice and freedom.

Newton and Brown were not alone in sharing this revolutionary dream, nor was it the sole provenance of the Black Panther Party. In the mid to late 1960s and the early 1970s, diverse Black revolutionary movements, from socialist-identified and internationalist groups like the Panthers, to cultural nationalists and Pan-Africanists, to religious organizations of every variety, to advocates for radical artistic and academic change, expressed a common faith in a Black-led revolutionary transformation of the world. Despite the bitter and sometimes fatal divides that too often would come to define these groups' relationships with one another, they shared one thing in common almost universally: their love for Malcolm X.

"A new militant spirit was born when Malcolm died," wrote Newton in *Revolutionary Suicide* (1973). "It was born of outrage and a unified Black consciousness, out of the sense of a task left undone."[13] Malcolm, wrote Newton, had "galvanized an entire generation," and the Black Panther Party itself "had been formed in the spirit of Malcolm."[14] Other leaders in what became known collectively as the Black Power movement agreed; examples of Black revolutionary leaders crediting Malcolm X and the Nation of Islam with inspiration for their actions are overwhelmingly abundant. Eldridge Cleaver, the Black Panther Party's minister of information, was a member of the Nation of Islam before joining the Black Panthers. His influential memoir, *Soul on Ice* (1968), made frequent use of the Nation's theology even as Cleaver insisted that "all the gods are dead except the god of war."[15] Cleaver was drawn especially to the apocalyptic language of Muhammad and Malcolm X: "The America out of which Elijah Muhammad calls his people is indeed doomed, crumbling, burning, if not by the hand of God then by the hand of man."[16] The Black Liberation Army member and famous fugitive Assata Shakur noted as a matter of course that, given her commitments to the Black struggle, "if I had any religion, it was Islam."[17] After all, she explained, "because of Elijah Muhammad and Malcolm X, the Muslim influence over our struggle has been very strong."[18] The words she relates from her fellow revolutionary Kamau Sadiki summarize the perception of Islam among Black militants during this time period: "A true Muslim is a true revolutionary. There is no contradiction between being a Muslim and a revolutionary."[19] H. Rap Brown (later Imam Jamil Al-Amin), the Student Non-violent Coordinating Committee (SNCC) leader who, along with Stokely Carmichael, gave the Black Power movement its original form, was drawn to Islam as a result of Malcolm X's depiction of the religion as militantly opposed to tyranny and oppression.[20] "More than any other person," wrote SNCC organizer, musician, and writer Julius Lester in 1966, "Malcolm X was responsible for the new militancy that entered the Movement in 1965 ... His clear, uncomplicated words cut through the chains on black minds like a giant blowtorch."[21] Yet, as Lester wrote in a *New York Times* book review of a collection of Malcolm's speeches in 1971, Malcolm's appeal was not primarily political, but spiritual: Lester compared him to "one of the Old Testament prophets. He is the voice of doom from the maelstrom of American history."[22]

The Religion of Black Power

Lester's comparison of Malcolm X to a prophet of the apocalypse was echoed in an insightful and influential essay written in 1968 by the civil rights activist Vincent Harding, "The Religion of Black Power," in which Harding describes a "resurgence of the Messianic theme" in the Black American religious tradition in the wake of Malcolm X's death.[23] Harding's essay is invaluable as a snapshot of the shifting emotional currents in the Black freedom struggle in the late 1960s. Harding was a long-time associate of Martin Luther King Jr., a devout Mennonite Christian who was committed to a philosophy of nonviolent revolutionary social change through mass civil disobedience. The "beautiful, pregnant time" of the early 1960s in which a "beloved community" of "freedom-loving believers ... willing to live and die in hope for what they believed, working with a steadily increasing company of white allies ... planned ... marched ... sang ... laughed ... stood up under the blows of their enemies and kept moving," was a "revelation" to him, and the remainder of his life's work was devoted to honoring this community of witnesses.[24] But the assassination of Malcolm X, he wrote, "had opened the way for his life to touch us more deeply than ever before."[25] Harding too followed the current of the "deep waters of disaffection, anger, rebellion, and pride" that began to define Black liberation movements.[26] King, he wrote, was similarly overcome by "anguish" over the hopelessness faced by Black Americans in urban centers as well as by the injustice of the ongoing war in Vietnam. Everyone, even committed veterans of the civil rights struggle, began to speak of "revolution."[27]

Indeed, King spent much of the final months of his life preaching on the apocalyptic themes Harding associated with Malcolm X. In his 1968 speeches, King warned America of God's coming wrath: "The judgment of God is upon us today," he inveighed in his final sermon on March 31, 1968, "and we could go right down the line and see that something must be done ... and something must be done quickly."[28] A month earlier, he had preached a sermon at his own congregation, Ebenezer Baptist Church in Atlanta, Georgia, reminding those in attendance of the Bible's assessment of nations that have neglected their responsibilities to the oppressed. "God has a way of even putting nations in their place," he declared.

> The God that I worship has a way of saying, "Don't play with me." He has a way of saying, as the God of the Old Testament used to say to the Hebrews, "Don't play with me, Israel. Don't play with me, Babylon. Be still and know that I'm God. And if you don't stop your reckless course, I'll rise up and break the backbone of your power." And that can happen to America.[29]

Writing of this period in King's public life, the Black theologian James Cone would reflect on how similar King's rhetoric had become to Malcolm X's, "standing before the day of judgment, proclaiming God's wrath and indignation upon a rich and powerful nation that was blind to injustice at home and indifferent to world peace."[30]

For King as for other Black leaders, this increasing resort to apocalyptic language reflected the growing frustrations of Black Americans, particularly in urban northern centers, about how the civil rights movement had failed to address meaningfully the dehumanizing conditions and racially based disparities faced by these communities. King was forced to address these frustrations personally in 1965 when he was heckled and dismissed in response to his attempts to advocate for calm in the midst of ongoing riots in Los Angeles.[31] This period of unrest, which would later become known to history as the Watts Riot or Rebellion, was catalyzed most immediately by the news that California Highway Patrolmen had physically assaulted and arrested four Black residents of Los Angeles: twenty-one-year-old Marquette Frye, his mother, Rena, his younger brother Ronald, and Joyce Gaines, an onlooker whom police alleged had spit at them after witnessing the arrests of the Fryes.[32] These assaults set the city on fire because they were not isolated incidents; deep and longstanding frustration over widespread conditions of poverty, segregation, dehumanization, and police violence seethed under the unrest. For those involved, the grievances that made the uprising necessary were obvious and concrete. Lucille Lacy, a woman arrested during the Watts Rebellion, described the reasons for her participation in the clearest of terms: being relegated to housing in which "rats in sewers [were] as big as cats" and the fact that her "11 year old [hadn't] had a school book since [he was] 5 years old."[33]

It is only in this context that we can understand why King himself described the late 1960s, despite the civil rights victories he had labored at great cost to achieve, as "a time of temptation to despair because it is clear now how deep and systemic are the evils [the movement] confronts."[34] The same conviction would lead to the emergence of the radical Black movements of the late 1960s, the self-identified heirs of Malcolm X. "Embracing and embroidering their memories of Malcolm," Harding wrote, Black militants "fashioned new dreams out of the hard materials of black urban life, faced the cruel centers of white American fear."[35]

Harding himself was moved and compelled by the changing rhetoric and tactics of the movement. In an essay published in the *Christian Century* in January 1967, Harding argued for the need for a new approach:

> If God is yet alive we cannot afford time to reminisce about the good old days of the civil rights movement when everybody knew the words of the songs. The time of singing may be past. It may be that America must now stand under profound and damning judgment for having turned

the redeeming lover of all men into a white, middle class burner of children and destroyer of the revolutions of the oppressed.[36]

And yet, his embrace of Black Power rhetoric was not unequivocal. In "The Religion of Black Power," published the following year, Harding gave voice to his ambivalence, his struggle to reconcile his commitment to nonviolent direct action with his recognition of the crucial contribution of Black Power.

The debates between civil rights and Black Power proponents, Harding argued, were fundamentally religious; although the religious character of the discussion was often "disguised," the ongoing conflict touched upon "issues of anthropology, incarnation, the nature of the universe and of God, issues of hope and faith, questions of eschatology and of the nature of the kingdom, problems concerning love and its functions"—that is, those "central issues of human life and destiny" addressed by religion.[37] Black Power, insisted Harding, was not *less* religious, only *differently* religious, than the earlier movement had been. In place of language of universal brotherhood and moral suasion, Black Power advocates stressed the need for love *within* the Black community as an antidote to ingrained self-hatred. The longing for community expressed by the Black Power movement, wrote Harding, had "deep religious moorings," previously expressed more than any other organization by the Nation of Islam in its persistent emphasis on building self-loving and self-sustaining Black communities.[38] Similarly, the language of Black Power drew upon the prophetic tradition of social justice and the condemnation of all systems of oppression.[39]

Most importantly, Harding saw the Black Power movement as the revival of a crucial, if submerged, theme in Black American religion: the promise of a Black messiah who would rise up "to deliver Black America from its bondage and White

America from its lethal folly."[40] He cited the Black Power activist and sociologist Nathan Hare's prediction of a "'Black Judgment Day around the corner' for America," and H. Rap Brown's demand that the nation "either 'straighten up' or face the fire of judgment" as intrinsically religious sentiments,[41] expressions of the "black Messianic hope" Malcolm X had brought up to the surface of contemporary Black thought.[42] The religion of Black Power, according to Harding, enshrined a millennial, messianic expectation. "Within the heart of Black Power stands the perennial tension between a salvation leading to swinging and singing and love, and a day of destruction demanded by a just God. Throughout the history of black American radicalism run the themes of repentance and atonement or judgment."[43]

Harding worried about the inherent volatility of this messianic vision, its incendiary nature. He was troubled over the loss of the central image of Christian nonviolence, that of the crucified Jesus, "the God who dies for his enemies, who rejects their terms and their weapons—and their kind of power," and questioned what, without that vision, would prevent the glorification of the same style of violent force utilized by those who oppressed the Black community.[44] What could, or would, set limits to the forces of Black judgment once they were sanctified and channeled into revolutionary struggle? Harding's concern was primarily moral: "For it may be that armed and marching black saints in Harlem are not likely to conceive of their task any differently than those who killed infidel Indians in New England, cut off unrepentant heads in old England, or now burn 'suspected' children in Vietnam. Is it given to black men any more than to whites to be self-commissioned executors of Divine judgment on evil-doers?"[45] He wondered if it were possible to distinguish the movement's valorization of "power" from the American obsession with weapons and might.[46] At the same time, he recognized and affirmed the insufficiency of continuing to pursue the same tactics when "even massive, disciplined nonviolent resistance will continue to meet increasingly violent (and/or sophisticated) repression."[47]

In the end, he asserted, "these two perspectives are badly in need of each other."[48] Harding described 1968 as a "joyously difficult time," diverse not only in political approaches but in the sacred powers brought to bear on the most important questions of life: "Allah and other gods of Africa enter into competition with Yahweh, Jesus, and Buddha … part of the affirmation of Black Power is 'We are a spiritual people.'"[49] In the chaotic clashes of ideologies and deities, new possibilities, new paths, new ways of being could emerge. Harding's own uncertainty about where the "religion of Black Power" would lead only reflected the mercurial—but alchemical—character of the moment. What it meant to be Black in America was changing rapidly, but it was not yet clear into *what* it was changing.

The Wrath to Come: James Baldwin in the Late 1960s and Early 1970s

As Harding made clear in "The Religion of Black Power," the proclamation of imminent divine judgment was a central theme in the statements of Black revolutionary movement leaders. Like Harding, these leaders often associated the contemporary shift to apocalyptic language with the Nation of Islam and Malcolm X. Perhaps the most vivid example of both of these points can be seen in the evolution of the work of the Black essayist and novelist James Baldwin. His powerful call for an honest response to American racism in *The Fire Next Time* (1963) had earned him acclaim and support from many in the literary world, but by the end of the decade, Baldwin had come to resent the role of "the Great Black Hope of the Great White Father" he felt he had been enlisted to play by the white establishment.[50] With the rise of the Black Power movement and following the assassinations of Black activists, including Malcolm X, Medgar Evers, Martin Luther King, and Lil Bobby Hutton, the language Baldwin used about power, love, struggle, and rage shifted dramatically. In *The Fire Next Time*, written during the height of the civil rights movement, Baldwin had eloquently described the power of love to "force our brothers [white Americans] to see themselves as they are, to cease fleeing from reality and begin to change it."[51] He had contrasted this vision of hope with the threat of "God's—or Allah's—vengeance" embodied in potential in Black separatist groups, especially the Nation of Islam.[52] However, by the time Baldwin wrote *No Name in the Street* (1972), he no longer believed in the same way that "the American state still contained within itself the power of self-confrontation, the power to change itself in the direction of honor and knowledge and freedom, or, as Malcolm put it, 'to atone.'"[53]

Baldwin's earlier work had always contained the threat of apocalyptic disaster—after all, the final words of *The Fire Next Time* (which give the volume its name) threaten divine retribution should the "relatively conscious blacks" and "relatively conscious whites" not join together to "end the racial nightmare."[54] And in his later period, Baldwin never completely abandoned hope in the promise of racial solidarity, justice, and communal healing. ("I really do believe in the New Jerusalem," he stated in an interview toward the end of his life. "I won't live to see it but I really do believe in it."[55]) Still, the shift in his overall emphasis in his writing in the late 1960s and early 1970s is striking.

What the Nation of Islam had represented in the early 1960s, Baldwin wrote in *No Name in the Street*, was "exactly what the Black Panthers" represented during the period in which he was writing.[56] Reflecting the changing mood of the time, he no longer described love as a sufficient force for overcoming power systems constructed to protect gains accrued through centuries of exploitation and oppression. "Political freedom is a matter of power and has nothing to do with morality."[57] Baldwin's hope for America's future had shifted from the promise of the repentant white conscience to the "energy" of the resisting non-white oppressed.[58]

> The excluded begin to realize, having endured everything, that they *can* endure everything. They do not know the precise shape of the future, but they know that the future belongs to them. They realize this—paradoxically—by the failure of the moral energy of their oppressors and begin, almost instinctively, to forge a new morality, to create the principles on which a new world will be built.[59]

This conclusion gave Baldwin no satisfaction. He still spoke of "helplessly lov[ing]" aspects of American civilization and desiring "to make the kingdom new, to make it honorable and worthy of life." It was "terrible to watch" white America refuse this offer of love. Terrible or not, however, the result was unavoidable: white Americans were "insist[ing] on their own destruction."[60] "An old world is dying, and a new one, kicking in the belly of its mother, time, announces that it is ready to be born … There will be bloody holding actions all over the world, for years to come: but the Western party is over, and the white man's sun has set. Period."[61]

In expressing his reluctant acceptance of the Black Power movement's vision of apocalyptic destruction and renewal, Baldwin turned to the biblical language of his Pentecostal youth. "I think black people have always felt this about America, and Americans," he wrote, "and have always seen, spinning above the thoughtless American head, the shape of the wrath to come."[62] More directly, a few years later, in "Where the Grapes of Wrath Are Stored," the third chapter of *The Devil Finds Work* (1976), he depicted the existential danger of America's unwillingness to grapple with its guilt in apocalyptic terms.[63]

The grapes of wrath are stored in the cotton fields and migrant shacks and ghettoes of this nation, and in the schools and prisons, and in the eyes and hearts and perceptions of the wretched everywhere, and in the ruined earth of Vietnam, and in the orphans and widows, and in the old men, seeing visions, and in the young men, dreaming dreams: these have already kissed the bloody cross and will not bow down before it again: and have forgotten nothing.[64]

Baldwin was consciously aware that in embracing this biblical language of divine judgment, he was drawing upon a long legacy of Black religious thought and practice. In *The Fire Next Time*, he had noted that the apocalyptic tenor of the Nation of Islam's and Malcolm X's pronouncements was "as familiar to [him] as [his] own skin,"[65] conveying a message "he had been hearing variations of" his entire life.[66] At the same time, Baldwin credited the Nation of Islam as responsible for the flourishing of this rhetoric and political vision. The question he posed in the early 1960s to his fellow Harlemites who had been won over by the Nation's preaching could have been posed just as well to him a decade later: "Why were they *hearing* it [assurance of God's condemnation of white people] now, since this was not the first time it had been said?"[67]

Baldwin's association of contemporary apocalyptic language with Malcolm X and the Nation of Islam is consistent with Black political and cultural thought more broadly speaking in the late 1960s and early 1970s: while many noted the historical importance of divine judgment in the Black American Christian tradition, many of these figures nevertheless associated the *current* use of this language specifically with Malcolm X and the Nation of Islam. The form this apocalyptic language took for Black Power advocates was specifically that of Malcolm X: Black judgment was God's judgment, embodied in the Black revolution. God was at work in the global, militant struggle of the non-white oppressed against their white oppressors.

"He Made Us Feel Holy": The Black Arts Movement

"Can you really imagine whole generations living and dying and never once having loved themselves?" the poet and activist Sonia Sanchez, one of the primary figures associated with the Black Arts Movement, asked rhetorically in a 1989 interview. "That's what we tried to change."[68] Born in Birmingham, Alabama, and raised in Harlem from the age of nine on, Sanchez had become involved in the civil rights movement through the New York branch of the Congress of Racial Equality (CORE) after attending the 1963 March on Washington for Jobs and Freedom—the occasion for Martin Luther King Jr.'s "I Have a Dream" speech.[69] During her time with New York CORE, Sanchez thought of the movement as primarily "necessary for the South."[70] This was not to say that Sanchez herself had not experienced racial discrimination in the North; a formative experience for her was having an offer of employment rescinded after the firm realized she was Black (an experience that left her so outraged that she, providentially, missed her subway stop and ended up wandering into the Schomburg Center for Research in Black Culture, where she read Zora Neale Hurston and other Black authors for the first time).[71] Despite her own "exceptional" status as a Black woman who had graduated from college and gone on to graduate school, she was aware of the "subtle segregation" that existed in New York City affecting, especially, access to housing and employment.[72] Still, she would have described herself, at this point, as a woman who "had most things that she really needed."[73]

It wasn't until she heard Malcolm X speak in person, at a rally co-sponsored by CORE, that she realized how deep, even in the

North, the need for liberation was for her people and for her personally. She began, surreptitiously, to attend Temple No. 7 in Harlem, where Malcolm was the minister and would preach. She vividly recalled his smile, and what it meant: "The smile said … 'I will protect you … I will love you above all' … We knew that man loved us." In that affectionate gesture, she saw him offer a promise to his young Black audience: "I will raise up … a generation, your generation, my generation that will begin to talk and preach truth in this country."[74] The word Sanchez used over and over again in her recollection of hearing Malcolm speak is "love": "we all loved him so very much."[75] Those who listened to him loved him for his honesty, for his brilliance, for his boldness. But most of all, she said, they loved that "he made us feel holy. And he made us feel whole. He made us feel loved, and he made us feel that we were worth something finally on this planet Earth. Finally, we had some worth."[76]

It was this realization—of her own beauty, her own infinite worth—that would be the animating force of her poetic contributions to the Black Arts Movement. It was also what brought her to the Nation of Islam. In *A Blues Book for Blue Black Magical Women* (1974), she extended an invitation to both Black men and women to join Elijah Muhammad and the Nation of Islam and to work together to build a Black Nation.[77] Her poetry from this period consciously plays with the Nation's theology, painting an apocalyptic vision of God sitting on a throne and judging the world.[78] Her exploration of the Nation's "mythologies" grew out of her awareness that her epiphany that she had worth as a Black woman was due to Malcolm, and, via Malcolm, the Nation. "He had been a vessel, but a lot of the information had come also through Elijah Muhammad in terms of his ideas."[79] As when she heard Malcolm X speak, she found in the Nation of Islam an uncompromising message of self-love: "you are a Black woman, and you are beautiful, and you are queen of the universe ... It was the greatest moral place for people who were trying to be correct, who were trying to be political, who were trying to be very much involved with their Blackness."[80]

Sanchez saw Malcolm X's and the Nation's message of Black self-love as the primary source of the new "Black aesthetic" of the late 1960s and early 1970s:[81]

> The turning of Black to beautiful was due to the theology of Elijah Muhammad's version of Islam which came into prominence in 1959. Black replaced white in that cosmology as the origin of good in the world and white replaced Black as the source of all evil. Thus Allah replaced Jesus or God, Black replaced Negro, self-sufficiency replaced dependency as the labels of reality. Through the charisma and intellect of Malcolm X and the overwhelming prophetic significance of the King movement, Black pride emerged as a social value on the lips of poets, in the lyrics of musicians, in the environmental trappings of Black life from hairdos to sandals, from jazz or Black classical music to Kwanzaa.[82]

The influence of the new "Black aesthetic" on the overall movement for Black liberation can be seen most explicitly in the influence of the movement of which Sanchez was a primary contributor, the Black Arts Movement.

The term "Black Arts Movement" describes what Lisa Gail Collins and Margo Natalie Crawford have termed "the art of Black Power,"[83] or, in the vision of the movement leader Larry Neal, "the aesthetic and spiritual sister of the Black Power concept."[84] Even among groups that eschewed or denigrated the identity-based Black nationalism associated with the Black Arts Movement (most notably, the explicitly internationalist and anti-nationalist Black Panther Party), it is important to recognize the shared milieu—including shared networks of relationships—out of which these different ideological strands emerged. Sanchez reflected on her time in San Francisco, the home of the Black Panther Party: "There was no division between the Black Panther Party, and the people at Black Studies, or [fellow Black Arts Movement pioneer, Amiri] Baraka or myself. We were all in the same area ... The division came somewhat later on."[85] The distinctions between the different groups involved in Black radical movements would become the source of violent conflicts (particularly between the cultural nationalist US Organization of Maulana Karenga and the Black Panthers), but the new "Black aesthetic" described by Sanchez was ubiquitous, a shared inheritance, as Sanchez noted, of the cosmology of the Nation of Islam, for which Blackness was sacred. The Nation's influence on the Black Arts Movement has too often been obscured, as Ammar Abduh Aqeeli has argued, in favor of a focus entirely on Malcolm X's Black nationalist rhetoric.[86] Sanchez's description of the shifting cultural sands of this period make it possible to understand the Black revolutionary movements of the late 1960s and early 1970s as, in Sanchez's words, "God-conscious activism," to the same degree as the civil rights movement has often been understood as an expression of religious faith.[87]

While the Nation's cosmology was a starting point, it was not, as Harding also intimated, an ending point; the Nation of Islam, via Malcolm X, opened the floodgates of a much broader imaginative world of sacral, revolutionary Blackness, incorporating diverse spiritual traditions of non-white peoples from around the globe and diverse political visions. Sanchez wrote of this generative, fecund period:

> And these brothers and sisters, their eyes opening like crystals, worked in America and the world, told us to take God out of the sky and put God in our hearts ... We heard the sacred in all of their handprints and footprints as they

reset the identity of African Americans and of people of color on the world stage from tragedy to the heroic celebration of themselves and their people … These poet-visionaries turned the river of memory and made the river turn black. Black. Black. Human. Human. Human. These poets were a *Cante jondo*, a deep song of Africa. The Caribbean. The Americas. India. The Middle East.[88]

Sanchez's telling of the story of the Black Arts Movement and the Black radical movements of this period aligns with the vision of Black religion defined by William David Hart in *Black Religion: Malcolm X, Julius Lester, and Jan Willis* (2008) as "Afro-Eccentric," a term Hart himself coined (a play, of course, on "Afrocentric"). An "Afro-Eccentric" view of Black religion counters what Hart describes as the "Standard Narrative of Black Religion" in which "the black Protestant church" is viewed as the normative form of Black religion,[89] and all other expressions of Black religiosity are viewed as deviant and "culturally suspect."[90] Hart emphasizes the "cosmographic creativity, spiritual restlessness, pilgrimage, and radical transformation" characteristic of Black religion, originating in the intercultural, global, pluralistic nature of African diaspora experience emerging from the "violent intercultural encounter" of slavery.[91] The tendency of commentators to portray the civil rights movement as religious and the Black Power movement as secular may derive, in part, from an unreadiness to recognize religiosity or spirituality outside of the "Standard Narrative of Black Religion." Sanchez's narration of her own history in the movement, however, radically challenges this view.

Her fellow leaders in the Black Arts Movement characterized their work in similar terms. The source of Black art, claimed the poet and playwright LeRoi Jones (Amiri Baraka) in a 1968 interview, was Islam. Art aims "to reveal, to manifest Divinity that man can understand, to make marks, to make symbols, to make signs, to make sounds, to make images that reveal Divinity, that reveal the presence of the One Force that animates everything."[92] It was Malcolm X who had led Baraka to see in Islam "a vehicle for the expression of truth on many levels about man, Black man, spiritual man's subjugation by anti-spiritual forces."[93] But, as in Sanchez's telling, this introduction to Islam was only the beginning of an opening to diverse spiritual visions of Blackness: Baraka began to explore West African, Yoruba religious practice around the same time he was delving into the mythologies of the Nation of Islam for artistic inspiration.[94] Larry Neal, in his seminal essay "The Black Arts Movement" (1968), used Baraka's play *Black Mass* (1966), which dramatized the Nation of Islam's story of Yacub and the creation of the white devil, as an example of how the movement recognized that "ethics and aesthetics must interact positively and be consistent with the demands for a more spiritual world."[95] *Black Mass*, according to Neal, was Baraka's "most important play mainly because it is informed by a mythology that is wholly the creation of the Afro-American sensibility."[96] This was an expression of what Neal called the "New Spirituality," which views "the world from the concise point of view of the colonialized."[97] This New Spirituality was intentionally and conspicuously pluralistic, as in Carolyn M. Rodgers's essay "Black Poetry—Where It's At" (1969), in which "the spiritual wisdom of our Egyptian/African forefathers," "NOMMO, JU-JU and the collective force of the positive spirits, moving in time with the universe," astrological signs, and "the love and spirit of the ancestors" are summoned as animating forces for Black poetry while Rodgers also proclaimed, "all praise is due ALLAH."[98]

Jesus, the Black Messiah?

In the midst of this exuberantly pluralistic spiritual renaissance, one religious tradition was often conspicuously absent: Christianity, the majority religion of Black Americans. This was not an oversight. "It seems," reflected Baraka, "that at this point Christianity has become a vehicle for the degenerate—it tends to cover truth rather than reveal it."[99] For the most part, the Black revolutionary spirituality of this period replicated the Nation of Islam's portrayal of Christianity as the religion of "Slavery—Suffering—Death."[100] Baraka could, however, think of one exception: "there are some Christian ministers who are moving to cut the layer of falsehood away from Christianity, like Reverend Cleage in Detroit, who begins talking about the Black Madonna and the Blackness of Jesus and trying to put Jesus into the right succession of prophets and identifying Jesus as merely one of the many prophets. And this is giving an Islamic temper to Christianity."[101] Reverend Albert B. Cleage Jr. (later Jaramogi Abebe Agyeman), the minister of the Shrine of the Black Madonna, formerly Central Congregational Church, on Twelfth Street in Detroit, was fully aware of the power of the new "Black aesthetic" and its origins in the Nation's mythology. Cleage's innovation of a novel religious framework, Black Christian Nationalism, consciously aimed to harness the power of what Harding termed the "religion of Black Power" to transform the church, and, through the church, the fate of all people of African descent. In the following three chapters, we will meet Cleage and the movement he set in motion: Black liberation theology.

4

The Rage of the Powerless

Reverend Albert Cleage and the Shrine of the Black Madonna

Rebellion: Detroit 1967

On March 26, 1967, Easter Sunday, an eighteen-foot-high mural of the Black Madonna was publicly unveiled at Central United Church of Christ in Detroit, Michigan,[1] replacing the stained-glass image of Pilgrims landing at Plymouth Rock that previously had been the focal point of the church's sanctuary.[2] The mural was painted by a local artist and activist, Glanton Dowdell, who had learned to paint while incarcerated in Jackson State Prison.[3] Based on the model of a young Black mother, Rose Waldon,[4] the painting was an expression of Dowdell's profound love for his community: "This is me," he said. "I can't divorce the Madonna from black women. I don't think that any of the experiences of the Madonna were more poignant or dramatic than those of any Negro mother, an ADC [Aid to Dependent Children] mother, a mother whose child goes wrong, anyone."[5]

For the church's minister, Rev. Albert B. Cleage Jr.,[6] the replacement of the image of the arriving white Pilgrims with the unapologetically Black faces of Mary and Jesus was a crucial component of the vision he had for the community he pastored. Following his lead, the painting had been commissioned

by the church's Heritage Committee as part of their commitment to "recapturing the glorious heritage of Black people."[7]
Later that year, Cleage was still in awe at the image and what
it represented for the congregation. "Instead of a sermon," he
reflected, "we could just sit here and look at the chancel mural
of the Black Madonna which we unveiled on Easter Sunday, and
marvel that we have come so far that we can conceive of the Son
of God being born of a black woman ... Our unveiling of the
Black Madonna is a statement of faith."[8] It had been the public
reveal of the mural, after all, that had served as the occasion for
Cleage's announcement of the launching of a new movement:
the Black Christian Nationalist movement.[9]

In informational materials about the Black Madonna mural,
the church explained the necessity of this initiative:

> For nearly 500 years the illusion that Christ was white
> dominated the world because Europeans dominated the
> world. But now, with the emergence of the nationalist
> movements of the world's colored majority, the historic
> truth is finally beginning to emerge—that Jesus was the
> non-white leader of a non-white people struggling for
> national liberation against the rule of a white nation,
> Rome ... The widespread repudiation by many black
> Americans of a white Christ has added to the attractive-
> ness of the Black Muslim movement. But many more
> black Americans, race-conscious enough to reject a white
> Christ, have been reluctant to embrace Islam ... The
> result has been the self-exclusion of most black militants
> from any religious affiliations whatsoever ... Rev. Albert
> B. Cleage, Jr., pastor of Central United Church of Christ
> and founder of the Black Christian Nationalist Move-
> ment, has been able to give new life and meaning to the
> Gospels and to the Christian calendar in light of Jesus'

role as a leader of a non-white people fighting for national liberation.[10]

Cleage, like many others during this period, had grown disillusioned with Christian integrationist leaders and the tactics of major civil rights movement organizations in the second half of the 1960s. Like these dissidents, Cleage had become increasingly attracted to the fiery rhetoric of the late Malcolm X and the Nation of Islam. Cleage heard in Malcolm's words something that he did not hear in King's: attentiveness to the "particular problems" of each particular audience, rather than repeating "the same speeches ... delivered a hundred times to Black people in a hundred different cities."[11] Malcolm's message spoke to the persistence of dehumanizing conditions and racially based disparities faced by these communities in a way that King's, he felt, did not. He gave voice to the anger over the intractability of racial injustice in the North that, in the later 1960s, was increasingly expressed in periodic eruptions of civil unrest: riots or rebellions, depending on one's point of view.

This was the background of the July 1967 Detroit uprising, or riots, which would propel Cleage into the national spotlight. Similar to the Watts rebellion and other examples of urban civil unrest in the mid- and late-1960s, the immediate cause was an incident of police harassment—in this case, a police raid on an unlicensed bar[12]—but the Black community of Detroit understood the true cause of the uprising, in the words of scholars Joe T. Darden and Richard W. Thomas, to be "white institutional racism in the form of urban renewal, expressways, and white suburban resistance."[13] By the end of the Detroit uprising, thirty-three Black people and ten white people had been killed, and thousands of Black residents of Detroit were displaced from their homes.[14] Police officers' actions during the period of unrest had confirmed the opinion of many within the Black community that the police served the role of an "occupying army" in Black neighborhoods,[15] especially as reports surfaced of "the execution-like slaying" of three Black teenagers in the Algiers Motel by members of the Detroit police.[16]

Only four months after Cleage had announced the launching of the Black Christian Nationalist movement in front of the mural of the Black Madonna, his church drew in unprecedented numbers of people inspired by the uprising. "More people joined the church in the months that followed the rebellion than in its entire fourteen year history," explained Alta Harrison (Fundi Difie) in a written history of the congregation. "Militants and cultural nationalists flocked to the church seeking direction during this turbulent period as there were few if any Black churches that held their doors open to this faction of the Black community."[17] It was during this time, wrote Harrison, that the name of the church was unofficially changed (the change would be made official in 1970) to the Shrine of the Black Madonna.[18]

Cleage had been an active leader among networks of radical Black activists and thinkers in Detroit for the entire 1960s,[19] and had been chastised by members of the Metropolitan Detroit Association of Congregational Churches earlier in the decade for his association with Malcolm X,[20] whom Cleage had invited to Detroit to give one of his most famous speeches, "Message to the Grass Roots," in 1963.[21] Malcolm X had drawn a stark contrast in his talk between what he characterized as the typical fare of Christian preachers, teaching "you and me, just like [with] novocaine, to suffer peacefully," and the revolutionary stance of his host: "As Rev. Cleage pointed out, they say you should let your blood flow in the streets. This is a shame. You know he's a Christian preacher. If it's a shame to him, you know what it is to me."[22] Still, it was the Detroit uprising, and his role in providing a spiritual home for those who seethed with the anger of the rioters, that cemented Cleage's role as the leader of Black militants in Detroit.

Edward Vaughn, the chairman of the Shrine of the Black Madonna's Heritage Committee, described the church's role during the uprising in detail in a document written by hand in 1968:

> Since the Detroit Rebellion of July 23, 1967, the Nation [the Black Christian Nationalist movement of the Shrine of the Black Madonna] has grown by leaps and bounds. The rebellion made us aware that in a time of crisis the Man will resort to the most bestial methods of repression. Black people suffered at the hands of the Detroit police, state police and National Guard troops. However, this brutality made us determined more than ever that Black people must be free—and we will. During the rebellion the Nation immediately set up a food distribution point for all Black people. We were one of the first churches in Detroit, Black or white, to do so. We helped our people find new homes as well as find friends and relatives lost during the struggle. Our church was offered and used for the funeral of a brave little Black girl, Tanya Blanding, age 4, who was murdered by trigger happy National Guard troops. After the rebellion we offered our church for a people's tribunal called by the Citywide Citizens' Action Committee to properly try police officers and National Guard troops who brutally executed several young Black men in the Algiers Motel during the rebellion. In spite of threats of every discription [*sic*] we had to do God's will— we had to do the things that the Black Messiah taught us. That is, bring the Black Nation together.[23]

The church's crucial role in responding to the rebellion led the community to expand its commitment to the principles of the Black Christian Nationalist movement first proclaimed by Cleage earlier that year. "On Sunday Nov. 19, 1967," Vaughn wrote, "a meeting of the entire Church Body was held to

consider plans for expansion ... The Body unanimously agreed
to establish the Black Nation in every corner of the globe where
Black people live."[24]

The leadership of the church during the city's unrest also
brought Cleage into the national spotlight; in 1968, Vincent
Harding described the Shrine of the Black Madonna as probably having "attracted more persons committed to Black Power
than any other single institution still connected to the Christian churches."[25] The latter part of the sentence is a substan-
tial caveat, given the fact that, as Harding noted, a connection
between religion and Black Power was typically not associated
with Christianity, but instead with the Nation of Islam, "the
best known indication of power inherent in this direction."[26]
As Cleage's first biographer, Hiley Ward, pointed out, writing
in the same year as Harding, "much of black nationalism has
been expressed in the Black Muslim movement for the past fifty
years."[27] His ideas, Ward opined, "could be the seeds of a major
new black Christian grouping or denomination to replace the
somewhat foreign Black Muslim influence among US militant
religious-minded blacks."[28]

The fact that Cleage's movement shared much with the
theology and program of the Nation of Islam was the result
of a gradual religious and political development. Cleage's origins were rooted firmly in the middle-class Black community
of Detroit; his father was the first Black doctor appointed as
the city physician, and a prominent member of the Black community.[29] Albert Cleage Jr.'s first political awakening occurred
as a young man, influenced by politically active Black clergy
in the city, especially Father Malcolm Dade, Reverend Charles
A. Hill, and Reverend Horace A. White.[30] In an interview with
Ward, Louis E. Martin, an active participant in the community's political struggles who knew the Cleages, claimed that
the young Albert Cleage diverged from his family as a young

man in his affinity for Rev. White's radical commitments and involvement in labor organizing: "The young boy, however, took interest. Horace [White] was radical as any—very radical it was then to champion the CIO."[31] In the mid-1940s, Cleage accepted a call to preach at Howard Thurman's interracial congregation in San Francisco, the Fellowship of All Peoples, an experience that Ward notes Cleage did not remember "with any fondness."[32] It confirmed him in his belief that an "interracial church is a monstrosity and an impossibility."[33] While there, he began to join in with the NAACP in campaigns against racial injustice.[34] After spending time in Los Angeles and a period accepting a call to preach in Massachusetts, Cleage returned to Detroit in 1950. Beginning in this period, Cleage increasingly identified himself with Black nationalist movements and radical Black thinkers.[35]

Throughout his decades-long career as a spiritual leader and community organizer in Detroit, Cleage played many roles, under many institutional names: Central Congregational Church, the Black Christian Nationalist movement, the Shrine of the Black Madonna, the Pan-African Orthodox Christian Church (PAOCC). In the words of historian Peniel E. Joseph, Cleage served as "the Pied Piper of the city's scoundrels—an assorted collection of militant youth, veteran activists, and the simply disgruntled."[36] Yet, he effectively organized this motley crew into political coalitions, mobilizing diverse groups of people in sometimes successful campaigns, to give some examples, against racially targeted school redistricting, urban renewal, and police brutality.[37] Through the Shrine of the Black Madonna, Cleage formed a political lobbying organization, the Black Slate, which was ultimately instrumental in electing a Black mayor of Detroit, Coleman A. Young.[38] He also founded a number of Black- and community-owned cooperatives, including a food market, housing co-op, a clothing and goods store, and, just a year before his death in 2000, a farm called Beulah Land.[39]

Despite the Nation of Islam's very public and unequivocal condemnation of Christianity, Cleage, a Christian pastor, turned to the Nation more than any other religious community as a source of inspiration.[40] In conversation with Ward, Cleage asserted that in the late 1960s, the "only organization seriously moving in the right direction is the Black Muslim Movement headed by Elijah Mohammed [*sic*]."[41] Cleage collaborated with representatives of the Nation of Islam in Detroit and elsewhere, for instance inviting Wilfred X, the minister of the Nation's Mosque #1 and Malcolm X's brother, to speak at the Shrine of the Black Madonna in support of the Freedom Now Party Cleage had co-founded,[42] and distributing food from a Nation of Islam farm in Michigan through the Black Christian Nationalist movement's co-op store.[43] In the public consciousness, Cleage was associated with the Nation of Islam and other non-Christian Black nationalists. A 1971 poem by Sonia Sanchez, for instance, described a new start for Black men patterned after Cleage and leaders in the Nation of Islam; she named Rev. Cleage alongside Louis Farrakhan and Elijah Muhammad as exemplars.[44] In some cases, Cleage had to explain that he was not associated with the Nation of Islam and was in fact a Christian; as an example, he was asked on a television appearance on *Tony Brown's Journal* in 1972 "if there is no difference between your organization and that of the Honorable Elijah Muhammad, why don't you join forces?"[45] For Cleage, the answer was simple: he was a Christian. And the message and program of the Nation of Islam, he asserted, could never reach the majority of Black Americans who, like him, were overwhelmingly "Christian in background."[46]

In a period of incendiary fury and rebellion, Cleage's embrace of rhetoric typically associated with the Nation of Islam earned him a place in the growing movement of radical Black dissidents. In a poem by another major figure of the Black Arts Movement, Nikki Giovanni describes the Shrine's mural of the Black Madonna as a symbol of Black resistance.[47] In another of her poems, "Reflections on April 4, 1968," the Black Madonna returns to wrestle with the god of white power, Zeus, as the poet rages over the murder of Martin Luther King Jr.[48] Sanchez, who recited her poetry at Detroit's Shrine of the Black Madonna for a Women's Day event in the early 1970s,[49] was also inspired by the power of the Black Madonna to shift Black women's perception of themselves: "You began to have in the churches, at the Shrines of the Black Madonnas … [a] Black Jesus Christ up there … People began to put up Black Marys and, and Black, you know, all of these things … And so, people said, Hold it. If they worship Black women, how have we become to be people who are not, women who are not worshipped and who are damned?"[50] But even as his message reached the increasing numbers of self-described revolutionaries and militants ascendent in the Black struggle for freedom, Cleage's growing visibility within the Black Power movement also had the effect of pushing him to the margins of the Christian community. In 1968, the Baptist Ministers' Conference held a press conference "denouncing Cleage's philosophy as 'the foolishness of separation.'"[51] Still, Cleage's hope for a version of Christianity remade in Malcolm's image was not entirely disappointed. For committed Black Christians who desired to remain in solidarity with the growing Black Power movement, Cleage and the Shrine of the Black Madonna led the way.

Cleage "has never received the recognition due to him" by academic theologians, argues Charles Lattimore Howard.[52] Despite Cleage's prominent role in the Black Power and Black Arts movements and the fact that there is every justification to identify Cleage as the founder of Black liberation theology, his role is often obscured. This is partially, Howard suggests, the result of scholars' discomfort with viewing Black liberation theology as a social movement rather than primarily an academic one.[53] Cleage had little interest in the academic study of religion and theology. He saw other early Black liberation theologians as generally engaging in irrelevant scholastic arguments of no real import for the Black liberation struggle,[54] although he expressed admiration for the subject of the following chapter, James Cone.[55] Howard asserts that reclaiming the example of Cleage would remind us of the important fact that Black liberation theology, in its beginnings, was "clearly connected to the liberating work that was happening right outside the classroom in streets."[56] Recent scholarship, particularly by the theologian Jawanza Eric Clark, the scholar of religious rhetoric Earle J. Fisher, and the political historian Angela D. Dillard, has illuminated Cleage's role in the formation of Black liberation theology.[57] Recovering Cleage's legacy enables us to view the emergence of Black liberation theology in its original context, which is to say, by way of the Detroit uprising. In Cleage's community's "strange fearlessness" during and following the unrest,[58] Cleage saw a movement of the Holy Spirit, a new possibility emerging for what it meant to be Black and Christian. It was, he wrote, "the most important thing that has ever happened in America."[59] In the midst of revolution, Cleage made his own Malcolm X's message of God's judgment incarnate in Black revolution. But for Cleage, that divine rebellion would mobilize under the banner of Jesus, the Black Messiah.

Rage, Anger, Hatred, Commitment: Cleage's Christian Theology of Revolution

For Cleage, Malcolm X was, like Jesus, a "savior" of Black people.[60] It was Malcolm, more than anyone else, thought Cleage, who had made a Black Christian Nationalist movement possible:

Brother Malcolm's message offered the only basis for salvation for black people. To identify an enemy, to understand him, to realize that he is violent and to recognize the fact that we are engaged in a power struggle—this was Brother Malcolm's message ... That's why this Church, The Shrine of the Black Madonna, is building a Nation, because we believe in Black Power. We are trying to organize for power ... We believe in it, and we believe that this was the message of Jesus as well as Brother Malcolm. That's why there is no inner conflict when we have a memorial for Brother Malcolm in a Christian Church which is dedicated to rebuilding the Nation of the Black Messiah.[61]

Cleage noted with admiration that the philosophy of Malcolm X was not static, as "he was able to adjust his analysis to fit new realities."[62] But Cleage was similarly inspired by the fundamental pivot on which Malcolm's thought turned: his faith in the awakening of his people to their own "humanity, to their own worth."[63]

This vantage point, borrowed from Malcolm X, empowered Cleage to plunge deep into the Black Christian tradition, bringing to the surface biblical texts and themes that had been submerged under language of reconciliation and universal brotherhood. Inherent in the traditional preaching of Black Christian clergy, Cleage declared, "was the faith that God must eventually shake white people over hell-fire ... White people were the oppressors. They were the sinners, they were guilty."[64] God required their repentance, and until then, God moved in the Black Nation to reclaim what had been stolen. "The Holy Spirit," he wrote, "gives us a sense of identification with the rage of suffering oppressed people everywhere ... It is rage, anger, hatred, commitment. It is divine discontent. It is the mystery of a magic moment when we are touched by a power which we cannot understand."[65] For Cleage, Malcolm X provided the missing key for understanding Black faith, rooted essentially in the Hebrew Bible and its story of a chosen people surviving and resisting its oppressors.

Cleage explained to his congregation that Black religion in the United States "is essentially based on the Old Testament concepts of the Nation Israel, God's chosen people, and our knowledge that the problems of the black Israelites were the same as ours. When we read the Old Testament, we can identify with a black people who were guided and loved by God."[66] This love for them meant that, in a real sense, God must be *against* their oppressors. Preaching on a text in the book of the prophet Jeremiah in which God promises the destruction of the Temple and the nation as a result of the people's injustice, Cleage inveighed: "All men in the sight of God have a right to dignity, and when somebody decides that he is going to build a civilization, a world, and deny black men the right to dignity, then God is going to act to destroy that very civilization and that very nation."[67] However, Cleage did not argue that God would intervene in history in the form of a *deus ex machina*. "People who are constantly waiting for divine intervention," he said, "find it very difficult to develop and keep leadership because leadership depends upon people who are expecting to do something for themselves."[68] Rather, he saw God as empowering the Black Nation in its building of communal power in order to liberate itself from oppression.

For Cleage, the life of Jesus of Nazareth was in absolute continuity with the Hebrew Bible's description of the struggle against oppression. Cleage preached the gospel of a revolutionary Black messiah, Jesus, who fought the white Roman Empire in order to resurrect the Black Nation. Cleage was unmoved by those who insisted that Christian theology required universal love and brotherhood of all people without respect to the imbalance of power between oppressor and oppressed. "When there is justice there can be love, peace and brotherhood," he declared in a sermon. "Only the oppressor can afford to talk about the preservation of law and order without justice."[69]

Cleage's language consciously echoed the Nation of Islam's theology of the white devil and Malcolm's vision of God's judgment borne out in global struggle against the white oppressor. Cleage was well aware that the imminent destruction of white supremacy, or, in the words of Malcolm X, "the end of time for the Western world, the European world, the Christian world, the white world," was the hinge upon which the Nation of Islam's theology turned.[70] Much of Cleage's public actions and speeches echoed Malcolm's theology of revolution, placed in a Christian context. The Black Nationalist Creed, adopted by Cleage's church in 1969,[71] is characteristic:

I Believe that human society stands under the judgment of one God, revealed to all, and known by many names. His creative power is visible in the mysteries of the universe, in the revolutionary Holy Spirit which will not long permit men to endure injustice nor to wear the shackles of bondage, in the rage of the powerless when they struggle to be free, and in the violence and conflict which even now threaten to level the hills and the mountains.

I Believe that Jesus, the Black Messiah, was a revolutionary leader, sent by God to rebuild the Black Nation Israel and to liberate Black people from powerlessness and from oppression, brutality, and exploitation of the white gentile world.

I Believe that the revolutionary spirit of God, embodied in the Black Messiah, is born anew in each generation and that Black Christian Nationalists constitute the living remnant of God's Chosen People in this day, and are charged by Him with responsibility for the Liberation of Black people.[72]

Cleage envisioned the Black Madonna as a companion image to that of the Black Messiah, the bearer of God's liberating judgment. He told his congregation that he wanted to commission two paintings of Christ to flank the painting of his mother: one of a Black Christ being crucified by his "white Gentile oppressors," the Romans, and another of Jesus as a "powerful black man" driving the money changers out of the Temple.[73]

God's Covenant People: Divine Blackness

Cleage's fundamental conviction was the same as Malcolm's: "nothing is more sacred than the liberation of black people." The latter quote was the title of an unpublished manuscript written by Cleage in the first years of the 1970s, much of which later was developed into his second book, *Black Christian Nationalism: New Directions for the Black Church* (1972). The same phrase was incorporated into the BCN (Black Christian Nationalist) Covenant, recited by members upon initiation into Cleage's religious movement.[74] In Cleage's teaching, ensuring the survival of Black people and the empowerment of the Black community took precedence over any other principle. "There is only one authority for a Black man," he wrote, "and that is the Black experience as it is influenced by the never-ending Black Liberation Struggle."[75]

On the one hand, as Jawanza Eric Clark has argued, the centrality of Blackness in Cleage's theology opened up possibilities of entirely new sources for Christian thought and practice, drawing upon West African and Black American history and culture.[76] But, on the other hand, Cleage's version of Black liberation theology remained firmly rooted in the Bible even as it diverged radically from normative Christian beliefs and prac-

tices. The Articles of Association for the Pan-African Orthodox
Christian Church (PAOCC), the ecclesiastical structure adopted
by the Black Christian Nationalist movement in 1978, begin
not with a statement about the Afro-centric commitments of
the organization but rather with the typical Protestant assertion, "We accept the Holy Bible as sufficient rule of faith and
practice."[77] Cleage defended this statement in a September 1978
sermon: "The Pan-African Orthodox Christian Church accepts
the Holy Bible as sufficient rule of faith and practice when interpreted by the Church with the guidance of the Holy Spirit ...
The Church teaches that the Bible is a history of God's relationship with the African Nation Israel and the Black Messiah
Jesus."[78] According to Cleage, what distinguished his church
from mainstream Black Christianity was this understanding of
the Bible as "a history of Black people."[79]

Cleage had learned from the Nation and from Malcolm
himself how ennobling and powerful the idea of divine Blackness—of Black people as God's holy, chosen people—could be,
especially when grounded in religious language and commitment. In a 1977 Christmas sermon, Cleage noted that when
Elijah Muhammad "started telling Black people they had a
history ... nobody else was saying it. When he said, 'You can
change. You do not have to stay a slave.' Nobody else was saying it."[80] And so, Cleage preached the Bible as the heritage of a
covenant people, whose God would always fight with them to
defeat their oppressors.

> Out of the whole world God chose Israel to covenant with,
> to say, "You will be my people and I will be your God."
> What else does a man need for dignity? He didn't go to
> the big nations with their big armies. He went to this little
> nation and said, "You are my chosen people." Perhaps if
> we could just remember that we are God's chosen people,

that we have a covenant with God, then we would know that God will not forsake us. Even in the midst of violence and oppression, we would know that we are God's chosen people. We could look the white man straight in the eye and say, "There is nothing you can do to destroy us, and you cannot take from us our dignity."[81]

It was this faith in the sacred identity of Black people, according to Cleage, that allowed Nat Turner to lead his rebellion against his enslavers, knowing that "when you fight you must believe that you are doing the will of God."[82] God's election of the Black Nation means that Black people are never alone in their efforts to liberate themselves. Far from it: "the struggle in which we are engaged is a cosmic struggle … the very universe struggles with us when we fight to throw off the oppression of white people."[83]

The main character of Cleage's religious universe was the Black community. While much of the early coverage of Cleage revolved around his insistence on the literal Blackness of Jesus,[84] Jesus himself was not viewed as uniquely divine by Cleage: God was only "incarnate in Jesus as God can be incarnate in anyone of you. It means God possessed him."[85] At the same time, the sacred identity of the *Black community* as potentially an embodiment of the revolutionary Holy Spirit was central to Cleage's thought, and this served as the foundation of Cleage's portrayal of Black people as the chosen people. In encountering the power of God in "Pentecostal experience," contact with God's Holy Spirit, "the church becomes the incarnation of God."[86] Because the community has met God, it can create radical change for the world: "We believe we've got power, because we believe that we're the incarnation of God—we are the Messianic Hope for the Twentieth Century."[87] For Cleage, the Holy Spirit was "the revolutionary power which comes to an exploited people as they struggle to escape from powerlessness and to end the institutional oppression forced upon them by an enemy."[88] Becoming the incarnation of God, then, meant entering into conflict, going into battle against the enemies of God's chosen people.

Cleage's assertion of a radical continuity between the beleaguered Black nation of ancient Israel (which, he said, represented "a mixture of Chaldeans, Egyptians, Midianites, Ethiopians, Kushites, Babylonians and other dark peoples, all of whom were already mixed with the black people of Central Africa")[89] and contemporary Black Americans led to an uncompromising emphasis on the Hebrew Bible as the primary source of knowledge of God's work in the world and as a guide for action. Cleage recognized that it was commonplace among Christian scholars and preachers to assert that "the 'authority of the Old Testament' is much less than the 'authority of the New Testament,'"[90] but he argued passionately that the goal of the church should be to "rediscover the historic roots of Christianity and strip from them the mystical distortions that are not basic to the concept of nation as revealed in the Old Testament and in the revolutionary teachings of Jesus."[91] For the purpose of inspiring revolutionary action, claimed Cleage, "the Old Testament is a Black-power document which no modern book can equal."[92]

In the books of the Hebrew Bible, Cleage saw conflict on every page: conflict between God's chosen nation and the oppressors who threatened its existence. Like Malcolm X, Cleage read the Bible anti-imperialistically, as a chronicle of the struggles of a colonized people against its colonizers. Cleage described the Bible as a series of historical events in which the Black Nation struggled for its freedom, focusing especially on Exodus, the Babylonian exile, the Maccabean revolt (notably, as the Books of the Maccabees are not usually included in Protestant editions of the Bible), and Jesus's life and death at the hands of the Roman Empire. These examples of biblical oppression and resistance, for Cleage, were the necessary key to understanding the signifi-cance of Jesus's mission: "We can understand Jesus more fully," he claimed, "by looking at Moses and the Maccabees than by looking at the Apostle Paul with his pagan concept of blood redemption."[93]

Rituals and educational materials used by the Black Christian Nationalist movement reinforce a strong connection between biblical characters struggling against oppressive domination and contemporary Black people. Notably, the PAOCC's self-defense force, likely patterned after the Nation's Fruit of Islam, is known as the Holy Order of the Maccabees, named after the priestly revolutionary family that led a successful rebellion against the Seleucid Empire's control of Palestine in the second century BCE.[94] Multiple funeral programs for deceased mem-bers of the Holy Order of the Maccabees include excerpts from the Books of the Maccabees describing the revolutionaries' "burning fervor for the Law" (1 Maccabees 2:50).[95] A ritual for the initiation of adult members into Advanced Training Groups contains a recitation of a list of biblical heroes in whom the "Revolutionary Power of God" was at work: Moses, Deborah, the Maccabees, and Jesus, "the Revolutionary Black Messiah." Immediately after making reference to these biblical figures, the names of African and Black American freedom fighters follow.[96] Similarly, in a Bible study workbook produced for the PAOCC's Alkebu-lan Academy for youth, the story of the Exodus is re-told over the course of eleven lessons geared toward portray-ing contemporary Black Americans as modern-day Israelites. The first lesson, after describing the unjust conditions experi-enced by the Israelites under Pharaoh, then asks, "What group of people today still live in oppressive conditions but do not realize the powerlessness they experience?" An answer is given in a child's handwriting in the copy of this workbook possessed by the Bentley Historical Library: "Black people."[97]

In Shelley McIntosh's account of developing an educational program for the children of Mtoto House, the residence in which children of the Shrine of the Black Madonna community were communally raised for two decades,[98] she describes how ritual and group meditation instilled in the children a sense of radical affinity with the covenantal community of the Bible. In a group devotional detailed by McIntosh, biblical themes are combined with Afro-centric terminology and meditation practices familiar to Buddhist and Hindu traditions in order to instill a communal spiritual experience of the presence of God among Black children as a community. A breathing meditation was followed by the Black Christian Nationalist movement's affirmations of faith expressed in call-and-response form:

Call: Like every child growing up in the Black Nation Israel, Jesus was taught the Covenant, the Law, and the Prophets.

Response: Like Jesus, we accept the Covenant, the Law, and the Prophets as the revelations of God, binding upon His Chosen People ...

Call: The Quest. Jesus sought the experience of God when he left Nazareth and walked the dangerous Jericho Road to Jerusalem to be baptized in the Jordan River where he heard the voice of God declare him to be the Messiah, and a dove lighting upon his shoulder symbolized the fact that he had received the Holy Spirit.

Response: Like Jesus, we too, seek the experience of God. Kutafuta, Kutamungu, Kugasana, Kujitoa.[99] We seek the experience of God.[100]

This spiritually eclectic meditation is characteristic of the PAOCC's approach from the mid-1970s onward, in which

deeper mystical experience in the pursuit of forming community was understood as the primary source of revolutionary
challenge to white power.

Cleage in particular emphasized instances in the Bible in
which the people's actual involvement in militancy was required
for the people's survival. He insisted that God would not intervene without human beings taking the initiative to throw off
their own oppressors. "I prefer to believe that God is not on
the side of evil," he wrote, "but is waiting for Black people to
get enough common sense to do what has to be done for themselves. In the Old Testament God helped the Black Nation Israel
fight for dignity, manhood, and nationhood."[101] At the same
time, the covenant people had to maintain hope in God's coming intervention against evil and injustice. "The hope of revolutionary change is tied to the mystical faith in the intervention of
God."[102] Cleage credited Elijah Muhammad's apocalyptic language with providing a necessary first step in the development
of a radical movement for Black liberation.[103] Cleage portrayed
his own thought as advancing beyond Muhammad's and Malcolm's, moving beyond the apocalyptic struggle between ultimate good and ultimate evil to a recognition of a power struggle
between human groups.[104]

Still, apocalypticism, the proclamation of a cosmic struggle
against a "satanic world," was fundamental to Cleage's message.
"If we are to do the will of God," he said, "we must somehow
break free of this evil satanic world and seek to do the will of
God and be recreated by God[,] by the church which God has
created upon earth."[105] In his poem "The Baptism of Fire," dis-
tributed in a BCN pamphlet in 1984, he wrote about the need
for a complete transformation of the world's corruption that
would begin with the community's direct, mystical encounter
with God.[106] Cleage's words echoed with Malcolm's insight:
that the cosmic struggle between the chosen, covenant people

of God and the forces of evil depended on human action and human struggle. Cleage longed and labored to make a spiritual home in which isolated, disempowered individuals could be brought together into a community capable of performing this divine task. As described by Bible study materials produced for the Shrine of the Black Madonna in 1976, the goal of seeking the experience of God's presence together in order to transform the world is the foundation of the Shrine's "apocalyptic nationalism," or the "belief that God will aid, help or intervene in a people's struggle." According to these documents, this was the heart of the faith of the ancient Black Nation Israel. Yet this belief in God's intervention was also paired with a commitment to action: "They found that God would *first work through them* and second with them if they were true to their covenant and gave total devotion, committment [*sic*] and obedience to the Torah, Law."[107]

Black Liberation Theology and Black Power

It was the Shrine of the Black Madonna's insistence on action that would so inspire one of the many Black Christians drawn into Cleage's orbit during the Detroit rebellion—a young, Black professor of theology "quietly teaching white students at Adrian College,"[108] around seventy miles away from the Shrine of the Black Madonna. James Hal Cone saw, in the Detroit rebellion and all over America, that "Blacks are no longer prepared to turn the other cheek; instead, they are turning the gun ... This is an era when many blacks would rather die than be slaves. Now the question is: What do the black churches have to say about this?"[109] The answer, Cone wrote at the time, was, in general: not much. But the Shrine of the Black Madonna, for him, was a shining exception. "The Rev. Albert Cleage of Detroit is one of the few black ministers who has embraced Black Power as a religious concept and has sought to reorient the church-community on the basis of it."[110] Cleage alone among the Christians, argued Cone, was doing what the Nation of Islam had already done, showing that there was a connection "between religion and the suffering of black people."[111] Cleage and the Shrine of the Black Madonna gave the young theologian hope that it was possible for the church to do the same, "to begin to relate Christianity to the pain of being black in a white racist society, or else Christianity itself will be discarded as irrelevant in its perverse whiteness."[112] Cone would continue what Cleage had started—bringing Malcolm's theology not only into the streets but into seminar rooms and syllabi.

5

Christ Means Black Power!

James Cone and Black Liberation Theology

Between Bearden and Black Power

"It's hard to know," the thirty-year-old James Cone wrote, "whether to laugh or weep" at American churches' lack of a compelling response to the white power system that spelled "death to black humanity."[1] While there were, of course, important differences, Cone hastened to note, between white churches, whose "very coming to be was an attempt to reconcile the impossible—slavery and Christianity,"[2] and Black churches, which had, at times, been "the home base for revolution,"[3] he was pained and outraged by the impotence of both in the face of the enormity of white racial terror. "Neither [the white or Black church] is notably identified with the tearing-healing power of Christ. Neither is a fit instrument of revolution."[4]

The bitterness in the young scholar's tone was palpable, and fully understandable for his readers only later, in view of the warmth with which—starting in the mid-1970s—he would habitually come to write about his earliest years among the Black community of Macedonia AME Church in Bearden, Arkansas. Growing up in Bearden, "a small community with approximately eight hundred whites and four hundred blacks," gave him a thorough education in both the cruelty of white racism and the power of Black faith.[5] The white residents of Bearden expected that Black people would all address them as "Mr." and "Mrs.," responding "by calling all blacks 'boy,' 'girl,' or by their first names."[6] Black residents of Bearden were expected to smile at all times and use the back door to enter public places.[7] Cone's recollection of his early life was marked by the "primal memories of terror and violence that were part of the reality of growing up in the Jim Crow South," but, he insisted, the ever-present threat of physical annihilation was not all that made growing up under segregation unbearable.[8] It was the fundamentally dehumanizing nature of the "social ethos" of Jim Crow that most powerfully shaped his understanding of white racism.

> As a child, I learned to wear a mask whenever I went to town in Bearden—careful always not to show my real self, for fear of offending white people. When I was around whites, I was mostly silent, spoke only when spoken to, and showed the deference expected of me: head down, never looking any white person in the eyes ... Whites were powerful and dangerous, and they could strike without warning; you had to be very careful and watch their every move, lest you unintentionally caused offense. So I kept my mask on until I got back to "Cotton Belt," the name for the black community where I grew up.[9]

In a world systematically designed to deny him any shred of self-respect or dignity, the young Cone, nevertheless, knew his own worth—thanks to the "profound love" of his parents[10] and to God's "frequent visits to the black community" at Macedonia AME Church.

From his father, Charles Cone, he received a rebellious spirit, a "conviction that survival for black people requires constant struggle, and that no black should ever expect justice from whites."[11] In the early 1950s, when James and his brothers were still at school, his father filed a lawsuit against the Bearden School Board "on the grounds that white and black schools were not equal," and, after the U.S. Supreme Court's ruling in *Brown v. Board of Education* in 1954 that school segregation was unconstitutional, Cone's father's suit was incorporated into the struggle for school desegregation. It was at this time, Cone later wrote, that

> Bearden whites began to talk about lynching Charlie Cone because he refused to take his name off the lawsuit. We were all afraid for my father's life and urged him to leave for his own safety. My father responded: "No white person is going to make me leave my own house. Let the sons of bitches come. They may lynch me; but with this double-barrel shotgun and my pistol, some of them will die with me." Fortunately the lynch mob never came, as had been announced. Legal complications prevented the Bearden schools from being integrated until the 1960s.[12]

Charlie Cone's relentless struggle to maintain his own and his family's dignity kept the family in poverty, as he refused to work at white-owned factories or sawmills, or to agree that Cone's mother, Lucy, work as a domestic servant or take money from white politicians to display their stickers on his property.[13] His father's model of "courage and resistance"[14] allowed the young James Cone to believe that he "could achieve great things in life, despite the barriers of white supremacy."[15]

From Cone's mother, Lucy, he received an abiding faith in God. Lucy "was one of the pillars of Macedonia, and a firm believer in God's justice," who would occasionally stop his father from speaking more when, expressing his despair, his "language moved toward disrespect for the mystery of God's presence in the world in the midst of oppression."[16] At church with his mother, he was introduced to the transformative power of Black spirituality. "At Macedonia African Methodist Episcopal Church (A.M.E.), I encountered the presence of the divine Spirit, and my soul was moved and filled with an aspiration for freedom."[17] At church, the "social ethos" of the white world was "reversed":

> After being treated as things for six days of the week, black folk went to church on Sunday in order to affirm and experience another definition of their humanity. In the eyes of the Almighty, they were children of God whose future was not defined by the white structures that humiliated them. That was why they called each other Mr. and Mrs. or brother and sister ... When the people of Macedonia had their backs up against the wall and all human resources appeared exhausted, they did not hesitate to turn to the Lord in prayer.[18]

Contrary to those who thought of Black Christianity as a "mere pain-killer," Cone saw how the church instilled dignity in its members and inspired them to fight for justice. "Every fight for justice and civil rights was initiated in and led by the church."[19]

And so it pained him, deeply, in the late 1960s, when the churches seemed so obviously to be lagging behind the Black revolutionary struggle. He did not, he said, "separate [himself] from the spirit and the truth of the black church," even as, for a time, he left the AME Church, angered at its conservatism.[20] But in the wake of the Detroit rebellion, it was not "the black church" that was responding to the needs of his soul. It was Malcolm X, and it was Rev. Albert Cleage. Only they gave him the resources to proclaim the message that had filled his heart: "in twentieth-century America, *Christ means Black Power!*"[21]

Black Fire: James Cone and
the Detroit Uprising

In 1967, Cone wrote in his memoir, "Detroit exploded and so did I."[22] Cone was not quite twenty-nine years old when the uprising "woke [him] out of [his] academic world."[23] The rebellion made the contrast between the content of the courses he was teaching at Adrian College—teaching theologians such as Karl Barth and Paul Tillich, reflecting the training he had received at Northwestern University's predominantly white Garrett-Evangelical Theological Seminary—and the realities of Black life, in which "black people were dying in the streets of Detroit, Newark, and the back roads of Mississippi and Alabama" all too clear.[24] In a lecture in 2016, two years before his death, Cone reflected on the profound shift in consciousness that occurred for him in the midst of the urban uprisings of the 1960s: "The blood of Blacks in America's cities—Watts, Detroit, and Newark—was crying out to God and to white America, crying out for their humanity to be recognized. 'We declare our right to be a human being,' Malcolm X said, 'to be respected as a human being on this earth, which we intend to bring into existence by any means necessary.'"[25] The rebellion in Detroit, closer to home than any of the other eruptions of unrest, was a turning point for his faith and for his theology. He seethed as he witnessed the typical white responses to the riots, full of condemnation for (Black) violence. Watching the events unfold, Cone felt a "*black fire*" kindle within himself that had to be let out in words. The Black Power movement enabled him "to give voice to the feelings of rage in the Negro community, and especially the rage inside" himself.[26]

It was during this period that Cone began to read Malcolm X, who "revolutionized [his] consciousness," transforming him into a "*black* theologian, angry and ready to do battle with white theologians."[27] It was "Malcolm's spirit of blackness" that "shook [him] up, turned [him] around, stirred [his] soul, stimulated [his] spiritual imagination, and reminded [him] to think for [himself] and for the people who raised and nurtured [him] into adulthood."[28] He found in Malcolm X what was missing in the theological outlook of his white colleagues, who "quoted to blacks Jesus' sayings about 'love your enemy' and 'turn the other cheek' but ignored their application to themselves ... In view of white people's history of violence against humankind," he mused, "how can their preachers and theologians dare to speak to the victims about love and nonviolence?"[29] He readily adopted the "Black aesthetic" lauded by the Black Arts Movement; he read Black poets, began wearing a dashiki, and grew his hair into an Afro.[30]

During the same period, he "also went to hear the Rev. Albert Cleage preach a Black Power gospel at the Shrine of the Black Madonna in Detroit." Cleage, wrote Cone, "was the only preacher [he] heard who had the courage to be unashamedly and unapologetically black."[31] In light of this preaching, Cone "began to read the Bible through the lens of Black Power, black arts, and the black consciousness movement."[32] What he found there electrified him: the "revolutionary Jesus leap[ing] off the pages."[33] In his first book, *Black Theology & Black Power* (1969), Cone would refer to only two counterexamples to the overall complicit state of white and Black religious communities: Cleage's church and the Nation of Islam.[34] Cleage, for his part, welcomed Cone's first two books, calling him his "very good friend Dr. James H. Cone," and characterizing Cone's task as the difficult one of "drag[ging] white Christians as far as they are able to go (and then some) in interpreting Black theology within the established framework which they can accept and understand."[35] Cone visited the Shrine of the Black Madonna in 1969 to speak about *Black Theology & Black Power*, later writing to the Shrine to express his thanks for a "glorious occasion to share with my people what it means to be black."[36] In 1974, Cone continued to cite Cleage's influence, describing him as a "prophet" and citing "good parallels" in the Hebrew Scriptures.[37]

Cone would never become a member of the Shrine of the Black Madonna; his church affiliation moved between the African Methodist Episcopal (AME) Church in which he had been raised, to the United Methodist Church, back to the AME, over the course of his life.[38] The foundation of his faith was the spirituality he had encountered at his childhood community, and the legacy of southern Black Christianity was always dear to him.[39] Yet in the late 1960s, this tradition was not enough: in order for his Christian faith to survive the complicity of the church with racial terror, he needed to preach the gospel of Black Power.

A Word to Whitey

During the summer after the assassination of Martin Luther King in 1968, Cone started writing. "I had to write to make sense out of King's assassination, the urban uprisings, the theology I had studied at Garrett, and the life I had lived growing up in Bearden."[40] He left Michigan to return to Arkansas for the summer, where he wrote from "7:00am to 12:00am" every day except Sundays in his brother's, Cecil's, office as the pastor of Union AME Church in Little Rock.[41] His first book, *Black Theology & Black Power*, published in 1969, was the result. The book, as he wrote in the introduction, was his "word to the oppressor, a word to Whitey, [written] not in hope that he will listen (after King's death who can hope?) but in the expectation that my own existence will be clarified. If in this process of speaking for myself, I should happen to touch the souls of black brothers (including black men in white skins), so much the better."[42] Cone, unlike Cleage, wanted to share the gospel of Black Power in terms that "Whitey" could understand, if not accept. He wanted to translate Cleage's and Malcolm's message into the specific vocabulary of academic Christian theology, using the sources he had studied in his doctoral program. "I knew that Black Power advocates, like Stokely Carmichael, and militant black ministers, like Albert Cleage, had no interest in debating white religious scholars or well-schooled white ministers. But I did … It was time to turn the white man's theology against him and make it speak for the liberation of black people."[43] Cone brought the provocative language of Malcolm X and Cleage into the world of systematic Christian theology. Unlike Cleage, Cone cared about the Christian theological tradition. Cleage rejected much of Christian theology as it had developed over time, starting even with rejecting the authority of the letters of St. Paul.[44] Cone wanted, like Cleage, to align himself radically with Black Power and with the legacy of Malcolm, but, unlike Cleage, he wanted to use the traditional sources of Christian theology as weapons in his battle against white supremacy.

Cone was not the first to try to bridge Black Power with mainstream Christian theology. Cone himself was involved with the Black Methodists for Church Renewal (BMCR), a group within the United Methodist Church pushing for greater identification with the Black Power movement; its 1968 "Black Paper," of which Cone was present for the drafting, asserted that the "Black Revolution is a fact! It is a call for black people throughout the nation and the world to stand on their feet and declare their independence from white domination and exploitation … Black power … is a call for us to respond to God's action in history which is to make and keep human life human."[45] Cone was likewise inspired by the 1966 Black Power statement of the National Committee of Negro Churchmen, which had proclaimed: "[The events constituting the rise of the Black Power movement], we believe, are but the expression of the judgment of God upon our nation for its failure to use its abundant resources to serve the real well-being of people, at home and abroad."[46] But Cone felt that both of these attempts "fell short" theologically. The statements, he argued, merely affirmed the Black Power movement without fully exploring the theological implications of doing so.[47] Cone, having been trained in systematic theology, understood the importance of a theological system based on clear principles. In the case of Karl Barth, the Swiss Reformed theologian about whom Cone had written his doctoral dissertation, an expansive, complex, and highly influential system of thought was built upon one essential principle: Jesus Christ as the revealed Word of God.[48] Cone, similarly, aimed to build a theological system based on that initial insight of Malcolm X's: divine, revolutionary Blackness.

It is impossible to understand Cone's early theology and the larger development of Black liberation theology without first taking into account Malcolm X's theology, and in turn how Malcolm was influenced by the theology of the Nation of Islam. Despite this, it is common among theologians today to emphasize Malcolm X's cultural/political influence on Cone rather than his theological influence.[49] This reflects Cone's own later characterization of his project, in which he tended to assign theological influence to Martin Luther King Jr. and cultural/ political influence largely to Malcolm X. Beginning with *Martin & Malcolm & America: A Dream or a Nightmare?* (1991) and until his death in 2018, Cone would repeatedly argue that "from King black liberation theology received its Christian identity … [whereas] Malcolm X … identified the struggle as a *black* struggle."[50] But when placing Cone's early theology in the broader context of the Black Power movement and Malcolm X's spiritual and theological role in the "religion of Black Power," it is clear that Malcolm X did not only offer Cone a cultural or political lens through which to read Christian theology, but also a theological worldview grounded in divine Blackness and divine Black judgment. A striking exception to the general trend of bypassing the theological influence of Malcolm X and the Nation of Islam in the literature on Black theology, however, is Mark L. Chapman's *Christianity on Trial: African-American Religious Thought before and after Black Power* (1996), which positions Cone, Cleage, and other early iterations of Black theology as consciously providing alternatives to the Nation of Islam and Malcolm X.[51] This chapter builds on Chapman's work by demonstrating the crucial importance of Malcolm's theological influence on Cone, especially in his articulation of divine Blackness and, relatedly, God's coming judgment against white oppressors.

Divine Blackness and Satanic Whiteness

The central theme of Cone's first book, *Black Theology & Black Power*, is the conflict between divine Blackness and devilish whiteness. While Cone's work would come to be associated with the biblical theme of the liberation of the Israelite slaves from Egypt,[52] references to the exodus in *Black Theology & Black Power* are sparse in comparison with its primary motif: the conflict between the Black Christ and the demonic powers of whiteness. In response to the question, "Is it possible for men to be *really* black and still feel any identity with the biblical tradition expressed in the Old and New Testaments?"[53] Cone turned first and foremost to Jesus Christ, who, as Cone paraphrased Karl Barth, is "the sole criterion for every Christian utterance."[54] Carefully using the respected sources of contemporary academic theology for his purpose, Cone borrowed language from Barth's own theological system about Jesus, describing him as the "man for others"[55] who is "God himself coming into the very depths of human existence for the sole purpose of striking off the chains of slavery."[56] Like Barth, Cone highlighted passages from the New Testament about the exorcisms of Jesus in order to indicate that Christ's life should be understood as a "deliberate offensive" against the powers of Satan.[57] Barth, in § 64.3 of his magisterial *Church Dogmatics*, had portrayed Jesus's miracles and exorcisms as "military actions, fulfilled by Jesus in the service of God" against the hostile powers of the world.[58] But, unlike Barth, Cone had a very specific instance in mind of where this "offensive" against Satan occurred. Where could we find the battle between Christ and the forces of evil? To answer that question, Cone responded, we must turn to "Malcolm X's designation" of "the beastly behavior of the 'devil white man.'"[59]

For Cone's primary academic theological source, Karl Barth, divine judgment against evil only *truly* occurred in the life, death, and resurrection of Christ. But for Cone, as for his true theological source (Malcolm X), the "constant battle between Christ and Satan … is going on now."[60] Cone was unequivocal about where this battle was raging in America: "Theologically, Malcolm X was not far wrong when he called the white man 'the devil.' The white structure of this American society, personified in every racist, must be at least part of what the New Testament meant by the demonic forces."[61] It was Malcolm's assertion of the divinity of Blackness and the demonic character of whiteness that provided Cone with the concept of Blackness and whiteness as fundamental symbols for a theological system. "In America, God's revelation on earth has always been black, red, or some other shocking shade, but never white. Whiteness, as revealed in the history of America, is the expression of what is wrong with man. It is a symbol of man's depravity."[62] By interpreting the biblical conflict between oppressive powers and the oppressed by way of the symbols of Blackness and whiteness, Cone declared that "the coming of Christ … means destroying the white devil in us."[63] As a result, as with Cleage and Malcolm, the Bible can truly be understood only by looking at God's work in contemporary conflict with oppressive forces: "God is with us now, actively fighting the forces which would make men captive."[64] Salvation, then, as Cone wrote in his next book, *A Black Theology of Liberation*, is determined by one's capacity to become "*black* with God" by participating in the struggle for Black liberation.[65]

Divine Wrath against White Oppressors

Cone's early theological writings resound with the apocalyptic tone of the "religion of Black Power" described by Vincent Harding and given its first extended Christian form by Cleage. Frustrated with other Black Christians' hesitancy to associate fully the Black revolution with God's own righteous judgment against evil, Cone defended his own embrace of the theme of Black apocalypse as a theological necessity. In his 1970 work, *A Black Theology of Liberation*, Cone was unequivocal in his articulation of God's wrath at work in America:

> Is it possible to understand what God's love means for the oppressed without making *wrath* an essential ingredient of that love? What could love possibly mean in a racist society except the righteous condemnation of everything racist? ... A God without wrath does not plan to do much liberating, for the two concepts belong together ... Living in a world of white oppressors, blacks have no time for a neutral God. The brutalities are too great and the pain too severe, and this means we must know where God is and what God is doing in the revolution. There is no use for a God who loves white oppressors *the same as* oppressed blacks. We have had too much of white love, the love that tells blacks to turn the other cheek and go the second mile. What we need is the divine love as expressed in black power, which is the power of blacks to destroy their oppressors, here and now, by any means at their disposal.[66]

Cone envisioned this same God who spoke in wrath to white Americans as speaking to Black Americans with consolation: "Even now I am present with you because your suffering is my suffering, and I will not let the wicked triumph."[67]

Cone conceded that reconciliation and love of enemies were also important themes in the Bible, but refused to acquiesce to the depoliticization of these concepts. Submitting to the violence of the oppressors, he claimed, was not Christian love for them. There are times, in a world that has been deliberately constructed to destroy and deny Black people's very being, that real confrontation, including rioting, was the "only possible expression of Christian love to the white oppressor."[68] To be aligned with God's action in the world and remade in the image of Christ is to act to cast out the demonic forces of oppression.[69] Cone was defiant and explicit in his expression of what this "casting out" of the white devil looked like: "The black experience is the feeling one has when attacking the enemy of black humanity by throwing a Molotov cocktail into a white-owned building and watching it go up in flames. We know, of course, that getting rid of evil takes something more than burning down buildings, but one must start somewhere."[70]

As in Cleage's sermons, Cone portrayed the Bible as a "history book" that relates the story of God's relationship with a chosen Black people, in God's "acts of grace and judgment as he calls the people of Israel into a free, liberated existence."[71] In the course of this history, God's fierce anger against oppressors may be frightening—Cone cited Hosea 13:8, in which God threatens to meet arrogant people "like a she-bear robbed of her cubs and tear their ribs apart"—but this signifies that there "is no divine grace in the Old Testament (or in the New Testament) that is bestowed on the oppressors at the expense of the suffering of the poor."[72]

It was passages such as these that inflamed Cone's critics, as, for instance, can be seen in a 1971 newspaper column by Father Andrew Greeley. Greeley was one of the most recognizable figures of the American Catholic left, a frequent contributor to progressive Catholic publications such as *America* and *Commonweal*, a successful novelist, a well-respected social scientist, and an outspoken critic of the Catholic Church's positions on birth control, divorce, and women's ordination. The outraged response from a white progressive such as Greeley illustrates why, as Cone later wrote, so many Black Christians had held back from articulating their views fully out of fear of raising a "red flag" for white Christians.[73] In the column, "Sees Resurgence of Nazi Mentality in America," Greeley singled out Cone as representative of the "self-proclaimed radicals of the left" and their growing insistence that "all whites are guilty of racism, all men are chauvinists, all old people have 'sold out.'"[74] Greeley described Cone's writings as "filled with hatred for white people and the assumption of a moral superiority of black over white," and he concluded his column by asserting that Cone and the unnamed "screaming women" of the feminist movement would have felt at home among the cheering crowds at the Nazis' Nuremberg rallies.[75] Referring specifically to Greeley's critique, however, Cone wrote in 1986 that "white reactions to black theology never disturbed me too much, because Malcolm X had prepared me for them."[76] Cone was not the first to articulate Black anger to the extent that he did; he was only following in the footsteps of Malcolm and his heirs in the Black Power movement. Cone was simply the most prominent figure to do so in the language of academic Christian theology.

As his theology developed, Cone began to stress the necessary balance of three competing themes in Black religion in America: justice, love, and hope.[77] He argued that while Martin Luther King Jr. had started out emphasizing justice as the primary concept that unified these three "central themes," concerns about the movement devolving into violence led him to emphasize love as the unifying concept that gave meaning to justice and hope. However, in the final years of his life, justice and hope once again rose to the fore in his rhetoric, leading to a resurfacing of the theme of divine judgment in his public addresses.[78] Within this framework of the three central themes of Black religion, Cone identified Malcolm X as representing "the most prominent theme in this trinity of divine virtues," that of justice, which was typically expressed in terms of faith in divine judgment against evil. "African Americans," Cone wrote,

> have always believed in the living presence of the God who establishes the right by punishing the wicked and liberating their victims from oppression. Everyone will be rewarded and punished according to their deeds, and no one—absolutely no one—can escape the judgment of God, who alone is the sovereign of the universe. Evildoers may get by for a time, and good people may suffer unjustly under oppression, but "sooner or later ... we reap as we sow."[79]

Malcolm X's theology of divine judgment, Cone wrote, was inextricably connected with this legacy of Black religion.

> [Malcolm] based his claim upon the biblical theme of justice and judgment and his analysis of the downfall of nations of the past. But whether Malcolm referred to the myth of Yacob, the Bible, or to history, his central claim regarding white America's doom was based upon his belief that "the all-wise Supreme Being" and "the great God of the universe" was also "the God of justice." White America's crime was slavery and segregation, hypocrisy and deceit. According to Malcolm, justice meant that *God* (not

Malcolm or the Muslims or black people) must destroy America for its sins.[80]

For Cone, Malcolm X was associated fundamentally with the proclamation of God's judgment against oppressors, which Cone credited to the influence of the Nation's doctrine of the "almighty black God [as] the source of all good and power" on Malcolm's thought, as well as its identification of whiteness with the devil.[81] Faith in divine Blackness allowed Malcolm to interpret "justice, love, and hope in the light of the all-important symbol of blackness."[82]

> In Malcolm's theology, God, Jesus, the prophets, and the "original Man" were portrayed as black, and the devil and all evil things were pictured as white … He was making a theological statement about God which is commonly found among peoples of the world whose religions portray God as being more than a mere extension of the ideology of the ruling class. In a society where blacks have been enslaved and segregated for nearly four centuries by whites because of their color and where evil has been portrayed as "black" and good as "white" in religious and cultural values, the idea that "God is black" is not only theologically defensible, but is a necessary corrective against the powers of domination.[83]

For Malcolm X, wrote Cone, the act of reading the Scriptures as a "symbolic, prophetic picture of what was happening in America" between the divinely chosen Black community and their white oppressors allowed for divine wrath against demonic whiteness to take on a central place in his theology.[84] "Malcolm's conception of the nightmare about which he spoke was strongly influenced by the biblical idea of the judgment of God. As a Black Muslim minister, he did not believe that America could continue its exploitation of the poor and the weak, here and abroad, and not experience the full force of the wrath of God as described in the Scriptures and as discernible throughout human history."[85]

The Apocalyptic Imagination of Black Religion

For Cone, however, Malcolm X's proclamation of divine judgment against white oppressors was only a starting point that allowed him to delve more deeply into the larger "apocalyptic imagination" of Black religion. The messianic, apocalyptic emphasis of Black religion, wrote Cone in *The Spirituals and the Blues: An Interpretation* (1972), dated back to slavery. He let the sources speak for themselves.

> "Oh my Lord, what a morning, when the stars begin to fall!" "When the sun refuse to shine, when the moon goes down in blood!" "In dat great getting up morning," "de world will be on fire," and "you'll see de stars a-fallin', "de forked lightning, de coffins bursting," and "de righteous marching."[86]

This was the vision, Cone explained, of a people who hoped "*against* the hopes of this world, against the self-erected gods of finite men."[87] This expectation was definitive of their "new, true personhood" that would be revealed, and, as such, "black identity is bound up with God's future judgment."[88] In other words, the centrality of divine judgment had a centuries-long legacy in Black religion, one that had largely been articulated in the distinctive language of Black American Christianity.

In response to critiques from other Black theologians and scholars (such as Charles Long, Gayraud Wilmore, and his brother, Cecil Cone) that his theology was too dependent on white theological categories,[89] Cone began to distance himself from his attempts to "twist and bend" European thinkers in service of Black theology.[90] Instead, Cone delved deeply into the study of Black cultural resources and history. In particular, in the spirituals Cone found a source for Black theology grounded in the "divine apocalyptic disclosure" of the Spirit to a suffering people.[91] Cone read the spirituals' retellings of biblical narratives as testimonies to divine encounter and Black survival. They "are not documents for philosophy; they are material for worship and praise to him who had continued to be present with black humanity despite European insanity."[92] In the spirituals' versions of the "Exodus, the Covenant, the prophets; and, most of all, Jesus' life, death, and resurrection," the encounter with God that divinized the Black community was made possible. "The authentic community of saints is bound up with the encounter of God in the midst of a broken existence, struggling to be free. God is the Community!"[93] The powers of Satan, personified in "the slaveholders, the slave traders, the drivers, the overseers," cannot negate God's identification of this chosen community with Godself.[94]

Delving into Black music, poetry, and folklore, especially in *The Spirituals and the Blues* (1972), *God of the Oppressed* (1975), and *The Cross and the Lynching Tree* (2011), Cone explored the roots of the conflictual theology of anger and protest he had encountered in Malcolm X's and Cleage's preaching. Here were the sources of those powerful images, expressions, dating back to the period of slavery, of God's unfailing covenant with an oppressed Black people: "God 'gwineter rain down fire' on the wicked … the liberated righteous will 'walk in Jerusalem just like John.' In black religious thought God's justice is identical with the divine liberation of the weak."[95] Black folklore and music would increasingly become the most important sources of Cone's theology from the 1970s onward, but his initial turn to the apocalyptic themes of God's judgment, of Christ's battle with the forces of whiteness, was in large part the legacy of Malcolm X.

The Black Messiah's Delay

In a 1968 poem, Black Arts Movement poet Marvin X (Marvin E. Jackmon) portrayed Malcolm as the one who had identified the "beast" of the Book of Revelation, and directed those who came after him how to defeat him.[96] Cone's and Cleage's theologies reflected this apocalyptic mood, shared by Malcolm himself, that current events "point[ed] toward some type of ultimate showdown … a clash between the oppressed and those that do the oppressing … between those who want freedom, justice and equality for everyone and those who want to continue the systems of exploitation."[97] At the time that Malcolm X made this statement, in an era of global decolonization and the height of the civil rights (and soon to be Black Power) movement, this statement had real credibility. Much of early Black liberation theology's embrace of the apocalyptic mood of Black Power was based in a similar expectation of radical, revolutionary change in American society. The theologies of Cleage and Cone, which were initially forged in the revolutionary moment of the Detroit uprising of 1967, were fundamentally shaped by this apocalyptic expectation, and the prevalence of the theme of divine judgment in the works of both thinkers was a result of this.

Over the course of the 1970s, everything changed. As Joshua Bloom and Waldo E. Martin Jr. argue in *Black against Empire: The History and Politics of the Black Panther Party* (2013), the late 1960s provided a unique moment of possibility for the widespread influence of Black revolutionary politics due to the existence of shared interests between Black radicals and white Americans opposed to the war in Vietnam—and, in particular, the draft. During these years, Black revolutionary politics were able to thrive despite consistently "brutal state repression." The political mood of the nation, however, changed following the end of the Vietnam War. Opportunities for coalition building with other movements and obtaining the support of powerful allies dramatically decreased, causing the same levels of violent state repression as experienced by the movement in the late 1960s effectively to root out Black militancy as a serious threat to institutional power in the United States during the 1970s.[98]

Supporters of the Black Power movement such as Cleage and Cone were forced, in the wake of the meteoric rise and fall of Black revolutionary politics, to revisit their prophecies of an imminent and decisive clash between white and Black Americans. As late as 1972, Cleage expressed hope that the urban uprisings of the late 1960s were merely "the first real indication of a growing revolutionary spirit" that would develop into a serious attack on institutions of white power,[99] but, in the same book, Cleage gave voice to a concern that revolutionary Black factions were "wasting the Holy Spirit,"[100] relying upon the comfort of radical aesthetics and rhetoric without "develop[ing] a program and an organization designed to confront" the enemy.[101]

By the late 1970s, Cleage was clear about his belief that the Black community had, in fact, wasted its moment of revolutionary opportunity. He expressed this recognition in words that conveyed profound disappointment and grief:

Black power was a kind of fantasy too. We started hollering Black power when we didn't have a thing to do anything with. We were going to holler Black power and holler Black power, holler Black power, hope somehow, mysteriously, Black power was a religion—that it would come true. Somehow God would do it for us. Black power never had the slightest opportunity of being realized, because we didn't have any power. It was a phase, a slogan, a sign, it didn't mean anything. We couldn't even work together, let alone have power. There's got to be unity to have power.[102]

As hopes in the Black Power movement faded, both Cleage and Cone were forced to revisit and revise their theological world-views. What was Black liberation theology without imminent apocalyptic hope? Was Malcolm's vision of God at work in the sacred, resisting, self-loving, non-white world majority dead?

6

The Twilight of Black Power

Black Liberation Theology in a Post-Revolutionary Era

The Grapes of Wrath: Apocalypse 1967

On August 30, 1967, the Shrine of the Black Madonna opened its doors to the Citywide Citizens' Action Committee (CCAC), an organization that formed in the wake of the riots, and of which Rev. Cleage was the chairman, to host a People's Tribunal. The CCAC wanted to hold a public trial—although, of course, not one with any recognized legal authority—for the policemen accused of killing three Black teenagers who had taken shelter from the violence in the Algiers Motel during the uprising. The justice system had failed to treat the defendants as serious subjects of prosecution, and the CCAC organizers were incensed by the prosecuting attorney's choice not to bring forward Black witnesses who could give testimony against the policemen.[1] "We decided," said Dan Aldridge, a graduate student at Wayne State University who was instrumental in the organization of the proceedings,[2] "that we would hold a tribunal so that the people could evaluate the evidence for themselves. The Black community needs to see that the type of justice we receive in Recorder's Courts is the same kind that is meted out in Mississippi."[3]

After the original location for the People's Tribunal, the Dexter Theater, backed out, Cleage volunteered his church. Aware that this would put the church in danger of white violence and harassment, the church's officers defiantly released a statement:

> We love our church and the building in which we worship. But even if granting permission for the People's Tribunal to be held here means the destruction of our building, as churches have been destroyed in Birmingham and all over the South, we still have no choice.
>
> We serve the Black Messiah, Jesus of Nazareth, who came to unite and free an oppressed black nation. Our free brothers have been brutally slain, and it is only right that the voice of truth, silent in the corrupt halls of justice, should ring out in the House of God.[4]

Cleage, in fact, noted that that the Dexter Theater's last-minute decision had actually enabled the tribunal to take place in a venue that appropriately reflected how sacred the gathering truly was. It was only right that the tribunal should occur "under the soulful eyes of the beautiful Black Madonna, the eighteen-foot painting by Detroit artist and CCAC co-chairman Glanton Dowdell," in the sanctuary of Cleage's church.[5] The tribunal, the jury for which included Rosa Parks,[6] was enormously well attended. By Cleage's account, "By 7 p.m. the sanctuary and Fellowship Hall were filled to capacity, and people were still coming from everywhere. More than 2,000 people were in the building, and others were outside trying to get in."[7]

Cleage was deeply moved, not only by the large quantity of attendees, but by the "strange fearlessness" exhibited by them, by the witnesses, the jury, and the Black community of Detroit.[8] It was clear to Cleage in viewing the tribunal that "fear [was] gone," ushering in "a new day" in which "Detroit is a new city, and black people have a new spirit."[9] Reading his early descriptions of this event, it is clear that the powerful transformation he saw in the Detroit Black community during this period was formative for him: it would serve as the model for the spiritual renewal of Black people in America. For Cleage, what he had witnessed in his church that day was sacred. It had made him think "of the painting of the Black Messiah, the strong black face under a crown of thorns, suffering, beaten, humiliated, but undefeated. And when a mother cried at the witness's story of the death of her son, the indignities he faced, the senseless cruelty of his dying, I could see the picture of 'Mary at the Crucifixion.'"[10] Yet despite the ongoing, endless, outrageous suffering, "in some strange new way we are forging a unity of the spirit which binds us together in love and in dedication to freedom."[11]

Reflecting on the tribunal in a sermon that would be included in *The Black Messiah* (1968), Cleage described this new stage in Black American life—of fearlessness—as the source of imminent reckoning for the United States. "Everything possible had been done by the police to intimidate [the witnesses at the tribunal]," he said, "and yet they testified and told the truth."

> Does that mean that as they sat here, their hearts were not pounding? Of course not. They knew that the man was going to brutalize them at the first opportunity, but that wasn't fear because what they did had to be done … It is not fear as long as you do what has to be done.
>
> America is set on a disaster course of conflict and violence. The black man cannot accept America as it is. The white man refuses to make the changes necessary for the black man to live in America with dignity and justice. These are two facts.[12]

The People's Tribunal crystallized for Cleage what he saw occurring throughout Black America: "We are not as we were a few years ago, a few months ago, a few weeks ago. Something has happened to *us*: not to America but to *us*, to the way we think, the way we fight, the way we work together." This change, he wrote, "is the most important thing that has ever happened in America."[13]

In Cleage's 1967 sermons during and following the Detroit rebellion, his tone was triumphant, full of hope for the possibility of real transformation, of real change, and certain that God was at work in the growing community of Black resistance. In "Grapes of Wrath," Cleage contrasted the typical white liberal Christian condemnations of Black rioting with the apocalyptic tenor of America's abolitionist hymns of old. "You remember the Battle Hymn of the Republic," he began. "White folks used to sing it."[14] Cleage was referring to the Civil War–era hymn, the lyrics of which were composed by anti-slavery activist Julia Ward Howe and published in the *Atlantic Monthly* in February 1862.[15] The hymn takes God's condemnation of unjust oppressors in the Bible and applies it to the Civil War, depicting the onward march of the Union army against the South as the righteous judgment of God.

America had forgotten, Cleage insinuated, the lessons of its past, and of the righteous violence and destruction that racial oppression could reap. Julia Ward Howe's hymn was characteristic; both white and Black abolitionists in the nineteenth century read the Bible's condemnations of empires like Egypt and Babylon as a warning to the new slaveholding empire of the United States. This view was emphatically expressed, for instance, by the Black anti-slavery activist David Walker in his *Appeal to the Coloured Citizens of the World* (1829). Walker asserted that the sufferings of the Israelite slaves under Pharaoh paled in comparison with those of Black slaves "under the *enlightened Christians of America*."[16] Walker threatened America with the same divine wrath manifest in the liberation of the Israelites from Egypt:

Oh Americans! let me tell you, in the name of the Lord, it will be good for you, if you listen to the voice of the Holy Ghost, but if you do not, you are ruined!!! Some of you are good men; but the will of my God must be done. Those avaricious and ungodly tyrants among you, I am awfully afraid will drag down the vengeance of God upon you. When God Almighty commences his battle on the continent of America, for the oppression of his people, tyrants will wish they never were born.[17]

White abolitionists, for their part, agreed. Sarah Grimké, for example, in an epistle to her fellow white southerners, argued that "God is in a peculiar manner the God of the poor and the needy, the despised and the oppressed."[18] Just as God had heard the cries of Israelite slaves in Egypt, God "knows the sorrows of the American slave, and he will come down in mercy, or in judgment to deliver them."[19]

As Cone noted in *The Spirituals and the Blues* (1972), the emancipation of the enslaved following the Civil War was understood by many Black Americans as "an act of God in history analogous to Israel's exodus from Egypt."[20] The Black activist Lucy A. Delaney, a formerly enslaved woman, expressed this view rapturously in her memoir, *From the Darkness Cometh the Light, or, Struggles for Freedom* (1891):

Slavery! cursed slavery! what crimes has it invoked! and, oh! what retribution has a righteous God visited upon these traders in human flesh! The rivers of tears shed by us helpless ones, in captivity, were turned to lakes of blood! How often have we cried in our anguish, "Oh! Lord, how long, how long?" But the handwriting was on the wall [Daniel 5], and tardy justice came at last and avenged the woes of an oppressed race! Chickamauga Shiloh, Atlanta and Gettysburgh, spoke in thunder tones! John Brown's body had indeed marched on, and we, the ransomed ones, glorify God and dedicate ourselves to His service, and acknowledge His greatness and goodness in rescuing us from such bondage as parts husband from wife, the mother from her children, aye, even the babe from her breast![21]

In 1870, the white radical abolitionist leader William Lloyd Garrison similarly described in a letter "our national visitation in 1861, when a just God laid judgment to the line, and righteousness to the plummet; and the hail swept away our refuge of lies, and the waters overflowed our hiding-place [see Isaiah 28:17]."[22] Garrison and other abolitionists saw the devastating mass casualties and destruction of the Civil War as God's judgment of America, a terrible but miraculous intervention that had occurred in plain sight of his entire generation. "Then the Union, which had been so constructed as to propitiate an imperious slave oligarchy, was by that same slave oligarchy cloven asunder; then there was 'a sound of battle in the land, and of great destruction' [Jeremiah 50:22], then 'Babylon was taken, and Bel confounded, and Merodach broken in pieces, and all their idols confounded' [Jeremiah 50:2]."[23]

America had forgotten, Cleage implied, what awaited those who ignored these divine warnings and these divine precedents. The late 1960s, in his estimation, was another turning point, perhaps an even greater turning point, than the upheavals of the 1860s. And this time, white liberals were not ready. Cleage noted of "The Battle Hymn of the Republic" sardonically: "I don't know if [white people] will sing it anymore." Cleage recited the song's famous opening: "Mine eyes have seen the glory of the coming of the Lord./He is trampling out the vintage where the grapes of wrath are stored./He has loosed the fateful lightning of his terrible swift sword./His truth is marching on."[24] He urged his hearers not to be afraid to embrace this very characteristic biblical portrayal of God, which, after all, white American Christians themselves had put to the well-known tune. "We

Divine Rage

don't have to be ashamed of it … We can sing that kind of song because that is the kind of God we worship."[25] Cleage continued reciting lines from the hymn, aware of the new meaning they took on in view of recent events:

> *I have seen him in the watchfires of a hundred circling camps.* I have seen him in a hundred watchfires of a different kind. *They have builded him an altar in the evening dews and damps./I can read his righteous sentence by the dim and flaring lamps./His day is marching on.* His day is on the way because we are participating in bringing it closer every minute and every day. *He has sounded forth the trumpet that shall never call retreat.* I don't think they are going to sing it anymore. *He is sifting out the hearts of men before his judgment seat* … He is sifting us … You were sifted during the riots. You had to make some kind of decision … *Oh, be swift my soul to answer Him! Be jubilant, my feet!* You know what he is talking about. *Our God is marching on.*[26]

The day of judgment had come, and God was marching with his people. "Everywhere," Cleage proclaimed in his New Year's message in 1968, "there is a growing black consciousness, black pride, black unity, and a growing commitment to black power … During 1968 black militant leadership must so structure and program this new commitment to Black Power that it constitutes more than a willingness to die in the streets. The success of black militants in this basic task will determine the course of the Black Revolution for the next decade."[27]

Collapse: The 1970s

The day of judgment, however, came and went without changing America. "The whole thing—collapsed," Cleage lamented in a 1977 sermon. "We wonder, 'What's happened?' It fell apart. It wasn't based on anything but a dream, and the dream was based on an incorrect analysis."[28] Nearing the end of the decade, Cleage surveyed the "collapse" of the Black Power, Black Arts, Black Studies, and Black Consciousness movements:

> Black Studies Departments all disbanded ... [Everyone] running around with their rifles and bullets and you couldn't even find them. All the poets—where did they go? Don Lee is still writing something—I don't know what it is. Amir[i] Baraka's gone back to the Communist Party and white women ... where'd we end up[?] We ended up on dope or ripping people off in the streets, urban centers falling apart. But, we still, we've come farther. Today we have better possibilities—Black leadership—We're in every-thing, we're messing with everything. We don't know what to do with it. We've come a long way in sixty years [since the Great Migration], but we have come to the end of the era.[29]

Cleage's characterization of the state of the Black Revolution at the end of the 1970s reflects what scholars have also noted about this period: the disintegration of Black revolutionary leader-ship and increasing disrepair in urban neighborhoods existed alongside unprecedented prominence and involvement of local Black leadership. "Black Power's demise as a national move-ment," wrote Peniel E. Joseph, "coincided with the deepening, from coast to coast, of America's urban crisis, which would con-tinue to unfold over the next decades. In the post–Black Power era African Americans took political control over metropoli-tan centers at the very moment that cities were, due to federal neglect, shrinking tax bases, and loss of industries, made most vulnerable to crime, poverty, and failing public schools."[30]

As the Black Power chapter came to a close, Cleage urged his listeners not to despair but, instead, to build a community that would not squander its moment of revolutionary opportunity a second time. As detailed by Cardinal Aswad Walker of the PAOCC in "Politics Is Sacred: The Activism of Albert B. Cleage Jr.," during the 1970s, Cleage retreated for the most part from the traditional modes of political activism that dominated his public role in the 1960s. Instead, he turned to the project of "training and developing a cadre of young adults to lead the church he founded with a theology of liberation committed to the full empowerment of black people as an expression of God's will."[31]

Cleage aimed to build a transformative communal structure that could liberate Black people from the psychologically debilitating frameworks of self-hatred and (white-derived) individualism which ensured that they would continue to "waste the Holy Spirit," as they had during the late 1960s. The power of God, argued Cleage in a sermon in January 1978, is easily squandered if the people who wield it remain the same, which is to say, if they remain the same psychologically as they were under enslavement (in both the case of ancient Israel and in contemporary Black America).[32] Cleage's decision to focus his efforts on building a church community derived from this assertion that revolutionary change would never be possible until communal spiritual transformation occurred. "You cannot organize unless you can change people, you cannot change people, unless you have a community and you cannot have a community that has power unless it's a community that's dedicated to commitment to God."[33] For Cleage, the source of this change, more than anything else, would be a transformative encounter with God: shared mystical experience. The rest of his life would be devoted to creating the conditions for this kind of spiritual transformation.

Cone's vision for Black liberation, too, would change—one only has to look at the epilogue of *The Cross and the Lynching Tree* (2011) to see just how much:

Blacks and whites are bound together in Christ by their
brutal and beautiful encounters in this land ... We are
bound together in America by faith and tragedy. All
the hatred we have expressed toward one another cannot destroy the profound mutual love and solidarity that
flow deeply between us—a love that empowered blacks to
open their arms to receive the many whites who were also
empowered by the same love to risk their lives in the black
struggle for freedom. No two people in America have had
more violent and loving encounters than black and white
people. We were made brothers and sisters by the blood of
the lynching tree, the blood of sexual union, and the blood
of the cross of Jesus. No gulf between blacks and whites
is too great to overcome, for our beauty is more enduring
than our brutality. What God joined together, no one can
tear apart.[34]

Cone's characterization of the relationship between Black and
white Americans differs strongly in tone from his earliest writings. In *Black Theology & Black Power*, for instance, he had stri-
dently asserted that "white people should not even expect blacks
to love them, and to ask for it merely adds insult to injury. 'For
the white man,' writes Malcolm X, 'to ask the black man if he
hates him is just like asking the *raped* ... "Do you hate me?"'"[35]

As dramatic as the differences appear between James Cone's
rhetoric in 1967 and 2011, these statements do not reflect a complete reversal of position but rather a gradual shift in emphasis
over time. Cone would never fully relinquish the prophetic, even
apocalyptic tenor of his earliest work, and during the rise of the
Black Lives Matter movement in the 2010s, he spoke with the
same fire as his younger self about the judgment facing white
Americans. Still, the trajectory of Cone's theological project on
the whole reflects a movement from a near-exclusive focus on

revolutionary anger to a broader treatment of Black faith, while never negating the potential of Black anger to serve as a conduit for God's justice.

Over time, the spirit of Bearden overtook the spirit of Black nationalism in Cone's theology. In a period of political despair, he argued, the Black community needed more than ideology. It needed heavenly faith, the faith of his mother, Lucy, and of Macedonia A.M.E. Church, a faith that transcended the unjust powers of this earth. "People get tired of fighting for justice," he wrote in 1975, "and the political power of the oppressors often creates fear in the hearts of the oppressed. What could a small band of slaves do against the armed might of a nation?"[36] Cone asked the same question about the Black community in the 1970s: "what can oppressed blacks today do in order to break the power of the Pentagon?"[37] His tone, like that of Cleage's sermons at the same time, conveyed a sense of loss and disappointment:

> Of course, we may "play" revolutionary and delude ourselves that we can do battle against the atomic bomb. Usually when the reality of the political situation dawns upon the oppressed, those who have no vision from another world tend to give up in despair. But those who have heard about the coming of the Lord Jesus and have a vision of crossing on the other side of Jordan are not terribly disturbed about what happens in Washington, D.C., at least not to the extent that their true humanity is dependent on the political perspective of government officials. To be sure, they know that they must struggle to realize justice in this world. But their struggle for justice is directly related to the coming judgment of Jesus. His coming presence requires that we not make any historical struggle an end in itself.[38]

It is telling that Cone, in this passage, depicted heaven as crossing over the Jordan River into the promised land—this was the same traditional language of Black devotion that Cone had in fact derided only six years earlier in *Black Theology & Black Power*. In 1969, he had argued that the "idea of heaven is irrelevant for Black Theology,"[39] and, citing the Black cultural nationalist Maulana (Ron) Karenga, he had agreed that Black people must "concern ourselves more with this life which has its own problems. For the next life across Jordan is much further away from the growl of dogs and policemen and the pain of hunger and disease."[40] The dimming prospects of Black revolutionary politics as a source of immediate, radical political transformation of the United States led Cone, like Cleage, to reassess his conception of *where* and *in what way* God was at work in the world. Cone, also like Cleage, retained Malcolm's original insight that God made God's presence known in the world through the Black community. But the ways in which Cone portrayed God at work in the Black community shifted. More and more, he turned to the faith of his childhood, interpreting Black folklore, music, and traditional church structures as sources of hope, vitality, survival, and resistance in the midst of persistent oppression. Cone continued to insist on the importance of Black political action as a site of divine action, but he placed this work within a more expansive context, affirming the full range of Black experience and celebrating the cultural and religious resources that enabled Black Americans to keep up the fight.

Albert Cleage: Mystical Experience and the Transforming Community

"Liberation ain't got nothing to do with the clenched fist," Cleage proclaimed in a 1978 sermon. "It's got to do with the mind. Mind, body and spirit working together in harmonious oneness."[41] Cleage's turn, in the later 1970s, to an internally focused strategy for the Black Christian Nationalist movement he had formed was rooted in his conviction that psychological and spiritual transformation of the Black community—which, he insisted, had been devastated by racist self-hatred—was a necessary first step in changing the world and its power structures. This transformation relied both on the creative innovation of new spiritual approaches, as well as investment in Black-led communal institutions: alternative, community-run sources of power.

From the 1970s onward, Cleage's Pan-African Orthodox Christian Church constructed a vast national system of "cultural centers, nurseries and youth centers, community service centers, law centers, health centers, political education centers, technological centers, housing complexes, KUA [a spiritual system that will be described below] educational centers, and a 4000-acre agricultural complex all rooted in the ministry and theology of a black church dedicated to personal and social transformation."[42] Some of these goals were laid out in the "BCN 10 Year Projection," written in 1972, which framed the need for these institutions as a matter of life and death for Black people. The plan articulated a "sense of urgency about the terrible future of Black survival as we see it" and described the building of Black communal institutions as a process of "putting together a Black Nation which in the end seeks to achieve total liberation for all Black people everywhere."[43]

The building of these institutions was described as a primary concern not only by the leadership in the PAOCC but as a fundamental principle stressed in the organization's educational programming. A 1993 workbook of the Alkebu-lan Academy (for youth education), entitled "Understanding My Faith," explained:

> Our Church is a *growing* **Black Nation**, with counter-institutions that give us the **POWER** to survive as a People with dignity and respect ... We *believe* God has given us the

ability to do whatever is necessary to take care of ourselves
and not have to beg for jobs, good schools, or healthy food,
or any of the other things we need to survive. We are also
getting the *skills* to develop these quality counter-institu-
tions! **A Black Nation is God's will** because it teaches us to
believe in our God-given worth and strength again![44]

Cleage's focus on Black-led community institutions reflected his
belief that the "Black Revolution" of the late 1960s and 1970s
had ultimately been foiled by the absence of a strategic, long-
term vision for building Black nationhood. "Black power wasn't
a concept that had in it any program for realization of power,"
he argued.[45] What was needed at the end of the 1970s was not to
integrate (which he deemed impossible) but "to build power so
that we can exist—so that we can survive. Now, our conditions
produced a slave mentality ... Only the church can liberate
Black people, because only the church can change Black people.
You've got to change—you've got to change the minds of Black
people before you can change the condition of Black people."[46]

The building of a vast network of community institutions was
necessarily bound to what his successor, D. Kimathi Nelson,
has described as a "psycho-spiritual change process," referred
to within the organization as the Science of KUA (derived from
a Swahili word for growth, or becoming).[47] Nelson explains
Cleage's vision for the Science of KUA as a program "to help
black people to rediscover the real and authentic self that was
made in the image and likeness of God so that they could act as
full human beings," enabling them to "become effective agents
of divine will in the world."[48] Nelson portrays Cleage's strategic
shifts in the 1970s as the first stage in a "transition from a strategy
of revolution to one of evolution and sustainability."[49] Over time,
Nelson writes, Cleage "became less focused on going out into
the world to change conditions," focusing instead on "drawing

seekers into the church/nation so that they could become part of an expanding transforming community movement."[50]

The term "KUA" in the PAOCC encapsulates this entire process, consisting of communal norms, rituals, sacraments,[51] meditation, personal transformation, and (finally) revolutionary action. A 1982 summary of the ideology of the Black Christian Nationalist movement succinctly describes the trajectory of the KUA process of transformation:

> THE WORLD SYSTEM is an enemy system. Our Struggle for Survival requires a recognition of the fact that we are outside of the System and we must Build a System of our own ... We must break the Chains of Operant Conditioning through Kua and the Group Process. The "Conditioned Self" accepts and then "represses" the white man's declaration of Black inferiority which renders us psychologically sick ... THE DIVINE SYSTEM requires a struggle for Enlightenment through Kua, "the Science of becoming what we already are." There is a Divine System in which we live and move and have our being, but of which we are seldom aware. It eminates [*sic*] from God who is the cosmic energy and creative intelligence which created and controls the universe. God can be experienced only by breaking through the limits of the rational mind and reaching a higher level of Consciousness where the power of God becomes available to us. This state of Enlightenment must be attained before we can reject individualism and integrate Spirit/Mind/Body. The "Experience of God" must be constantly renewed by regular participation in the rituals of the Transforming Community (the Kua Processes), sacramental worship, confession, and mortification of the Ego ... THE TRIUMPH OF THE DIVINE SYSTEM on earth is the objective of all of our struggles!

We seek to bring the world into submission to the will of
God. Our participation in the Transforming Community
then becomes a revolutionary struggle for social change
and the building of a Pan-African World Community.[52]

Cleage's belief that cultivating immediate contact with the
divine was the only way to effect this transformation was
based in his conception of God. As opposed to the "traditional
anthropomorphic [human-like] conception of God," he argued,
the Bible itself had "no conception of" this anthropomorphic
understanding of divinity.[53] Cleage insisted that the religious
ideas of the Bible "can only be understood in the light of the
history and culture of Africa," given the dominance of African
civilizations in the region in which the early religious ideas of
Israel were formed.[54] Cleage understood his concept of God as
rooted in indigenous African traditions in which "individuals
actually feel that they are possessed by God."[55] In light of African religious concepts, Cleage argued, Jesus's statement that "I
am in God and God is in me" denotes a field of shared energy.[56]
God, as the "cosmic spirit of which all things were created," can
be encountered by the community when it places itself "in the
SACRED CIRCLE under the power of God hoping that they
will be transformed, changed."[57] So, then, for Cleage, revolution
and mysticism were simply "two sides of the same thing."[58] He
saw the community's pursuit of the encounter with God as what
enabled it to harness the "power to do the things that [God]
gave Jesus the power to do ... to help people change, to restore
people, to help, to give people a new sense of what they're worth,
of what they can be."[59]

Cleage's strong identification of the PAOCC's mission with
mystical experience brought him into contact with a diverse and
sometimes surprising array of contemporary spiritual trends,
which Cleage described as part of a "consciousness revolution,"

often representing what would today be referred to as New Age spirituality.[60] Cleage cited and agreed with criticisms of this movement as at times expressing narcissistic, individualistic, and escapist values. At the same time, he pointed to the consciousness revolution as illustrating a growing awareness that "people have such a terrible need, such a terrible need to fill the empty vacuum which is their life."[61] These increasingly popular spiritual practices showed without a doubt that "people are looking for a God they can experience for themselves."[62] That, Cleage said, was exactly what the PAOCC was doing: "The Pan-African Orthodox Christian Church uses all the techniques that the consciousness movement is trying to use separately and apart from the church because basically they are Christian techniques. They are techniques that developed out of the Christian faith, out of the Christian church, out of the teachings of Jesus, out of the Bible, out of the experiences of the Black Nation Israel."[63]

KUA practices and rituals reflect diverse influences, as in the case of a KUA healing ritual that involves a practice of laying on hands on the sites of each of the "seven chakra energy centers."[64] As hands are laid on the site of each chakra, the participants recite a different "KUA Affirmation" describing an event in Jesus's spiritual journey and mission. "With spiritual preparation and faith that the Power of god [sic] can act through us," explains the introduction to the ritual, "we are able to transmit HEALING ENERGY into the body of others by 'Laying on of Hands'. The individual is opened, sensitized and enabled to internalize the Seven KUA Affirmations, making them the foundation of faith and commitment, controlling and changing behavior."[65] Shelley McIntosh, in her development of an educational curriculum for children in the PAOCC, borrowed many awareness practices and meditations from psychotherapist John O. Stevens's book *Awareness: Exploring, Experiment-*

ing, Experiencing (1971),[66] and also included the practices of yoga and breathing meditation in the ritual and educational life of the community.[67] In a 1978 sermon, Cleage summarized this spiritually eclectic approach: "You have to be changed in a group—encounters, confrontations, meditations, Yoga—all of the kind of things that enable a person to gain control of his own mind."[68]

Cleage never abandoned the spiritual revelation of "Brother Malcolm": "nothing is more sacred than the liberation of black people." The mark of Malcolm X on Cleage's version of Black liberation theology remained present in the unshakable certainty that God is present in the struggle for Black empowerment, for Black dignity, for Black self-love. From the 1970s onward, however, Cleage was realistic about how long and gradual the process of transformation ahead would be for his community. "In the Nation we talk about building Beulahland," Cleage said in 1984 of the independent farm complex the PAOCC succeeded in making into a reality in 1999. "You can say well it is off, it takes time. That is true … [But] if we could get Beulahland, it would be the first stage in a whole process by which Black people can change the way we live."[69] The world in its injustice needs to change, yes. The white power structures need to be torn down. But in a time of political disappointment and despair Cleage believed that his community needed to recognize that a revolution would be long in coming. First, as Cleage expressed in 1984 in a poem, they needed to be transformed by an encounter with the power of God whose very being was their own.[70]

James Cone: Black Salvation as Story and Survival

James Cone wrote *Black Theology & Black Power* in his brother's church office, stopping his work only to sleep and, on Sundays, when he would join in the worship of Union A.M.E. Church in Little Rock, "listening to [his] brother preach and the congregation sing, pray, and testify, reminding [him] what [he] was writing about and for whom [he] was writing."[71] While writing, he listened to the music of "Mahalia Jackson and B. B. King, Aretha Franklin and Bobby 'Blue' Bland." It reminded him, as he wanted it to, of his childhood, of the two poles of his community's survival, the church and the juke joint, the spirituals and the blues.[72] So it pained him, in the intense debates that occurred among both Black and white Christians following the publication of the book, when Black critics (especially Charles H. Long, Gayraud Wilmore, and Cone's brother, Cecil Cone) took his work to task for being too influenced by white theologians, closer to the spirit of Barth than to Bearden.[73] That had not been what he had meant to do: he had meant to sing "a new theological song, a blues song, messing with theology the way B. B. King messed with music. I used Barth's theology the way B. B. used his guitar and Ray Charles used the piano ... I wasn't following Barth; he was simply an instrument I played and left behind whenever it got in the way."[74]

And yet, still, Cone knew there was an "important truth" behind what his critics were saying.[75] He was "shaken" by the critique, and, in order to respond to it, to learn from it, he "soaked [himself] in 'the world [he] came from'—the world of the spirituals and the blues, folklore, and slave narratives, and found the language of freedom and liberation black slaves and ex-slaves sang and talked about."[76] Ultimately, and most profoundly, this meant a return to Macedonia A.M.E. Church, which began to surface frequently in his work during the mid-1970s. It also meant an increasing distance from less mainstream expressions of Black nationalism, including the Nation of Islam and the Shrine of the Black Madonna, the two religious communities he had singled out for praise in *Black Theology & Black Power*. "Because of my commitment to the faith of the black church, I refused to adopt too quickly a black religious nationalism that seemed unconnected with the life-experiences of black church people."[77] (Some critics have argued that Cone's increasing focus on the mainstream Black Protestant Christian tradition had the effect of obscuring the religious diversity of the Black community;[78] Cone would likely argue in response that he could only speak out of his own experience.) Returning to the "life-experiences of black church people" as the primary source for his theology caused Cone to diverge from the emphatically Pan-African aspects of Black nationalist thought preached by Malcolm X and Cleage, as well as their much harsher treatment of Black Christianity and what they perceived as the destructive, "otherworldly," subservient faith preached in mainstream (Methodist, Baptist, or Pentecostal) Black churches. As Mark Chapman has argued, Cone's attitude toward mainstream Black churches took on a different shade depending on his conversation partner. Cone "acted as a defender of the faith" when speaking to anti-Christian Black nationalists, and as a critic when speaking to people who represented traditional Black religious institutions.[79]

In *God of the Oppressed* (1975), Cone explained the distinction between his initial and current approaches to writing Black liberation theology:

> In previous books and articles, I have discussed the intellectual foundation of Black Theology and have sought to show theologically that any analysis of the gospel which did not begin and end with God's liberation of the oppressed was *ipso facto* unchristian. In this present work, I do not abandon the intellectual search but simply integrate it with the existential and social formation of my faith as it was and is being shaped in the black community. I hope that this approach will not only help to clarify my perspective on Black Theology, but more importantly will help to

join the black theological enterprise more firmly with the true source of its existence—the black community.[80]

The turn to more traditional sources in the mid-1970s aligned with his different goals for Black liberation theology in an era after revolution no longer seemed imminent. In *A Black Theology of Liberation* in 1970, Cone had declared the goal of Black liberation theology to be "identifying God's presence with the events of liberation in the black community."[81] Over time, he would come to describe his theological work as pursuing a more expansive task: bearing witness to the manifold ways in which Black people's encounter with God in America gave them "the courage and strength to make it through."[82]

Black people's encounters with God were indeed conveyed in the apocalyptic vision of God's future judgment of oppressors,[83] but they were also present in the blues' chronicles of real "life, its trials and tribulations, its bruises and abuses," which expressed no faith in immediate salvation.[84] It was also, Cone declared emphatically, *love* that had gotten his people "through suffering and through life undefeated," even as rage remained an essential aspect of that love.[85] This commitment to love in a universal sense, Cone argued, was an enormously important aspect of mainstream Black religion (especially in Methodist and Baptist preaching); it was the seed that grew into Martin Luther King Jr.'s faith that "the rule of love would be established among all races of people."[86] By delving deeply into the historical sources of Black religion as a source for his theology from the mid-1970s onward, Cone came to portray God's manifestation in Black revolutionary action as one aspect of a broader testimony of Black people's encounters with the divine Spirit on American soil.

Cone's focus on the mainstream Black churches can best be understood in the context of his concern with "the miracle of survival" of Black people in America.[87] Although not exhaustive, although not perfect, although he never recanted the harsh criticism he made of Black churches in his early work, these institutions represented, according to Cone, what the "vast majority of blacks" believe or have believed. They were the bearers of the legacy of survival, in all of its beauty and in all of its challenge.[88]

Spirituality and Survival

The turn toward spirituality—of mysticism or of church community—in both Cone's and Cleage's writings in the 1970s was not a coincidence. In the absence of lasting revolutionary political change, the central and urgent question became what spiritual resources were available, were crucial, to survive. Cone and Cleage were not alone in this turn toward the contemplative, or in the struggle to reconcile the revolutionary theology of Malcolm X with the consolations of direct experiences of the divine. At heart, there was no true contradiction: Malcolm's commitment to the struggle was born the night he saw God face to face in his Norfolk prison cell. In practice, however, as we shall see, it has not always been easy to reconcile the revolution and the longing for God.

7

Of Malcolm and Merton

Black Power Contemplatives

Waking from a Dream of Separateness

On March 18, 1958, the Trappist monk and internationally acclaimed writer Thomas Merton had a profoundly transformative experience "at the corner of Fourth and Walnut, in the center of the shopping district" in downtown Louisville, Kentucky.[1] "I was suddenly overwhelmed," he wrote, "with the realization that I loved all those people, and they were mine and I theirs, that we could not be alien to one another even though we were total strangers. It was like waking from a dream of separateness, of spurious self-isolation in a special world, the world of renunciation and supposed holiness."[2] Merton had been at war with himself for the past ten years, since his autobiography, *The Seven Storey Mountain* (1948), had become, in the words of the historian James T. Fisher, "one of the great success stories in the history of American publishing ... Merton became a great American Catholic celebrity."[3] Merton and his writings were suddenly ubiquitous, and in high demand.

His gradually increasing longing for contemplative solitude that, as he described in his autobiography, had led him to Catholicism and then to the monastic life, ironically became harder and harder to achieve as a result of his successful recounting of this journey. Young men "flocked" to join him at the Abbey of Gethsemani near Bardstown, Kentucky, eager to follow in his footsteps. Merton repeatedly requested from the abbot of the monastery, Dom James Fox, to be transferred to a more cloistered, reclusive religious community, but the abbot refused: "he felt Merton was not fully stable, and his writings provided a major source of the monastery's income."[4] At the same time, Merton's frustrated desire for greater solitude was paradoxically entwined with a relentless need to reach out toward the world, to make himself known in his writing. As the novelist Mary Gordon put it succinctly in her illuminating book on Merton: "he had taken a vow of silence and had a compulsive need to write."[5] At the end of *The Seven Storey Mountain*, Merton lamented the continued existence of this "shadow" or "double" within himself, "this writer who had followed me into the cloister." He was "supposed to be dead," but there he was, "generat[ing] books in the silence that ought to be sweet with the infinitely productive darkness of contemplation."[6] Merton's famous "Fourth and Walnut" experience of awakening from the "dream of separateness" was the moment in which he admitted to himself, for better or worse, that he longed for connection. Over the course of the next decade, before his death from accidental electrocution on a visit to Southeast Asia in 1968, he would put this desire into practice in his increasing engagement with the social movements of the 1960s, including the Black Power movement.

While Merton was increasingly drawn into radical political circles—through letters and visits, while remaining committed to his vow of stability at the Abbey of Gethsemani—prominent activists in the struggles for liberation of the 1960s and 1970s were also consistently drawn to *him* and to his spiritual writings. Albert Raboteau relates how Martin Luther King Jr. and Merton corresponded in the months leading up to King's

assassination, searching for a time for King to visit the abbey.[7]
But Merton's appeal extended also to more radically affiliated
movement figures. Eldridge Cleaver, the Minister of Information of the Black Panther Party and a one-time member of the
Nation of Islam, first encountered Merton's writings when his
teacher, Chris Lovdjieff, who gave lectures on history, religion,
and philosophy at San Quentin prison during the time Cleaver
was incarcerated there, introduced them to him.[8] As Cleaver
related in his memoir, *Soul on Ice* (1968), he had been reluctant to
read about Merton's choice for monastic life, "because a prison
is in many ways like a monastery ... We were appalled that
a free man would voluntarily enter prison—or a monastery."[9]
Cleaver was at first skeptical of Merton's spiritual journey; his
own use of religious language extended only to the struggle.
In the theology of Elijah Muhammad and Malcolm X, Cleaver
found weapons to wield against those who had "chained [him]
in the bottom of a pit."[10]

Still, Cleaver was struck by Merton's open-hearted description of the Harlem ghetto in *The Seven Storey Mountain*. Cleaver
enjoyed it "so much [he] copied out the heart of it in longhand"
and used it frequently in later lectures.[11] In the passage in question, Merton had described with indignation the degradation
he found in Harlem, angrily lamenting that "in this huge caul-
dron, inestimable natural gifts, wisdom, love, music, science,
poetry are stamped down and left to boil with the dregs of an
elementally corrupted nature, and thousands upon thousands
of souls are destroyed ... washed from the register of the living, dehumanized."[12] In this section of the book, Merton was
reflecting on the only period in his life in which he had directly
encountered racial injustice: his time volunteering at Friendship
House, a Catholic interracial ministry, in Harlem. The encounters he had there, as he wrote in *The Seven Storey Mountain*,
"nearly tore [him] to pieces": he was overwhelmed by the genu-

ineness of love and joy that paradoxically thrived in the midst of slum conditions.[13] Reflecting on his relatively comfortable life in his journal, he asked: "How can I write about poverty, when, although I am in a kind of way, poor, yet here I am in this happy country club?"[14] In the passage that Cleaver would read, he converted his astonishment and guilt into righteous anger.

Merton's words, Cleaver wrote, reminded him of Elijah Muhammad's and Malcolm X's in their "protest against tyranny."[15] In the final balance, Cleaver "vibrate[d] sympathetically" with the monk.[16] "Welcome, Brother Merton," he concluded. "I give him a bear hug."[17] Other prominent activists, including two who will be discussed in this and the next chapter—Julius Lester, a prominent SNCC organizer and Black Power advocate, and José "Cha Cha" Jiménez, the founder of the Young Lords Organization, a Puerto Rican gang-turned-political organization patterned after the Black Panther Party—were strongly influenced by Merton. Lester, like Cleaver, was impressed during his initial reading of Merton by the "purity" of Merton's love for the world, his feeling for the suffering of others, even as he was writing from behind monastery walls.[18]

Merton's appeal to these figures is, at first, surprising. *The Seven Storey Mountain*, taken at face value, is the memoir of the spiritual journey of a young white man raised alternately in France, the United States, and Britain, focusing on his time studying at bastions of educational privilege, Cambridge and Columbia. It details his journey from illusions of devoting himself "to the causes of peace and justice in the world"[19] to his purported end point, becoming a monk and joining those who were "free from the burden of the flesh's tyranny ... clean of the world's smoke and of its bitter sting ... raised to heaven and penetrated into the deeps of heaven's infinite and healing light."[20] Merton did, as Cleaver noted, describe his growing awareness of racial disparities in Harlem, but at the end of the book, Merton noted only in passing walking accidentally into the "Jim Crow waiting room ... full of Negroes" at the Louisville train station before making his way to Bardstown and to the monastery, safely removed from the world and from the violence of the segregated South in which his new home was planted.[21] In time, these contradictions would become clear to Merton, and the tension between his yearnings for solitude and his solidarity with all human beings would dominate his later writings. A time would come in which he would feel obligated to engage with the revolutionary theology of Malcolm X and his heirs, even as it challenged and threatened the foundations of spiritual solitude he had sought at Gethsemani. And yet even his early, non-political writings spoke to radical activists such as Cleaver, Lester, and Jiménez in how they communicated longings for transcendence, for healing, for transformation.

Like Merton himself, radical readers of Merton struggled to bridge their political commitments with these spiritual needs. As the victories of radical movements waned in the 1970s, the desire for what Merton (following the Catholic spiritual tradition) called contemplation became an increasing priority for many movement veterans. The theological legacy of Malcolm X that began with Malcolm's profound spiritual experiences in prison, encountering God in the face of a non-white man, came full circle in the 1970s. Emerging from the traumatic violence of racial terror, of government and police suppression, of movement conflicts, many participants in the liberation struggles of the period turned to the search for mystical or contemplative spirituality. Following the paths of Thomas Merton and two SNCC organizers and Black Power advocates—Julius Lester and Gwendolyn (Robinson) Zoharah Simmons—in the late 1960s and afterward, this chapter explores the contradictions and connections between the revolutionary theology of Malcolm X and contemplative spirituality.

Thomas Merton and
the Black Struggle for Liberation

The location of Merton's 1958 epiphany—downtown Louis-ville—was more appropriate than he likely realized at the time. The words that Merton used to describe his own voluntary exile ("separateness," "alienation," "isolation") from the broader human community also could be applied to the legally sanctioned, involuntary separateness, alienation, and isolation that defined the Louisville shopping district in the late 1950s. As the Louisville-based educator and activist Lyman Johnson wrote, the racial boundaries of the city in which he had been born and raised were eminently clear. "Restaurants, schools, hotels, libraries—even the parks—were all segregated."[22] In 1960, Merton learned about these restrictions by reading Robert Penn Warren's *Segregation: The Inner Conflict in the South* (1956). In his journal, Merton expressed his appreciation for the book. Warren described, he wrote, the "reality of the south to which I belong—without ever thinking of it."[23] But as the national spotlight on the horrors of racial injustice increased, Merton began to think about it: to reflect publicly on the spiritual challenge facing white America. In two collections of essays, *Seeds of Destruction* in 1964 and *Faith and Violence* in 1968, Merton engaged in extended dialogue with Black thinkers; in the case of the former, his major influence was James Baldwin, and in the case of the latter, his most important interlocutors were Malcolm X and his heirs: SNCC chairmen and Black Power advocates Stokely Carmichael and H. Rap Brown.

Though wholeheartedly committed to an ethic of Christian nonviolence, Merton in *Faith and Violence* was unequivocal in granting the Black Power movement its central claim: that the protest movement of the 1950s and early 1960s had proved inadequate in the face of unacceptably persistent racial injustice. He wrote: "The partial failure of liberal non-violence has brought out the stark reality that our society itself is radically violent and that violence is built into its very structure."[24] Simply engaging in protest, he claimed, was no longer sufficient; it did not do enough to "eradicate" the "basic violence and unjustice" of American society.[25]

Merton devoted considerable attention to the statement of SNCC chairman H. Rap Brown that "violence is as American as cherry pie."[26] Merton understood this statement as a damning diagnosis of the American psyche. While white liberals worried about what Merton termed "the violence of the hood waiting for us in the subway or the elevator," the true violence of American society was *white-collar violence, the systematically organized bureaucratic and technological destruction of man.*"[27] Merton recognized that this language originated from Malcolm X in the connections it drew between persistent anti-Black discrimination in the United States, global economic systems built upon exploitation, and imperialist aggression all over the world, including in Vietnam. Merton praised Malcolm's development of a powerful vision of solidarity shared throughout "the formerly colonial, under-developed world, filled with black, white, yellow, red, brown and mestizo populations (in other words the majority of the human race), against a highly developed affluent technological society which cannot really help the others in their struggle for liberation because it needs them to remain in a state of economic and political tutelage."[28] In Merton's view, the Black Power movement's exposure of the pervasiveness of this oppressive global system issued a profound and necessary spiritual challenge to white Americans.

Still, Merton was not personally enthusiastic about the apocalyptic tone of Black Power rhetoric. He preferred the religious language of the civil rights movement in the late 1950s and early 1960s. "Where the powerful believe that only power is efficacious, the non-violent resister is persuaded of the superior efficacy of love, openness, peaceful negotiation and above all of truth."[29] But Merton worried: was nonviolence, in the end, only an idolatrous ideal? He was concerned that white Christian activists had converted the genuine insights of Mohandas Gandhi, Martin Luther King Jr., and others into a self-serving ideology that would act to justify the maintenance of a violent status quo or, even more egregiously, offer a rationale for the moral superiority of white, allegedly "peaceful" Christians over and against members of oppressed groups who were fighting for their lives and for the survival of their people. The Black Power movement was forcing Christians to recognize that their "Christian calling does not make [them] superior to other men, does not entitle [them] to judge everyone and decide everything for everybody."[30] Instead, it was inviting them to join with the rest of humankind in "facing the mysterious realities of the world with the same limitations as everybody else, and with the same capacity for human failure."[31]

Merton did not, in the limited time left to him, resolve the tension between his contemplative calling and the demands of justice. In 1967, after finishing an article about Malcolm X that would come to be included in *Faith and Violence*, Merton wrote in his diary: "I realize I don't fully know what I am talking about. Perhaps I overestimate him … Perhaps already beginning to be corrupted in a new way."[32] He fretted, as he so often did, about his "imprisonment" (he himself puts the word in quotes) in the monastery, but also the falsity that a "romantic escape" to join the revolutionary struggles of the Third World would entail.[33] Merton's dominant mood in reflecting on the state of the country and the struggle for racial justice in his journal during this period was despair. He asserted, as he did in his public essays, that there was no justification for complaining about the Black Power movement given "the infinitely organized muteness and absurdity of the U.S. civilization which surpasses every other facticity."[34] But his support for social movements—in both their nonviolent and increasingly militant forms—was reluctant, hesitant, distant. "The kind of protest that is available seems to be plainly useless," he wrote; but as for "revolutionary violence," "what will it accomplish beyond a tightening of police repression?"[35] A motif repeats throughout his journal entries: "I don't know what to do."[36] Over and over again, Merton reflected on the possibility and the impossibility of leaving, of the value of a life of prayer and contemplation, of the urgent needs of the world. He worried that he spoke too often about social issues; he was glad, for instance, when another white commentator admitted he was right to predict urban rioting in the early 1960s, but "was it necessary for me to reply?"[37]

Merton's journals testify to an unresolved interior struggle between a desire to hear the apocalyptic call of the times and a persistent concern about being swept away from the spiritual rootedness he believed necessary to confront the true evils of the world in a meaningful fashion. Merton was not alone in this grappling, nor in the inconclusiveness of his strivings. As the initial revolutionary fervor of the movement faded, the need to reconcile revolutionary rhetoric with contemplative grounding became increasingly important for a number of those engaged in the struggle.

The God's-Eye View from the Outhouse:
Julius Lester

In 1973, Julius Lester—the former SNCC organizer, nationally renowned folk singer, and prominent advocate of the Black Power movement—returned to the South, the first visit since his time working there with SNCC.[38] Lester was a southerner: although he was born in St. Louis, Missouri, his family moved to Nashville when he was nine years old, and even after years of living in the North, he would continue to think of himself as a product of the South.[39] "The South shaped and formed me and its speech remained on my tongue; its slow, easy rhythms were the rise and fall of my breathing."[40] It had formed him irrevocably in other ways, too. He found it hard to explain to northerners what it had been like, growing up as a Black child under Jim Crow.[41] When he taught courses to students in Massachusetts on the civil rights movement, speaking about his southern childhood would bring "globules of pain like phlegm" into his throat, and tears, unbidden, would flood his eyes: "I am aware of a massive trauma of anger and terror within me. This is not the melodrama of rhetoric; it is the consequence of surviving in a land where terror was as omnipresent as sunlight and sunshine."[42]

In Atlanta on that first trip back since his time in SNCC, Lester met up with a number of former organizers who still lived in the city. It was hard to see them again, acclimated to what looked to Lester like disappointingly middle-class mores. "Most of them seemed to be living the same lives that would have been theirs if they'd never sung 'We Shall Overcome.'"[43] What had happened, he wondered, to the "meaning" that the movement had given their lives, their vision of a radically different future they had dreamed together? "Could any of us sing 'We Shall Overcome' now without being ashamed of ourselves for once having believed it?"[44] They had not been transformed, Lester reflected, not the way that the movement had tried to transform them. That was one reason, he wrote, "why 'the movement' did not succeed."[45]

This is an unsettling statement from someone who, at one time, was seen as one of the ablest communicators of the message of the Black liberation struggle to the country. In a review in the *New York Times* of Lester's *Look Out, Whitey: Black Power's Gon' Get Your Mama!* (1968), Truman Nelson credited Lester with "teaching us how to speak and write as free artists—not because America permits us to say certain things, but because America is forcing us to be revolutionary again."[46] Lester's book, Nelson wrote, was a "magnificent example" of the ways in which the Black revolution was forging not only new political paths, but a new artistic vision of the world that "could generate the tidal force to sweep aside all the tired and dead matter on our literary shores, the litter we try not to see or to smell because we are too close to it."[47] Lester first joined the movement as a singer, performing freedom songs at SNCC rallies. In 1964, during the Freedom Summer (a coordinated campaign to register voters in Mississippi and organize the Mississippi Democratic Freedom Party to seat delegates at the Democratic National Convention that August, in opposition to the all-white, segregationist delegation of the Mississippi Democratic Party), Lester joined the movement officially, traveling to Mississippi "to sing in freedom schools, at mass meetings, and to hold workshops on Negro music."[48] In the late 1960s, he was instrumental in forging a new internationalist direction for SNCC, traveling to North Vietnam and Cuba with Stokely Carmichael and other SNCC leaders, positioning the organization as part of a global, revolutionary anticolonial struggle after the pattern of Malcolm X's own internationalism.[49] Yet by 1968, he wrote, he had "drifted away" from a movement that, in his judgment, had "ceased to be viable."[50]

Lester wrote two memoirs, in 1976 and 1988, both of which are strongly ambivalent about his time in the civil rights and Black Power movements. There are many ways in which the two memoirs diverge, especially in their religious orientation—both are essentially spiritual autobiographies, similar in style to Merton's own but written with different end-points in mind. In *All Is Well* (1976), Lester described himself as a "crypto-Catholic."[51] Lester's destined Catholic identity is revealed in episodes such as an instance in which he snuck away from his family to take a peek at the interior of a Catholic church as a child[52] and in his final, "awe-struck" revelation, on a visit to Merton's Abbey of Gethsemani detailed on the last page of the memoir, that all the seeming absurdities of Catholic doctrine ("the Immaculate Conception … the Virgin Birth, the Crucifixion, Resurrection, and Assumption") could all be true if God were God. Filled with joy, he realized: "I cannot save the world: I cannot change the world. All I can do is say Lord, Here I am."[53] In *Lovesong: Becoming a Jew* (1988), written after his conversion to Judaism, Lester portrayed himself instead as destined, from childhood, to reclaim the Jewish heritage of his maternal great-grandfather, Adolph Altschul.[54] The discrepancies in the religious narrative unfolded by Lester in these two autobiographies reflect the crucial importance for him of the spiritual journey he embarked upon following his departure from SNCC; it quickly became the most important aspect of his life. In contrast, his explanations in the two memoirs of his experiences in the movement closely correspond. In both, he stressed his internal ambivalence, pain, and alienation during his time with SNCC.

He had not wanted to join the movement, he wrote repeatedly. He wanted to read Merton and be a mystic.[55] He joined because he felt he had to, after the bombing of Sixteenth Street Baptist Church in Birmingham, Alabama, that killed four young Black girls. "History claimed me for Itself; I became a revolutionary."[56] In both memoirs, he described this choice as a turning away from the vividness of his inner life, a choice shaped by duty, not desire. "I forgot Merton and became a part of my times."[57] This was, for him, a heartbreaking trade, and his memories of the movement were dominated by fear and distress. He related his inner turmoil hearing the "raw emotion" in the voices of young people singing the freedom songs he was leading.[58] "We were too young to carry the pain of all those lives, too young to live, day and night, knowing that in any car behind us or coming toward us might be white men with rifles to kill us."[59] He found the person he became after years under the sustained pressure of racial terror hard to recognize in retrospect. In *All Is Well*, he included a letter he wrote in 1967, after his trip to North Vietnam, in which he had written:

> To kill is often an act of love. And I learned that from a beautiful, shy young girl who is a guerilla in South Vietnam. She's killed 25 G.I.'s and I knew when I met her that she knew about a love I haven't experienced yet, and look forward to. I look forward to the day when I will place a person in my rifle sight, squeeze the trigger, hear the explosion and watch that person fall. And after the shooting has stopped, I will continue that act of love that began when I started to hate, by helping others to build a country that will exist for its people and not vice versa.[60]

He read the letter over again, in the mid-1970s, with horror: "Those words do not sound like any person to whom I would give my name, or even want to, but they are mine."[61] More recognizable to him was the memory from a few weeks after his trip to Hanoi, at the home of a friend in Sweden, of lying on the floor listening to John Coltrane and feeling "reunited" with the South and the people who had given him life. "Those spirituals, whose essence Coltrane stood at the center of, had been sung by the ancestors beneath the midnight skies, and they were lines to another reality, The Reality, and that was prime. The ancestors had known, despite the whips and constant presence of Death. They had known and had sung, 'If anybody asks you who I am, tell 'em I'm a child of God' … I was their child."[62] But how could he reconcile these longings, his strivings to be a "poet-saint-mystic" with his political commitments, with the revolution? He could not figure it out. "Was I mad for trying to be Rimbaud, St. Francis, and Che Guevara?"[63]

Lester would become one of the strongest critics (from within the fold) of the trajectory of the Black liberation struggle during this period. In 1970, as Lester began to distance himself from the Black Power rhetoric he had earlier championed, he identified the shift in the movement in the late 1960s with Malcolm X, whose words were designed, he wrote, "to frighten whites and anger blacks."[64] At the same time, however, he expressed sustained affection and admiration for Malcolm, and reserved his strongest criticism, counterintuitively, for Martin Luther King Jr. Malcolm, he wrote, did not intend violence with violent rhetoric, but instead (relying upon an anecdote shared by Coretta Scott King) Lester hypothesized that Malcolm had used extreme language in order to force white people to work with King.[65] The move toward violent rhetoric in the later 1960s, he argued, was of an entirely different character: not an articulation of the need for self-defense, not strategic, but instead a "principal part of [the] program."[66] Lester interpreted this shift as understandable, a reaction to the "psychic, cultural, and physical" violence Black Americans were forced to endure. But it was also, in his view, a regrettable reaction to King's failure to offer an adequate spiritual vision of nonviolence after the pattern of Gandhi.[67] Lester did not view King as sufficiently contemplative, criticizing him for not fasting in jail.[68] Lester advocated instead for a vision of *satyagraha* (soul-force, Gandhi's concept of nonviolence) in which violent self-defense is permissible, but only as a last resort in order to preserve one's physical survival, a decision "which must always weigh upon one with excruciating pain."[69]

Lester's critique of King, in contrast with his praise of Malcolm, appears, at times, incongruous with his criticism of the revolutionary rhetoric Malcolm X inspired, and his enthusiasm for nonviolent direct action. As unexpected as these statements at times can seem, they are consistent with Lester's personal history, with how Malcolm X had touched him and shaped him even as he came to embrace a philosophy closer to King's. "Unlike Malcolm," Lester argued in another 1970 article, "[King] did not immerse his being in the soul of his people."[70] He remembered how, working as a welfare investigator in Harlem in the early 1960s, he and a few others had secretly whispered to each other about Malcolm X outside the hearing of their white boss. "Anything a white man hated that much couldn't be too wrong."[71] Malcolm X, like John Coltrane, had helped him root himself in love for his Black identity. In 1966, he had been one of the first publicly to articulate the rise of Malcolm X as the paradigmatic figure for the movement:

> More than any other person Malcolm X was responsible for the new militancy that entered The Movement in 1965. Malcolm X said aloud those things which Negroes had been saying among themselves. He even said those things Negroes had been afraid to say to each other. His clear uncomplicated words cut through the chains on black minds like a giant blowtorch. His words were not spoken for the benefit of the press. He was not concerned with stirring the moral conscience of America, because he knew—America had no moral conscience. He spoke directly and eloquently to black men, analyzing their situation, their predicament, events as they happened, explaining what it all meant for a black man in America.[72]

Malcolm X offered Lester a language of struggle that did not demoralize him in his pain, in his trauma, he and all who "still get headaches from the beatings they took while love, love loving … [dying] from trying to change the hearts of men who had none."[73] Lester could not stop being thankful for Malcolm X, even as he began to speak in terms of *satyagraha* and love for enemies.

Lester's abiding affection for Malcolm X and his love for

Thomas Merton, in the end, sprung from the same source: his crying out in the wilderness of the Jim Crow South for God's sustaining presence. Out of all of his memories of his time in the movement, Lester wrote, the most vivid was of an afternoon in May 1966, in Lowndes County, Alabama, during the formative period of Black Power. The memory is not about the work in which he was engaged, building, along with Stokely Carmichael and others, the Lowndes County Freedom Organization (also called the Black Panther Party, not to be confused with the originally Oakland-based organization of the same name). Instead, it was of going to the outhouse. Rare moments of quiet like this, Lester wrote, brought peace that was hardly imaginable in the midst of the conditions he witnessed daily. "We hated that people lived with bent shoulders and bowed heads, hated that people lived in houses in which they had glued newspapers up for wallpaper, hated knowing that the children in those houses were condemned never to know what their possibilities were and who they could have been. My Mind did not understand why white people killed over something as innocuous as voting, or why hatred was more compelling than love."[74] But in moments like the one in the outhouse—"the warm breeze soft on my exposed buttocks," listening to a man plow a field, the birds chirping overhead—he felt suddenly, and overwhelmingly, at one with God. "The poverty and the pain and the death all around me vanish as if they had never been."[75] Following his time in SNCC, Lester worked to regain these moments of peace by returning to the contemplative path—and to Merton. In 1975, in a poem published in *The Catholic Worker*, Lester described a visit to Merton's grave at Gethsemani's cemetery, and reflected on how, in death, Merton was simply a monk sharing the silent repose of his brothers buried with him.[76] Lester longed for that anonymous solitude, as out of reach as it had been both for him and for Merton himself during the turbulent years of the 1960s. Lester's time in the civil rights and Black Power movements was undeniably traumatic, illustrating vividly the vulnerability of contemplative spirituality to the brutal violence of racially based domination. And, at the same time, Lester emerged, perhaps despite himself, as a mystic whose spirituality was deepened and elevated by its realization of the awful cost of revolutionary solidarity.

A Path for Wounded Spirits: Gwendolyn (Robinson) Zoharah Simmons

As Gwendolyn Robinson prepared to move from her home in Memphis to Atlanta to start her freshman year at Spelman College, her grandmother, whom she called "Mama," had one firm request: "Soon as you get there, join a church."[77] Robinson listened, and asked around to find a Baptist church.[78] In Memphis, she and her family were members of the Gospel Temple Baptist Church,[79] part of the nurturing "all-black world" in which Robinson had been raised.[80] Her church, like her school and her neighborhood, had been a "very affirming and supportive" place,[81] something she stressed in a 2012 oral history interview that she "always like[s] to mention"[82] when describing growing up at a time and place in which "Jim Crow was in full force."[83] She would later reflect that over the course of her years in the movement, she would for some time lose sight of how crucial her traditional Black Baptist church home had been in shaping her awareness of her own dignity and her commitment to the struggle for justice.[84] This temporary "forgetting" reflects the fact that Robinson's journey through the civil rights and Black Power movements contained all of the winding turns of these movements themselves; she was an instrumental actor in the nonviolent mass movement of the early 1960s as well as the turn to Black Power politics in the later 1960s. Her spirituality, too, mirrored these shifts, moving from the Black Baptist church home of her childhood, to the interracial "beloved community" of SNCC's Freedom Summer, to the Nation of Islam, to, finally, the Islamic mystical tradition of Sufism and a reappraisal of King's theology of nonviolence. Her life story gives voice not only to the political evolution of the movement but to the spiritual challenges faced by those who fully committed themselves to the struggle.

Robinson was raised primarily by her paternal grandparents, visiting her mother—who, after her relationship with Robinson's father ended, had to work full-time—on weekends.[85] Robinson's mother had felt like a "big sister" to her, while Mama, "kind and loving and full of the joy of life," was her primary caregiver.[86] It was Mama, a "great storyteller," who passed down to her stories of the horrors of enslavement, labor exploitation, and anti-Black violence of the American South.[87] Her grandmother would cry as she told Robinson stories of Lucy,[88] Mama's own grandmother, who had been tormented by her owner, her half-sister: they shared a father in Lucy's first master. Lucy's sister would insert "long darning needles between Grandma Lucy's fingernails and nail beds while my great-great-grandmother bled profusely and begged for mercy."[89] From Mama, the young Robinson also learned about the continued horrors of sharecropping following emancipation, and Mama's stories grew especially harrowing as she turned to the topic of the people she knew who had escaped from plantations in Mississippi. These fugitives had been, in practice, enslaved to the plantation owners who exploited and cheated them and kept them in debt, holding them at gunpoint when they tried to flee.[90] "Don't *ever* go to Mississippi," Robinson's grandmother warned her. "It's the *worst* of the worst for black people."[91] Robinson's readiness to follow her grandmother's other piece of advice—find a church in Atlanta—would ultimately lead her to disobey this warning.

The church she found was West Hunter Street Baptist Church, whose pastor was Reverend Ralph Abernathy, one of the co-founders of the Southern Christian Leadership Conference (SCLC) and Martin Luther King's best friend.[92] Robinson was familiar with the "spirit-filled" style of Baptist preaching, but the message she heard from Rev. Abernathy's pulpit was new: "I was being summoned to a pacifist's war against racism, injustice, denial of rights, and assaults against my dignity and personhood."[93] Not only Rev. Abernathy but also Dr. King himself would deliver sermons at the church, and she began to visit Ebenezer Baptist Church to hear King preach from his own pulpit.[94] Robinson was ready for the message of King and Abernathy—her first year at Spelman had introduced her to African American history and literature through a course by two white professors, a Quaker activist, Staughton Lynd, and a Jewish woman from New York, Esther Seaton: "the material was just mind-blowing."[95] The course opened up to her a whole new world of possibility beyond the middle-class life she had envisioned achieving as a result of her matriculation at Spelman.[96] By the time she heard King and Abernathy preach, she was already prepared for their invitation to the struggle; "thrilled," she was ready to join King's "nonviolent army."[97]

This decision was not welcomed by her family. For her first year at Spelman, she kept her visits to the SNCC office secret and did not attend demonstrations. But after the March on Washington in 1963 (which she did not attend, but watched on TV, due to her family's disapproval), she increased her involvement, and was elected to serve on SNCC's board for the Atlanta-area Black colleges and universities.[98] She concealed her involvement, until her first arrest prompted Spelman to call and inform her grandmother: "the gig was up then ... my grandmother was threatening to come there and kill me."[99] Undeterred, Robinson pressed on, initially refraining from telling her grandmother what would most disturb her: her intention to travel in the summer of 1964 to join the Freedom Summer.[100] When her grandmother found out, she was furious: "They're going to kill y'all," she told Robinson. "That's the Klan down there. Are you crazy?"[101] But Robinson was insistent. Her family cried as a friend came to pick her up on the way to the bus station, and Mama told her solemnly: "If you leave, don't ever come back." On the Greyhound, Robinson cried the whole way.[102]

It did not take long for Robinson to encounter the horrors about which her grandmother had warned her. Two weeks into her orientation in Mississippi, two white volunteers (Michael Schwerner and Andrew Goodman) and one Black volunteer (James Chaney) were lynched by the Ku Klux Klan in Philadelphia, Mississippi, with the involvement of the local deputy sheriff.[103] She was horrified; she had met Chaney only a week before he was murdered. The protection she thought that having white volunteers travel with Black volunteers would afford her had not protected him, and, she realized, would not protect her. "It was like, 'Oh, these people really will kill us? ... we really could lose our lives here. This is, this is no joke.'"[104] Robinson was assigned to Laurel, Mississippi, a place deemed too dangerous to send white volunteers, to be a teacher in the Freedom School.[105] "I just thought, 'We're never going to get out of here alive.'"[106] But having defied her family, she did not think she could back down and admit that their fears had been justified.[107]

When the project director in Laurel, Lester McKinney, was arrested and forced to sign a pledge not to return to the county for five years, Robinson was unexpectedly asked to take his place as the head of the project.[108] But she soon found that she, like the people around her whom she was organizing, had a profound capacity to "[run] with it," to "catch" on and do the impossible.[109] In the sixteen months in which Robinson embedded herself in the Laurel community, she oversaw a staggering number of initiatives: mock voter registrations, the Freedom School, day-care, a community center, a housing project, literacy training, food and clothing distribution, and organizing demonstrations, marches, and direct actions.[110] Artists, theater troupes, and musicians—including, she remembered, Julius Lester—visited Laurel and played to packed audiences.[111] "I just have a wonderful overall memory of that period," she would later reflect.[112]

In the midst of the meaningful work she was accomplishing, however, the violence did not abate. The Freedom House, the base of the project in Laurel, was firebombed by the Klan—but SNCC members stayed in the building, continuing their work despite the burn marks on the walls.[113] When Robinson led a group of teenage girls in an action to desegregate a local restaurant, the sheriff took out his gun and threatened her.[114] At the point of his gun, she fell back on prayer:

> He leveled a gun at my chest and told me to turn the demonstrators around or he would fire. I was so afraid, but the demonstrators were mostly kids, and I felt that I had to stand up to him, not show my fear. I kept walking toward him, whispering a prayer as I walked. For some unknown reason, he let me and the scraggly line of demonstrators pass him and carry out our demonstration until we dispersed. He laughed and, holstering his gun, said, "Gal, you sure is crazy; you gonna git your damn self kilt one of these days." I thought, *I'm working God overtime today!*[115]

At the time, in response to these violent threats, Robinson continued to speak in the language of Gandhian nonviolence inculcated by the movement. A letter written by Charles Hartfield, a teenage boy and Mississippi resident who was organized into political involvement by SNCC,[116] relates an incident in January 1965 in which Robinson locked herself in a car during a demonstration, when the police manhandled protestors and reporters, smashing the latter's tape recorders. Hartfield wrote that Robinson told him that the police had threatened to hand them over to the Klan if they did not disperse. She explained to Hartfield that she was not afraid of being beaten by police, but was only afraid of "the evil" that had the power to turn human beings into demons: "she did not hate those men but she pitied them, because she could understand that they have been traped [*sic*]."[117]

Robinson's commitment to this theology of nonviolent resistance would come to be tested by the sheer intensity of violence she and other SNCC organizers and volunteers would experience. The Klan "started a reign of terror in Jones County," burning crosses and threatening local ministers who allowed the SNCC workers to use their churches.[118] The breaking point for Robinson came at the end of her time in Mississippi—it was, in fact, the reason that her time in Mississippi came to an end—when she and around a thousand others were arrested at a large statewide demonstration in Jackson. Not having jail capacity for so many people, the arrested demonstrators were kept in pens built for livestock at the local fairgrounds, where they were held for fifteen days, beaten severely and frequently.[119] "We were brutalized very badly ... lots of beatings, and, um, all kinds of terrorizing."[120] She saw two people in the fairgrounds almost beaten to death. Young girls—thirteen, fourteen years old—who had spontaneously joined the march were sexually assaulted by their white jailers.[121] Robinson was traumatized, "shell-shocked," and the executive secretary of SNCC, James Forman, insisted she leave Mississippi and move to New York for her own well-being.[122] It was during this time in New York, as she attempted to recover from the terror she had experienced, that she was introduced to the Nation of Islam.[123]

Robinson had first heard of Malcolm X in Laurel, after someone had mailed a record of Malcolm's speeches to the partially burned-out Freedom House. "We have a little record player there," she remembered, "and I put the record on and Malcolm X is talking about the ballot or the bullet. And I've never heard anything like this. I am totally mesmerized. I'm scared to even listen to it, it's so incendiary, you know, compared to anything else I know."[124] By the time she had fled Mississippi to New York, Malcolm X was already dead, but Harlem was a home in which his memory was held sacred. She began attending Amiri Baraka's Black Arts Repertory Theater and listening to the Nation's street preachers and their message, which astonished her, "that blacks needed their own land in this country, we deserved it."[125] While she, as she explained in an interview to the historian Ula Yvette Taylor, retained reservations about the Nation's teachings on gender even during her time as a member of the Nation of Islam, she was increasingly interested in what they had to say.[126]

Robinson would return to work with SNCC in the South—this time, in Atlanta—and she would bring with her this "whole 'nother song I've never heard before" with her.[127] There, she found like-minded people, including the man who would become her husband, Michael Simmons, who had known Malcolm X and whose brother was Elijah Muhammad's national secretary.[128] The SNCC workers in Atlanta—who collectively would become known as the Atlanta Project—would lead the way for SNCC to take on a Black Power orientation inspired by Malcolm X and the Nation of Islam:

> My coworkers in the Atlanta Project of SNCC and I wrote the first position paper in the organization that promoted the concept of Black Power and the idea that it was time for the whites of SNCC to leave the black movement, return to their own communities—which were the sites for the creation and continuation of racism and white supremacy—to create progressive change there. There-

fore, long before the Black Power cry became public,
SNCC staff in the Atlanta Project, influenced by Malcolm
X and his mentor, the Honorable Elijah Muhammad, as
well as by our own analysis of the endemic nature of white
supremacy and racism in U.S. society—even among our
white SNCC colleagues—had embraced a form of political
black nationalism and a rejection of racial integration as
the solution to the African Americans' problems.[129]

The historian Clayborne Carson portrays the Atlanta Project as
pivotal in shifting the overall direction of SNCC, resulting in
the passing, after rancorous debate, of a resolution in December
1966 that expelled white workers from the organization.[130] The
Atlanta Project's position paper mentioned above by Robinson
argued fervently that an "all-Black movement" was necessary
in order to combat the racist assumption that Black people cannot organize themselves, to prevent the "white liberal establishment" from using its power and wealth to set the movement's
course, and to allow for Black organizers to assert their own
self-determination.[131] Following the lead of Malcolm X, the
paper insisted on an internationalist, anticolonial framework
for combatting anti-Black racism in the United States: "Black
people are a semi-colonialized people, victims of a domestic
colonialism. Our introduction into this country occurred during the same time as the partition of Africa and Asia by the
European powers, so that the American institution of slavery
was, too, a form of Western Colonialism."[132] As a result, "our
struggle for liberation and self-determination can only be carried out effectively by Black people."[133]

SNCC's transformation into an all-Black organization was
experienced as both traumatic and liberating by different participants. Robinson described the frustration she felt as an influx of
white SNCC workers after the Freedom Summer led to a famil-

iar situation of Black SNCC staff members having to justify their
need for resources to white workers at the national headquarters.[134] For her, the expulsion of white members, at the time, had
represented new possibilities of power and self-determination
for SNCC. But for two other Atlanta-based SNCC workers, the
white, married couple Dorothy and Bob Zellner, who had been
part of SNCC since its beginning, the decision was tragic. The
expulsion from the organization left the Zellners "devastated,"
uncertain how to continue the dangerous work of organizing in
the South without remaining part of the SNCC community to
which they had given their lives.[135] The Zellners' particular grief
in losing their SNCC family was later recognized by Gwendolyn
(Robinson) Simmons, after learning from Bob Zellner about his
alienation from the white community: "his folks were members
of the Klan. He *couldn't* go home. I mean, they'd threatened to
kill him."[136] But, at the same time, the Zellners could understand
what had happened. "Everybody's always crying over the poor
white people," Dorothy Zellner said in an oral history interview
in 2015.[137] But, she argued, the expulsion of white people from
the movement should not have been a surprise, not after the
Democratic National Convention refused to seat the Mississippi
Democratic Freedom Party delegates in 1964, not in the midst
of such a "profoundly ... racially disturbed country."[138]

Expressions of Zellner's ambivalence over her expulsion can
be found in other sources, both Black and white. Julius Lester,
for example, described the experience of attending the December 1966 debate over white participation in SNCC while sitting
next to a white, female volunteer for whom he had developed
romantic feelings. "I understood the political necessity for the
decision," he wrote, "for it established the right of black organizations to determine their membership, a right which had
always been allowed whites. However, SNCC did not make a
political decision as much as an emotional one, evicting the

aliens from the city and stoning them outside the gates."[139] The
pressure to separate from white activists, comrades, and part-
ners was widely prevalent during this period, not just in SNCC,
but in many radical Black movement circles. The memoir of
Hettie (Cohen) Jones, Amiri Baraka's wife, chronicles the
breakdown of their marriage during this same period as Baraka
gradually reached the decision to divorce her as a rejection of
interracialism. On the one hand, Baraka's slow abandonment of
their family was heartrending. On the other, she "viewed as crucial the collective release of black anger; I wanted that to happen
even if my own awkward position continued. I'd seen enough
of the South and Harlem and Newark to believe, I thought, in
Malcolm's 'by any means necessary.'"[140]

Robinson's experiences in SNCC—the intensity of the violence she faced, and the ways in which she saw white paternal-
ism functioning even within the organization itself—had led
her on a path far afield from the message she had first heard
rapturously from the pulpits of Abernathy and King. "I began
to see Dr. King as an accommodationist, a moderate, a deal
maker with the establishment, hierarchical, sexist, a preacher
who was out of step with what the new times called for—Black
Power—and perhaps a renunciation of nonviolence ... Malcolm X's words were resonating with me now; his statement
'Any Negro who teaches Negroes to turn the other check in the
face of attack is disarming that Negro of his God-given right,
of his moral right, of his natural right, of his intelligent right to
defend himself' had become my anthem."[141] Malcolm's words
"were a strong cup of black coffee to the sleeping, an antidote
to the psychic and mental poison that was killing black people
figuratively and literally."[142] The journey that had begun with
her grandmother asking her to find a Baptist church had led her,
ultimately, to join the Nation of Islam.

While Simmons (no longer Robinson) "went into the [Nation

of Islam] because of its black-nationalist ethos and its economic 'do for self' motto," she "became very attracted to Islam as a religion after joining."[143] She had joined the Nation as part of a commitment to a revolutionary Black struggle, but she found in Islam itself a spiritual depth that brought up more fundamental questions about her time in the movement and the terror she had experienced. The Atlanta Project's work collapsed over the course of a couple years; funding "dried up" as SNCC took on a more nationalist and exclusive direction, and volunteers left the organization.[144] Simmons continued her involvement in movements for justice, organizing local low-income women in the Midwest with the National Council for Negro Women, and, afterward, on the staff of the American Friends Service Committee researching government surveillance of social justice organizations.[145] As Simmons's work transitioned from the life-or-death struggle of SNCC to longer-term commitments, she was, at the same time, exploring more deeply the spiritual questions that had "always" been with her. "Even early on," she reflected in an interview, "I had questions that I now understand that were always there, you know, about who are we? Why are we really here? What is this all about? Because now thinking about it, I saw a lot of poverty and suffering ... why is God letting this happen?"[146]

In 1971, Simmons would meet Bawa Muhaiyaddeen, a Sri Lankan Sufi master who would become her teacher on this "inward path."[147]

I was graced by God to meet a Sufi mystic, Sheikh Muhammad Raheem Bawa Muhaiyaddeen, who by his teachings, his example, and his very being introduced me to Islam, an Islam of justice, truth, beauty, and grace. The Islam that my Sheikh taught and exemplified is a gender, racial, and religiously egalitarian Islam. It is an Islam that teaches that all human beings are created from a divine ray of God, are all God's children and are completely equal in God's sight.[148]

Simmons was uncertain about how the Black nationalist fervor, her passion for revolutionary justice—that which had brought her to Islam in the first place—could align with the mystical path about which Bawa Muhaiyaddeen spoke. When she asked him about this, about the relationship between the struggle and the inward path of transformation, he "looked at [her] so lovingly and he said, 'my dear daughter, you are a small lamp trying to do the sun's work ... if you get what I have brought, you will become a sun.'"[149] Simmons was deeply moved, but continued to struggle with his response:

> I really grappled with it for quite a while. I mean to the point of tears, because the movement and the struggle was such a part of my life that I said I can't give this up for anything. But on the other hand, what he was teaching me about the soul and why we really had come was also very appealing. So there's that tension that exists still to this day after all these years. I'm still grappling with those two things.[150]

How could she reconcile the message of Bawa Muhaiyaddeen—that the "One Benevolence will show its compassion through its three thousand gracious attributes, and all lives will be seen as one's own life,"[151] even including "each enemy or person we dislike"[152]—with the rage against injustice she had found so profoundly humanizing in the message of Malcolm X and the Nation of Islam?

The tension remains. Simmons's "grappling" with these equally important concerns, however, can be seen in her reappraisal of King's own mystical-political vision of nonviolence. She recalled visiting Phnom Penh in the wake of the Cambodian genocide with the American Friends Service Committee, "to see the mountain of skulls and bones there."[153] Once again, as in Mississippi, she was face to face with the full extent of radical evil, the human capacity for terror and destruction. With the benefit of her Sufi training, Simmons said, she now can appreciate more deeply what this signified:

> Not only do we have to change things legally, politically, structurally. We also have to change things in people's hearts and their spirits … I think that's what helped me to come around to understanding Dr. King's message in a way that I had not and I had rejected … It brought me sort of full-circle back to nonviolence as the only real way to bring about a change that doesn't leave corpses piled mountains high, or even just wounded spirits and souls and bodies … It's not the easy way, but it's the only way that you might be left with people who can work together … and move forward without the pain and all you have when it's been warfare or massacres and the like.[154]

Revisiting King's life and work, Simmons praised King's gradual development of a prophetic vision of "an international non-violent movement stretching across the globe in the developed and developing world bringing pressure 'to bear on the capital and governmental power structures [of the West].'"[155] Simmons recognized both the struggle and the appropriateness of remaining politically active while, at core, committing to spiritual transformation: "I am still in movements, still doing work … Bawa has made it plain that we're not to go sit on a mountaintop somewhere and just meditate … We are, as the Muslims say, God's vice-regents, so we are to do good work in the world, but we have to be very clear that our major work is to become human beings, which is the *insan kamil*, the divine beings that we were created to be."[156]

God and the Revolution?

For Merton, Lester, and Simmons, the question of how to bring together political struggle and contemplation would persist—but it would not disappear. Malcolm X endured as a fixed presence in their questionings, their wrestling, even as he could not remain alone, and John Coltrane, or Bawa Muhaiyaddeen, or Martin Luther King Jr. needed to be heard as well. The stories of Lester and Simmons demonstrate the role Malcolm X's vision of God's presence in the non-white revolution would increasingly play in social movements: one possible element among others in facing the spiritual devastation of entrenched global oppression.

His vision would resonate not only for future generations of Black activists, but of revolutionaries of every stripe. As his revolutionary theology inspired a larger and more diverse set of movements, its spiritual articulation would take in many different forms. "God means revolution," chanted Cha Cha Jiménez and those attending the People's Church (*Iglesia de la Gente*), the community created when the Puerto Rican Young Lords occupied the Armitage Avenue United Methodist Church, in 1969. In the first years of the 1970s, too, queer liberation activist Sylvia Rivera, who had worked with both the Young Lords and the Black Panther Party, would kneel down with her fellow "street queen" Marsha P. Johnson nightly before candles of patron saints and pray for divine protection and defense. Even as hopes for an immediate "revolution" that would upend life in America as we know it faded, the radical movements brought into existence by this dream kept alive the faith that God was there in the struggle.

8

People's Churches

Other Heirs of Malcolm X

The Radical Jesus Is Winning:
José "Cha Cha" Jiménez and the
Other Heirs of Malcolm X

Cha Cha Jiménez's mother, Eugenia, wore black for an entire year of his childhood: it was a *promesa* she had made to God to get her husband, Antonio, to stop drinking.[1] Migrants from rural Puerto Rico, the couple and their children had been displaced over and over again within the city of Chicago. They were forced out of the Near North Side, then drifted "northward two or three blocks at a time" in Lincoln Park, as a result of federal slum-clearance policy which tore down barely habitable slum buildings only to allow private developers to replace them with luxury apartments far beyond the financial capacity of the original residents.[2] Doña Eugenia's piety was, during Jiménez's childhood, a rare source of stability in a world otherwise pervaded by volatile ethnic conflicts, violence, addiction, and desperation. Sensing her husband slipping away into the alcoholism that had killed two of his uncles, she convinced Don Antonio to join *Los Caballeros de San Juan* (The Knights of Saint John), a Chicago-wide Catholic organization that by the 1960s, according to Michael Robert Gonzales, had become "the city's largest

Puerto Rican religious and social club."[3] Doña Eugenia, herself a member of *Las Damas de Santa Maria* (The Ladies of Saint Mary), the sister organization of *Los Caballeros*, was an active organizer of the local Puerto Rican Catholic community, lobbying for the Mass to be celebrated in Spanish at a local parish and leading daily neighborhood recitations of the rosary and Spanish-language catechism classes from the Jiménez home.[4] Just as Doña Eugenia had used her close connections to the local Catholic community to protect her husband, so too with her son: when she saw Cha Cha begin to get "into trouble" along with local neighborhood boys, she arranged with a local priest to have him sent, tuition-free, to St. Teresa's, a predominantly white (German, Polish, and Italian) Catholic school.[5]

Jiménez flourished at St. Teresa's, where his earlier "mischievousness" was transformed into "piety."[6] He had become an altar boy at the Spanish Mass at St. Michael's, a local Redemptorist parish, and continued this role at St. Teresa's, where he also spent his free time helping out, "shoveling snow, sweeping, mopping and waxing the floors, and dusting the pews in the chapel."[7] He had "made up his mind" about the future: he wanted to be a priest.[8] But Jiménez found it hard to disassociate himself with the neighborhood gang culture, particularly the protection that gang affiliation could provide from others' attacks. In one incident, members of local "European [white ethnic] gangs" targeted and chased him down the street until he made it into the Puerto Rican area of Lincoln Park.[9] Combined with the "anti-Puerto Rican feeling" to which he had become accustomed at St. Teresa's, Jiménez struggled to resist the pressure to affiliate with a gang out of "self-defense."[10] Invited by a neighborhood friend to a meeting at which a new gang, the Young Lords, was formed, he saw his involvement at first as only "nominal."[11]

That changed when the only possible alternative future Jiménez could imagine was foreclosed to him. As he completed eighth grade at St. Teresa's, he applied to the Redemptorist seminary in Wisconsin to begin his path to the priesthood. He lacked, however, a necessary recommendation from the pastor of St. Teresa's, as, unbeknownst to Jiménez, the pastor had been on a bus at which he and a classmate had thrown eggs toward the end of the school year. The pastor wrote the seminary requesting that Jiménez be denied entry. Jiménez returned to public school, located in the very neighborhood in which the Young Lords operated.[12] Jiménez lived his life for the next half decade in and out of incarceration, first in juvenile detention and then in prison,[13] and he became president of the Young Lords in the mid-'60s due to being "trusted" for having spent so much time in prison.[14] By 1968, he had reached a low point—prevented by court order from visiting his wife and newborn daughter, he had become "really depressed" and addicted to heroin.[15]

Determined to overcome his addiction, Jiménez asked for religious books to read during his time in solitary confinement. One changed the course of his life irrevocably: *The Seven Storey Mountain* by Thomas Merton. Unable to leave his cell to attend Mass, he began to practice mental prayer and meditation and reflected on his need to start a new life. He asked for a priest to be brought to his cell, and, through the bars, he confessed his sins and received absolution.[16] During this same period, a prison librarian who was a member of the Nation of Islam began sharing "political books" with him, including the writings of Martin Luther King Jr. and Malcolm X.[17] The life of Malcolm X in particular, which he connected with the legacy of the Puerto Rican nationalist leader Pedro Albizu Campos, charged his imagination.[18] It was also during this time that he first heard of the work of the Black Panther Party, and thought to himself, "we need something like that in the Puerto Rican community."[19] These two sources of inspiration—Thomas Merton's memoir of his spiritual conversion, and Black revolutionary politics—

would shape Jiménez's radical next step, the reorganization of the Young Lords into an organization dedicated to communal empowerment and self-determination.

Jiménez was not alone among non-Black activists inspired by the example of Black revolutionary politics. The Young Lords were only one organization that explicitly drew on the Black Power movement—its politics, its aesthetics, its worldview, its messianic vocabulary—as a model for revolutionary change. Participants in the constellation of liberation movements that emerged during the late 1960s and 1970s in the United States frequently credited Black political organizations and figures (especially Malcolm X, Stokely Carmichael, and the Black Panther Party) with pioneering the tactics and style their own movements had adopted. The original spirituality of these radical Black politics, rooted in the apocalypticism of the Nation of Islam and Malcolm X's revolutionary theology, took on different forms as it found new homes in different cultural and religious contexts. This is true also of the diverse Christianities with which these movements came in contact. The Young Lords, as one example, was comprised of many members, like Jiménez, with a Puerto Rican Catholic background, influencing the organization's combination of revolutionary politics with veneration of Jesus as an advocate of the poor.

The Young Lords are only one example among many liberation movements during this time period that developed revolutionary ideologies in dialogue with Christianity. This is true even among movements often associated with hostility toward Christian institutions, such as gay and queer liberation movements, which, along with the story of the Young Lords, this final chapter will explore in depth. While queer activists were often resentful of the role Christian churches had played in the oppression of sexual and gender minorities, many of the leaders of the Stonewall riots and queer liberation longed not for the elimination of religion but for its transformation into a source of liberation and protection from anti-gay/trans violence. The same would be true, for instance, of the American Indian Movement (AIM), which would reclaim traditional ceremonies and reject the Christianization forced on indigenous peoples in the United States but would also center leaders of the Native American Church, a syncretistic Christian/traditional religious body, as spiritual guides for the movement.[20] An AIM leader and Sicangu Lakota woman, Mary Brave Bird, who credited her adoption of traditional Lakota and pan-indigenous ceremony with her political and spiritual transformation, was at first "uncomfortable" with the strong presence of Jesus in the rituals of the Native American church: "Wasn't this an Indian, not a white man's religion?"[21] Over time, she came to appreciate the co-existence of indigenous and Christian spiritual practices.[22] As these examples demonstrate, revolutionary politics in the 1970s became differently—but not less—religious than the protest movements of the 1960s, and Christianity remained an important source of symbolic and spiritual power for many involved. For many in these movements, Malcolm X remained the prototypical revolutionary but also the generator of new spiritual possibilities.

La Iglesia de la Gente: The Young Lords and the People's Church

During the week of Christmas in 1969, the lesbian activist Martha Shelley, along with other members of the newly founded Gay Liberation Front, had organized 24-hour-a-day vigils outside of the New York Women's House of Detention in support of Black Panther Party members Afeni Shakur and Joan Bird, who were then incarcerated there.[23] But on New Year's Eve, hearing about what was happening in Spanish Harlem, Shelley left the

vigil and took the train uptown. She wanted to see it for herself: the Young Lords had forcibly occupied the First Spanish
United Methodist Church (FSUMC) after trying, unsuccess-
fully, to convince the Cuban-American pastor, Rev. Humberto
Carranza, to enable them to use the space for their community
programs, especially serving free breakfast to neighborhood
(largely Puerto Rican) children.[24] The overtures of the activists,
who had begun regularly attending the church and attempting
to plead their case with the church leadership, became increasingly less welcome to the pastor and the board, prompting Rev.
Carranza on December 7 to call the police. The officers rushed
into the church with billy clubs, arresting thirteen Young Lords
and wounding five to the point of needing hospitalization; four
police officers also reported injuries. In response, on December 28, during the Sunday service, Young Lord leaders nailed
the doors of the church shut from the inside with railroad
spikes and announced they were occupying the church. They
then escorted out any church members who wanted to leave
through the one remaining door. The occupation—the People's
Church—remained in place until January 7.[25] Martha Shelley
described the event after the fact:

> They left peaceably after being served with an injunction—
> but during their stay 200 children were fed hot breakfasts
> daily. Over 100 children were given complete physical
> examinations. The Young Lords held classes, poetry read-
> ings, film showings, and a New Year's Mass by a radical
> priest. And the church was open to all the people.[26]

The Young Lords appealed to the congregation to join them in
this work of serving the community ("This church is open for
three hours on Sundays, and wouldn't it be nice for it to be open
five days a week with a day-care center so that parents could go to
work and leave their children in a safe place? Why isn't this place

feeding the hungry? Isn't that a credo of Christianity?"),[27] and many, did, in fact, agree and stay. Mickey Melendez describes being touched, despite how his earlier religious commitments (he was also a former altar boy) had evolved into a "faith in revolution" as a college student, by the church members' reaction to their message: "I 'knew' about revolution, nationalism, and socialism ... But the congregation's belief, based on faith alone, dwarfed my action. Theirs had no explanation, no basis, and no science to back it up. And still they were resolved to continue."[28]

Melendez's alienation from Christianity was not unusual for the Young Lords. As Johanna Fernández notes, most of the Lords "came to see Christianity as an ideological instrument of conquest, colonialism, and repressive state rule in Latin America, distinguishing it from the radical origins of the church of Jesus."[29] But the latter part of that statement is as important as the first: the Young Lords critiqued Christian institutions in a manner that centered Jesus as a radical icon. When Shelley entered the People's Church, she noticed the entwinement of radical and religious rhetoric immediately: "The church was hung with the children's drawings, and with revolutionary posters and slogans: 'The doors are open to the people's church.' 'Jesus Christ helped the poor.' 'All power to the people.' 'A Vietnam yo no voy, porque yanqui yo no soy' (I will not go to Vietnam because I'm not a Yankee)."[30] Fernández writes that, prior to the occupation, one member of the Young Lords had brought a poster into the church portraying Jesus as a revolutionary, an AK-47 rifle slung over his shoulder.[31] During the occupation, the Young Lords' minister of education, Juan González (yet another former altar boy), preached about Jesus, who "walked among the poor, the poorest, the most oppressed, the prostitutes, the drug addicts of his time."[32] The Latin American Catholic context, as Melendez notes, was not lacking in examples of Christian communities serving as a voice for social justice: he cites the Medellín conference at which the Catholic bishops of the region expressed their support for human rights movements as well as examples of Cuban, Mexican, and Puerto Rican religious leaders who campaigned against injustice.[33] He also notes the role of Christian communities in the Black freedom struggle as an inspiration.[34] Like these other communities, "we wanted that same responsiveness from the church for the Puerto Rican community in New York."[35]

Their most direct inspiration for the occupation of the church in Harlem, however, had been the first People's Church. The Chicago branch of the Young Lords, under the leadership of Cha Cha Jiménez, had occupied the Armitage Avenue Methodist Church in June 1969, in response to the church board declining their request "to rent church space for a daycare center and a Panther-style children's breakfast program and health clinic."[36] Unlike Rev. Carranzo later that year, however, the pastor of the Armitage church, Rev. Bruce Johnson, had supported the Young Lords unequivocally and declined police assistance, enabling the church to become the Lords' national headquarters.[37] "The church was renamed the People's Church, a new symbol of the cross bursting the chains of bondage was created, and a new creed appeared at the church door," proclaimed an article in *Y.L.O.*, the Lords' newspaper.[38]

> The Good News of Jesus Christ is that each man is of worth as a special creation of God. And Christ's resurrection means that there is no power or establishment which can control a man who claims his own dignity.
>
> This is your faith & your Church! Claim them both and join us in this dream.[39]

Three months later, Rev. Johnson and his wife, Eugenia (Jean), were tragically murdered in their sleep, a case that has never been solved. At a memorial service held at the People's Church

the same day they were found, Cha Cha Jiménez eulogized Rev.
Johnson and Eugenia Johnson, describing how, in contrast with
the vast majority of "churchmen" who were "static, like boats
tied to the dock, going nowhere, doing nothing," the Johnsons
forged a new path for the church: "We need people who will
move across the waters toward the sunlight of freedom, the new
land in the sunlight. If people do that, if they ever arrive at the
land of freedom and they look back across the water, they will
see the bodies of Bruce and Jean Johnson near the land. They
will see how close our two friends had come to freedom."[40] The
church broke out into a chant:

> The bread is rising ** Bread means revolution ** God
> means revolution ** Murder is no revolution ** Revolu-
> tion is love ** The radical Jesus is winning ** The world is
> coming to a beginning ** Organize for a new world ** The
> liberated zone is at hand. RIGHT ON![41]

Despite the openness of the Young Lords to Christian symbols, stories, and communities in their organizing, their model
remained firmly that of Malcolm X over that of Martin Luther
King Jr. "The fact that the white power structure that opposed
him in life can honor Dr. King in death is perhaps indicative
of the shortcomings of his ideology," an article on the fourth
anniversary of Malcolm X's assassination in the first issue of the
Young Lords' newspaper reflected. While King, the newspaper
asserted, did not fundamentally pose a challenge to American "liberalism," the "gun" offered by Malcolm X to the Black
revolutionary struggle did.[42] "Malcolm X, an Orthodox Muslim," wrote Umar Muntu Bakr of the Young Lords' ministry of
defense in *Palante*, the New York chapter's newspaper, "was one
of the few brothers to rise out of the degradation that all Blacks
and Puerto Ricans experience in Babylon."[43] Bakr noted that
Malcolm X's call for community ownership of land and insti-

tutions was the origin of the parallel call in the Young Lords' program and the tactics used by the organization.[44] By 1970, however, Bakr argued, it had become clear that revolution was the only way that Puerto Ricans could gain control of their land. Here, too, Malcolm led the way. Unlike most "amerikkkans," Bakr wrote, Malcolm X understood the cost of freedom: "Revolutions are bloody and Malcolm realized that aside from war veterans, very few amerikkkans know what mass killing looks like ... People in amerikkka have become hung-up on death and physical violence although their whole world is based on violence."[45] Bakr called on his readers to stop playing revolutionary by only discussing revolutionary politics ("how you going to spend your time when there are no more 'Books of the Month'?"), and announced a five-day festival in honor of Malcolm X starting on May 19, 1970, what would have been Malcolm's forty-fifth birthday.[46]

The Young Lords would eventually fracture, like the Black Panther Party also did, over disagreements about what this call to revolution actually entailed. In 1971, the Young Lords leadership would choose to redirect the energy of the organization away from "survival programs" like those offered at the People's Church towards a nationalistic, revolutionary struggle in Puerto Rico itself, an effort that, in Fernández's summary, ending up reaping "no significant success—symbolic or otherwise—that might have increased their membership base or reputation and influence among potential sympathizers on the island."[47] By 1972, the remaining leadership abandoned these efforts and embraced an explicitly Marxist-Leninist-Maoist line that, along with continued relentless government suppression, contributed to the disintegration of the Young Lords Organization.[48]

And yet, the kind of liberatory spiritual community created by the Young Lords at both the first and second People's Church—as well as in their other creative actions and neighborhood organizing—was a model for other movements. The Gay Liberation Front visitor to the People's Church, Martha Shelley, left the church in Harlem with her imagination full of possibilities about "what GLF could do with a church or a loft or a brownstone. What it would be like when GLF has its community center, how we could serve our people … what we might learn from the Young Lords' experience."[49] At the same time that Shelley wrote this, Sylvia Rivera, another Gay Liberation Front activist who would become involved in the Young Lords, was, along with her friend Marsha P. Johnson, thinking about the same thing: how to create a communal and spiritual home for the vulnerable community of "street queens"—who today would be described as transgender sex workers—to which she belonged.

The Saints of Christopher Street: The Spirituality of Queer Liberation

At the STAR House on Second Street in New York's Lower East Side, fifteen to twenty-five self-identified street queens crammed into four rooms nightly, making use of every available surface, including the bathtub, for a place to sleep.[50] There was no electricity in the apartment; the landlord had turned it off, so they lived by candlelight. "We'd cook up these big spaghetti dinners," Sylvia Rivera remembered, "and sometimes we'd have sausage for breakfast, if we were feeling rich."[51] It was a dream, Rivera recalled, living together in this safe and caring refuge from a violent world. It was a dream that had nourished her and the other queens through all they had suffered, through police harassment, through poverty, through racism, through the omnipresent dangers of sex work, through the community's rejection, through addiction, through rebellion and protest, through homelessness and heartbreak. It was a dream that she

could barely summon growing up, she said, "basically ... without love," after her mother's suicide, and a dream she could not
have imagined as a child sexually exploited and abused by family members.[52] But among her sisters, she began to be able to
envision that dream. "I remember nights when the queens used
to sit around and smoke in our little hotel rooms," Rivera wrote.
"We'd party and dream of some day when we could walk down
the street and say: 'Fuck the cops, we're here, and we're going to
stay here.' We'd dream that dream over and over."[53]

Rivera and her friend and co-founder of the STAR House,
Marsha P. Johnson, had embodied that dream in June 1969,
during the Stonewall riots, when they, along with other queens
and queers, had fought back against a police raid at the Stonewall Inn in Greenwich Village. "The queens knew how to fight,"
Rivera noted pointedly.[54] Johnson agreed: they weren't afraid.
"I'd been going to jail for, like, ten years before the Stonewall,"
she explained. "They'd say, 'All yous drag queens under arrest,'
so we, you know, it was just for wearing a little bit of makeup
down Forty-second Street."[55] The riots had not been Rivera's
and Johnson's introduction to political action. "Before gay
rights, before the Stonewall," reflected Rivera, "I was involved
in the Black liberation movement, the peace movement ... My
revolutionary blood was going back then."[56] Over the course of
her time organizing with queer liberation movements, Rivera
would continue to work in coalition with other radical groups.
In 1970, Rivera would become involved with the Young Lords:
"I became one of them. Any time they needed any help, I was
always there for the Young Lords."[57] She met with Huey Newton
in 1971, as Newton (like the Young Lords) grew to recognize the
struggle for queer liberation as parallel to the Black struggle.[58]
Both Rivera and Johnson were closely involved with the work of
numerous radical queer organizations such as the Gay Liberation Front, the Gay Activists Alliance, and the Queens Libera-

tion Front. They would become most known, however, for the organization they themselves founded: the Street Transvestite Action Revolutionaries, STAR, the very heart of which was the STAR House on E. Second Street.

The building was a "slum building," barely habitable when they first moved in.[59] They had begun STAR's work by organizing a sit-in at New York University's Weinstein Hall when the university had caved to students' parents' pressure and ended gay dances hosted regularly at the location. In response to the demonstration, the Gay Liberation Front and the organization Gay Youth held a fundraiser for STAR to help the organization rent a house.[60] Despite this initial show of support, Rivera recalled receiving little help from other queer activists in renovating and maintaining the space. "When we asked the community to help us," she later told an interviewer with tears rolling down her face, "there was nobody to help us. We were nothing. We were nothing!"[61] An exception was she and Johnson's friend Bob Kohler, a Gay Liberation Front activist who helped paint the apartment and "put wires together."[62] Kohler was deeply committed to expressing solidarity with different oppressed groups, and had begun his activism with the Congress of Racial Equality (CORE).[63] In the wake of the Stonewall riots, Kohler publicly took his fellow "butches" (masculine-presenting gay men) to task for distancing themselves from the drag queens who had faced the brunt of police violence during the uprising: "I learned something this past Summer, something I can't put into words yet, but whatever it is, it helped me to stand in front of the Village Voice on a Gay picket line and say Fuck You to the Closet Cases and Straights who looked at me aghast for standing up to be counted ... It helped me to realize that Drag Queens are more than a part of my culture—they are a part of me."[64]

Kohler, however, was an exception to the norm. The gay community's neglect clearly unsettled Rivera, even years later,

showing her broader feelings of hurt about her place in movement circles. She and Johnson had often felt out of place, and at
times, actively unwanted. "In these struggles," recalled Rivera
in a 2001 speech, "in the Civil Rights movement, in the war
movement, in the women's movement, we were still outcasts.
The only reason they tolerated the transgender community in
some of these movements was because we were gung-ho, we
were front liners. We didn't take no shit from nobody."[65] Johnson told an interviewer in 1972 that she experienced what she
called "oppression" especially from gay men, while gay women,
on the whole, she found to be more welcoming. "Once in a while
I get an invitation to [the lesbian organization] Daughters of
Bilitis, and when I go there, they're always warm. All the gay
sisters come over and say, 'Hello, we're glad to see you,' and they
start long conversations. But not the gay brothers. They're not
too friendly at all toward transvestites."[66] Johnson's impression
of the generally hospitable reception she received from lesbians
is all the more tragic given what eventually caused the end of
STAR: the public and embittered fallout between Sylvia Rivera
and a group of radical lesbian feminists in 1973, when the latter condemned the drag queens and transvestites (as they then
self-identified) participating in the Pride march as "female
impersonators" degrading women.[67] Heartbroken over what she
felt was betrayal by a movement she had helped found, Rivera
attempted suicide in Johnson's and her shared home, where she
was found by Johnson. As they waited for Rivera to be brought
to the hospital, Johnson told her: "you're not crossing that River
Jordan without me, you and I will cross together."[68]

Rivera and Johnson's sisterhood, at the STAR House, was
opened up to others, especially young people in danger. "We
tried," Rivera remembered. "Marsha and I and a few of the other
older drag queens. We kept it going for about a year or two. We
went out and made that money off the streets to keep these kids

off the streets. We already went through it. We wanted to protect them. To show them that there was a better life. You can't
throw people out on the street … We had kids from Boston,
California, everywhere."[69] The deep commitment Rivera and
Johnson made to each other was reflected in the common life of
the community, which was bound together not only by shared
experiences of trauma, danger, and exclusion but also by ritual
and prayer. Rivera recalled:

> We'd all get together to pray to our saints before we'd go
> out hustling. A majority of the queens were Latin and we
> believe in an emotional, spiritualistic religion. We have
> our own saints: Saint Barbara, the patron saint of homo-
> sexuality; St. Michael, the Archangel; La Calidad de Cobre
> [sic], the Madonna of gold; and Saint Martha, the saint of
> transformation. St. Martha had once transformed herself
> into a snake, so to her we'd pray: "Please don't let them see
> through the mask. Let us pass as women and save us from
> harm." And to the other three we'd kneel before our altar
> of candles and pray: "St. Barbara, St. Michael, La Calidad
> de Cobre [sic]: We know we are doing wrong, but we got
> to live and we got to survive, so please help us, bring us
> money tonight, protect us, and keep evil away." We kept
> the sword of St. Barbara at the front door and the sword
> of St. Michael at the back door to ward off evil. We were
> watched over.[70]

As Joy Ellison and Nicholas Hoffman have noted, Rivera's
description here of the STAR House's nightly prayers reflects the
influence of Santería, an Afro-Caribbean syncretistic tradition
with both West African (Yoruba) and Catholic components.[71]
Rivera's description of the young, mostly Latina queens turning to saintly protection in the midst of danger echoes stories
of queer Latino diaspora communities across the United States.

Lázaro Lima shares a story, for instance, of a Cuban-American drag queen, la Señorita Mar Tini, performing in 1994, during the AIDS crisis, as La Caridad del Cobre, the Virgin of Charity, the patroness of Cuba and one of the sacred guardians summoned by the STAR House residents.[72]

While Rivera, who was half Puerto Rican and half Venezuelan, had practiced these traditions from her youth, Marsha P. Johnson's enthusiastic participation in these rituals, however, requires a bit more explanation. Although she had been raised attending an African Methodist Episcopal church and had a normative Black Protestant upbringing, she chose to identify specifically with Catholic religious practice. "I practice the Catholic religion," Johnson shared, "because the Catholic religion is part of the Santería of saints, which says, we're all brothers and sisters in Christ."[73] Johnson, as her friend Randy Wicker pointed out, was "deeply religious," and could be found frequently prostrating herself in front of the statue of the Virgin Mary at Ss. Peter and Paul Church in Hoboken, New Jersey. Her tastes were religiously pluralistic; she would attend Greek Orthodox, Roman Catholic, Baptist, Jewish, and other religious services.[74] But more than any other tradition, she affiliated with Catholicism, and in particular its saints. Sylvia Rivera described an incident in which Marsha P. Johnson came over to her house "dressed like the Virgin Mary, in white and blue, and she was carrying a wooden cross and a Bible."[75] Johnson would do things like this, Rivera explained. "Marsha lived in her own realm, and she saw things through different eyes."[76]

Johnson had lived in her own realm for quite some time, beginning with the profound spiritual relationship she forged with Jesus as a teenager. "I got married to Jesus Christ in church when I was sixteen years old," Johnson recalled, "still in high school, and I haven't married anybody in the church since then, because I believe he's the only man I can truly trust. He's like the spirit that follows me around, you know, and helps me out in my hour of need, and listens to my problems, and never laughs at me! He takes me very seriously."[77] Easily evoking comparisons with medieval female saints like St. Catherine of Siena or St. Joan of Arc, Johnson regularly had visions. "In one of them," she said, "there were ten suns shining in the sky, gorgeous and freaked out, like the end of the world. I love my saints, darling, but sometimes the visions can be scary."[78] Her eccentric spirituality was recognized and revered by many in the community. "Marsha had a following around town," explained Tommy Lanigan-Schmidt, "of people that—like, I'd go to the Flower District, and they have these big tables where they sort, like, lilies and things. Marsha would be sleeping under them. And I saw this more than once. And I would say to the guy there, 'why is she here?' And the guy would just say, 'well, she's holy!'"[79] Wandering through the Village bedecked in flowers and plastic fruit and with costume earrings in her hair,[80] she was a strange sight, but also a welcome one. "Friends and many people who knew Marsha," shared Randy Wicker, "called her Saint Marsha, because she was so generous, and she was such a good person. A little queen would come up and say, 'Marsha, that brooch is so beautiful!' And Marsha would say, 'Oh, you like it?', and take it right off, and give it to her."[81] Rivera herself had experienced Johnson's extravagant generosity in their first meeting, when Johnson had pulled the eleven-year-old Rivera off the streets, introduced herself, and took her out to eat. "A very strong sistership was born," Rivera remembered.[82]

While it is Marsha who continues to be revered as the "Saint of Christopher Street,"[83] Sylvia Rivera had her own deeply held religious commitments. In the last years of her life she was an avid member of New York's Metropolitan Community Church, one of the first LGBTQ+ religious communities in the world, where Rivera directed the food pantry. Rivera had met the leader of the community, Reverend Pat Bumgardner, at a demonstration, and accepted an invitation to visit the church, where she received what Reverend Pat called a "hero's welcome," something, she noted, Rivera had not always received from the gay community. Reverend Pat describes holding Rivera's hand as she neared her death of liver cancer at St. Vincent's Hospital, while Rivera dug her nails into Reverend Pat's arm, pleading with her to use the church basement as a shelter for homeless LGBTQ+ youth (the shelter was later formed, and was named Sylvia's Place).[84] Rivera continued to engage in Santería-inspired rituals and practices, as she had since childhood. "My saints protected me," she said, reflecting upon her lifelong struggle to survive.[85] In 1992, Marsha P. Johnson's body was retrieved from the Hudson River in what was officially ruled a suicide but some still suspect may have been a homicide. Sylvia Rivera, devastated by her friend's death, ended up homeless for a time, living on the Christopher Street Piers, but still made sure to keep "candles burning on an altar to Marsha inside her makeshift home."[86]

The religious character of Johnson's and Rivera's activism might, at first glance, be unexpected, given the typical portrayal of queer liberation movements (and liberation movements of this period in general) as secular or anti-religious. It is true that, out of all of the radical movements that formed during this period, it is unsurprisingly easy to spot anti-religious sentiments in contemporary radical queer publications. However, even in this case, this anti-religious rhetoric often conceals a desire for a different *kind* of religiosity. Thus, for instance, Leo Louis Martello inveighed in the Gay Liberation Front's newspaper, *Come Out!*, in 1969 that "religion has always treated sex as a 'sin'. It has brainwashed millions into believing that a biologically normal drive is 'evil.' It has ruled by guilt."[87] What a cursory reading of this passage does not reveal is that Martello was actually a pioneering Wiccan who wrote a regular column entitled "The

Gay Witch" for *Gay*, another gay newspaper.[88] Both the poetry and prose of these periodicals convey spiritual yearnings that are authentic to the experience of a tremendously oppressed and persecuted minority. A striking example is a poem by Sandy DeWine, published in *Come Out!* in 1970. The poem is dedicated to an Argentinian student, Diego Viñales, who was seriously injured after jumping out a window attempting to flee a police raid at a gay bar in Greenwich Village, landing on a spiked fence. The poem expresses DeWine's outrage and pain about Viñales's near martyrdom in the language of Catholic devotion, imagining St. Christopher (of Christopher Street in the Village) being transformed into the mutilated martyr, St. Sebastian, and depicting Viñales's mother as the Madonna in a modern-day pietà.[89] A Gay Activists Alliance member and United Church of Christ minister, Roy Birchard, wondered in an article in the Metropolitan Community Church's newspaper in 1972 if queer people's lived experiences of persecution and suffering might allow them to illuminate aspects of the Bible that at the time remained in darkness, allowing the Scriptures once again to "speak with prophetic force."[90] DeWine's poem demonstrates that this work was already very much underway.

For Birchard, the figure who had initiated this new spiritual awakening was, of course, Malcolm X. The "experience of the black struggle," Birchard wrote, gave witness to the "incredible psychological liberation which comes when the oppressed see that they have been the victims of power games, not of an immutable fate which has condemned them to permanent inferiority."[91] So, when "Malcolm X and SNCC said go organize your own people, some of us began to wonder who 'our people' were."[92] Malcolm's revolutionary language found echoes in the militant queer liberation groups with which Johnson and Rivera associated, and can be heard in their own analysis of their activism. "I was a radical, a revolutionist," Rivera said in a later interview. "I am still a revolutionist ... I remember when someone threw a Molotov cocktail [at Stonewall], I thought: 'My god, the revolution is here. The revolution is finally here!'"[93] Johnson, similarly, described STAR's work in language used by the Black Panther Party, who themselves drew on Malcolm X's assertion of the right of armed self-defense: "STAR is a very revolutionary group. We believe in picking up the gun, starting a revolution if necessary."[94] At the same time, Johnson was also comfortable with more conciliatory language: "How many years has it taken for people to realize we're all brothers and sisters and human beings in the human race?"[95] The more radical wing of the gay/queer movement was deeply concerned with connecting their organizations with Black Power and other revolutionary struggles. "We are one of many oppressed groups," wrote Allan Warshawsky and Ellen Bedoz in *Come Out!* in 1970. Their organizing as queer people, they argued, must be understood as part of a broader revolutionary movement: "Our participation in Movement actions (e.g., the Moratorium [to End the War in Vietnam], Panther rallies) is a beginning. Each time we appear at a Movement function identified as GLF we reinforce the bonds between us."[96]

Revolutionary rhetoric such as this co-exists in queer periodicals from the time with a variety of spiritual approaches. A few pages after Warshawsky's and Bedoz's article in *Come Out!*, for instance, a passage by the Oglala Lakota writer Black Elk is reprinted that relates a vision Black Elk had of "seeing in a sacred manner the shape of all things in the spirit, and the shape of all shapes as they must live together like one being. It is the story of all life that is holy and is good to tell, and of us two-leggeds sharing in it with the four-leggeds and the wings of the air and all green things; for these are children of one mother and their father is one spirit."[97]

The co-existence of the revolutionary language of the Black

Panther Party alongside statues of St. Michael and St. Barbara for Johnson and Rivera, then, should not be a surprise, no more than the co-existence of Thomas Merton and Malcolm X in Cha Cha Jiménez's life story should be. The revolutionary period in which these movements were forged was a time of political and spiritual ferment: creative and novel, volatile and destructive, diverse and challenging. The decentering of traditional Christian religious institutions in the movement heralded by Malcolm X did not mean a "de-Christianization" of the movement. If anything, quite the opposite: new languages of Christianity's relationship to politics emerged at this time, alongside diverse other religious traditions' transformations of their stories and symbols. Today, at a time when the most active organizations at work for Black liberation and other struggles for justice are not generally associated in the public consciousness with Christianity, we can learn from these earlier examples to look more closely, beyond affiliation with traditional religious institutions, for signs of spiritual transformation at work on the ground.

Coda

"They Don't Know That Their Hearts Are Breaking"

Malcolm X in Minneapolis

On February 21, 2021, the 56th anniversary of Malcolm X's assassination, as the wind blew intermittent flakes of snow around them, a group of Minneapolis residents gathered together in front of a former Speedway gas station that, during the uprising in the city in May and June 2020, had been seized by locals, covered with murals, and converted into a space of communal gathering. The first half of the gas station's name, "Speed," had been painted over with the word "People's"—People's Way. The abandoned gas station is part of the intersection occupied by community members and renamed George Floyd Square.[1] During the February gathering, large placards with twenty-four demands (including funding for local youth and more measures to ensure police accountability) leaned against the building next to murals of George Floyd, the 46-year-old father of five murdered in the square's location by a police officer, Derek Chauvin. Chauvin had placed Floyd in a chokehold under his knee as Floyd suffocated for almost ten unbearable minutes. Floyd's death, which had been caught on video, horrified many white American viewers, who, homebound during the Coronavirus-19 lockdown, witnessed anti-Black violence in all its ugliness in a manner many had previously managed to avoid. Polls

showed a dramatic increase in support of the Black Lives Matter movement—a grassroots movement against police brutality,
anti-Black violence, and systemic racism that had begun eight
years previously, and which till then had never been supported
by a majority of polled Americans.[2]

The movement received its name in 2012, when a young
activist named Alicia Garza wrote a "love note to black people" on Facebook following the announcement that George
Zimmerman—who had killed a Black teenager, Trayvon
Martin, in Sanford, Florida—had been acquitted.[3] The letter
ended with the declaration that despite the ongoing and systemic devaluation of Black life in the United States, "our lives
matter."[4] While the name for the movement sprung from this
early collaboration between Alicia Garza and two other young
Black activist women, Patrisse Cullors and Opal Tometi, it is
not confined to a single organizational structure. Rather, as the
Washington Post journalist Wesley Lowery put it, "Black Lives
Matter is best thought of as an ideology. Its tenets have matured
and expanded over time, and not all of its adherents subscribe
to them in exactly the same manner."[5] As Lowery and others
have pointed out, the movement itself did not gain a broad level
of national attention until the outbreak in August 2014 of mass
demonstrations in Ferguson, Missouri, after the fatal shooting
of another Black teenager, Michael Brown, by the police officer
Darren Wilson. The protests in Ferguson began with a spontaneous uprising and developed into an organized national call
for people from all over the country to come to Ferguson to join
with and support the demonstrators, lending a national focus to
the growing movement.[6]

Brown's death was a "breaking point" for many Black Americans, argues Keeanga-Yamahtta Taylor, a scholar of African
American Studies at Princeton University, due to the particular
"inhumanity" with which Michael Brown was treated (his body

was left in the street for four and a half hours after he was murdered) and the notably militarized response of the police to Black protests in Ferguson.[7] At the same time, Taylor notes, Brown was also one person among too many other instances of police killings of Black Americans. Police murders of Black people, argues Taylor, "are only the tip of the iceberg when it comes to the US criminal justice system" in its treatment of Black lives as disposable and Black pain as unworthy of attention. These acts of police violence take place in the larger context of longstanding disparities in the United States "between Blacks and whites in employment, poverty, housing quality, and access to education" rooted in a history of discriminatory laws and practices.[8] Still, these deaths, as vivid illustrations of white Americans' indifference to Black life, became powerful symbols of the failure of "postracial" America during the years of Barack Obama's presidency.[9] "The spotlight now shining on pervasive police abuse, including the ongoing beatings, maimings, and murders of Black people, destabilizes the idea of the United States as colorblind and thus reestablishes the basis for strengthening regulatory oversight and antidiscrimination measures."[10] If Brown's death was a "breaking point" for many Black Americans illustrating the nonexistence of post-racial America, Floyd's was a wake-up call for white Americans during the racially charged atmosphere of Donald Trump's tenure in the White House. By February 2021, at the gathering outside the People's Way, however, most of white America had moved on.

For some in Minneapolis, however, the uprising after Floyd's murder was the start of a transformative and lasting movement. "I think so much about what we did this past summer, this Freedom Summer," one young woman seated in front of the People's Way shared, "and how quickly we all were on the streets, you know, we were all fighting while our city was occupied, because our brother was murdered right here, another one of our brothers was murdered."[11] Multiple other speakers shared their experiences of homelessness, of incarceration, of racism, and recalled the memory of Malcolm X as a champion of Black humanity. "They can't bastardize Malcolm X like they bastardized Martin Luther King," one woman shared. "They can't take Malcolm X's words out of context like they can Martin Luther King. They can't say, 'Oh, Malcolm X wouldn't like that, Malcolm X wouldn't want you burning down buildings.' Hell yeah, Malcolm X would be out here for us burning down buildings!"[12] As other speakers emphasized, the attacks on property that had been part of the uprising had a meaning beyond mere destruction. During the uprising, the first seated woman recalled, "we were helping people, we were doing what we can to extend all the resources we have to keep each other safe and alive," and while they were doing so, people on television, she said, were accusing them of looting selfishly. "It's like, no, we're trying to get what we've been needed, and what has been denied to us for decades, for centuries."[13] The real meaning of the uprising, so another woman shared, was very simply: "Fuck anything but Black joy ... We don't want, just, like, affordable housing. We don't want just, like, to be able to buy the food that will keep us full for the week, like, we want joy, and we *deserve* that, yo, we deserve that all the time, and if Black people are joyful, everyone's gonna be fucking joyful."[14]

What the gathering was describing was not just a political transformation, but a spiritual one. "We speak of our freedom like it's a fucking mantra," the first woman went on.

Wake up in the morning, have your ritual and remind yourself why you have this breath. Remind yourself who laid this path that you get to walk on ... You gotta love yourself enough to see that everyone here, all of y'all people ... all of y'all are parts of me that I don't know, and I

love you … Even people in their towers, even people who
got everything they think they need, they don't know that
their hearts are breaking. There's a lot of rich people who
kill themselves … We are co-signing other people's pain
every time we are merely thinking about getting ours. So,
our joy … is so important and the joy of all our kin is just
as important … Malcolm X said this, "the future belongs
to those who prepare for it today." And we prepare for it by
making sure that everybody got what they need.[15]

The woman's words, spoken against a background of murals
with the names and faces of the murdered, drew on a long legacy
of communal empowerment and care powerfully communicated by Malcolm X and his heirs. She reminded those at the
gathering and those watching the live stream: the anger of rioters can be seen, from another angle, as the love of community,
the assertion of humanity. Activists had wrestled with the ten-
sions implicit in this equation before, and they were wrestling
with them again.

From the Detroit rebellion to the Minneapolis rebellion,
from the 1964 Freedom Summer to the 2020 Freedom Summer, from the Black Arts Movement to the artists graffitiing the
walls of a communally seized gas station, Malcolm X's theology
of revolution, along with the civil rights movement's theology of
nonviolent direct action, have been shaped, tested, challenged,
and transformed not only in theory but in practice, by actual
human beings—more often than not, young people—starving for joy, connection, meaning, balm for their broken hearts.
Their stories, then and now, whether inspiring and hopeful,
whether disquieting and painful, need to be heard, and need to
be shared.

Acknowledgments

This book originated in questions raised for me by my involvement with communities engaged in the work of justice, especially Su Casa Catholic Worker Community, the JOIN for Justice Organizing Fellowship, and Jewish Voice for Peace—Boston. I feel privileged to have been able to experience (in Hannah Arendt's term) the "public happiness" of communal, social, and political action through these organizations and through friendships with the extraordinary people I have met through this work. I have to begin by thanking them.

Many thanks are due to my editor at Orbis Books, Jon Sweeney, for his faith in this project and his openness to my ideas and vision for the book. I am very grateful for Orbis's support and honored to have the book with a publisher so committed to the pursuit of a more just world and church.

For the dissertation research that eventually was adapted into this book, I was very lucky in my committee: my advisor, Jeannine Hill Fletcher, and my readers, Mark Chapman and Bryan Massingale. Their support, encouragement, questions, and suggestions made the dissertation a stronger, better argued, and more complete project, and I have striven in the book to honor their comments and contributions. Thank you also to other faculty who supported and encouraged me during my time as a doctoral student and candidate at Fordham University, especially Kathryn Reklis, Brenna Moore, John Seitz, and Patrick Hornbeck.

My heart is filled with gratitude for my Fordham family, our magical, inspiring, supportive, silly, thoughtful, prayer-filled, hilarious little crew. "This is how movements start!" Vanessa Williams (and Sean), Mary Kate Holman, Jim Robinson, Eric Martin (and Anna), Gregory Tucker, Christopher Sprecher, and Lisa Holsberg (and Peter): I love you all madly.

Thank you to the staff of both the Schomburg Center for Research in Black Culture and the Bentley Historical Library at the University of Michigan. Having the opportunity to examine Malcolm X's and Albert Cleage's personal papers was truly a gift.

To so many beloved friends, especially Julie Frega (and Nathan, Oliver, and August), Alana DiPesa Truelove (and Tom and Juniper), Joey Kingsley, Emily Kobel, Chantal de Alcuaz, Josie Beavers, my sweet and silly godson, Jude Paruq Beavers de Alcuaz, Nora Wintermute, Jonathan "Dewey" DeWeese, Emma Mahern (and Eduardo, Oscar, and Rosa), Erica Concors (and Ann-Marie), Elisha Baskin (and Yuval and Akko), Emilia Diamant, Aliya Sabharwal (and Alex), Kirsten Lamb (and AJ), Shireen Ahmed, and Steph Yang (and Gaby). I'm so grateful for all of you in my life!

And to my best friend, my dearest Matthew Cortese, SJ: *thank you* is inadequate. You have been both my *hevruta* and my *anam cara* since we first wandered into each other's lives in the autumn of 2005 in the chaplains' office. So much of my mind and my heart is a reflection of your friendship, and I love you.

To my family: thank you to my parents, especially for allowing Meg and me to take refuge in Vermont during many periods of intensive work, and to my sisters, Rachel (and partner Rox) and Jessica, and their respective animals: Artie, Amelie, Buffy, and Beanie; and Theo, Finn, Tonks, Obama, Maeve, Dax, and Sisko.

To my sweet little dog, DeWitt: thank you for all the cuddles and silliness over the course of writing this book. You are the very best noodle in the world and I love you.

Finally, to my wife, my Meg: I love you so much. I always think of you when I read or teach James Baldwin's description of what it means "to be loved, baby, hard, at once, and forever, to strengthen you against the loveless world." Thank you for loving me, and for always believing in me throughout this journey. You are my very favorite person.

Notes

Introduction

1. Diane Nash, "August 1961, National Catholic Conference for Interracial Justice, Detroit, Michigan," in *Women and the Civil Rights Movement, 1954–1965,* ed. Davis W. Houck and David E. Dixon (Jackson, MS: University Press of Mississippi, 2009), 164.

2. David Halberstam, *The Children* (New York: Fawcett Books, 1998), 327.

3. Nash, "August 1961, National Catholic Conference for Interracial Justice, Detroit, Michigan," 164.

4. Halberstam, *The Children,* 327-29.

5. Halberstam, *The Children,* 327.

6. Nash, "August 1961, National Catholic Conference for Interracial Justice, Detroit, Michigan," 164.

7. Halberstam, *The Children,* 267-89.

8. *Freedom Riders,* directed by Stanley Nelson Jr. (Firelight Media for PBS American Experience, 2010).

9. Halberstam, *The Children,* 37-38.

10. Halberstam, *The Children,* 47-49.

11. Halberstam, *The Children,* 49.

12. M. K. Gandhi, *Non-Violent Resistance (Satyagraha)* (Mineola, MN: Dover Publications, 2001), 39.

13. Gandhi, *Non-Violent Resistance,* 6-7.

14. Gandhi, *Non-Violent Resistance,* 78-79.

15. John D'Emilio, *Lost Prophet: The Life and Times of Bayard Rustin* (Chicago: University of Chicago Press, 2003), 50.

16. D'Emilio, *Lost Prophet,* 230.

17. D'Emilio, *Lost Prophet,* 230-31.

18. Nash, "August 1961, National Catholic Conference for Interracial Justice, Detroit, Michigan," 166.

19. "Student Nonviolent Coordinating Committee Founding Statement," *The Sixties Project,* Institute for Advanced Technology

in the Humanities (IATH), University of Virginia at Charlottesville, http://www2.iath.virginia.edu/sixties/HTML_docs/Resources/Primary/Manifestos/SNCC_founding.html. For more on this statement in context, see Clayborne Carson, "Student Nonviolent Coordinating Committee," in *Organizing Black America: An Encyclopedia of African American Associations*, ed. Nina Mjagkij (New York: Routledge, 2001), 647.

20. Clayborne Carson, "Rethinking African-American Political Thought in the Post-Revolutionary Era," in *The Making of Martin Luther King and the Civil Rights Movement*, ed. Brian Ward and Tony Badger (New York: New York University Press, 1996), 115-27.

21. Dorothy Zellner, Interviewee, Emilye Crosby, John Melville Bishop, and U.S. Civil Rights History Project, *Dorothy Zellner Oral History Interview Conducted by Emilye Crosby in Baltimore, Maryland*, 2015, transcript, 72. https://www.loc.gov/item/2016655416.

22. Joseph R. Washington Jr., *Black Religion: The Negro and Christianity in the United States* (Boston: Beacon Press, 1964), 27.

23. Stokely Carmichael and Charles V. Hamilton, *Black Power: The Politics of Liberation in America* (New York: Vintage Books, 1992), 51-52.

24. Halberstam, *The Children*, 507.

25. Halberstam, *The Children*, 523-26.

26. Peniel Joseph, *Stokely: A Life* (New York: Basic Books, 2014), 21.

27. Joseph, *Stokely*, 244.

28. It should be noted that there is debate among scholars about the use of the term "nationalism" in describing what is typically referred to as Black nationalism. Even one of Black nationalism's most important theorizers, E. U. Essien-Udom, expressed concern about the imprecise nature of this term with regard to the diverse movements and trends it is used to describe. Essien-Udom defined nationalism in general, and Black nationalism in particular, as "the belief of a group that it possesses, or ought to possess, a country; that it shares, or ought to share, a common heritage of language, culture, and religion; and that its heritage, way of life, and ethnic identity are distinct from those of other groups. Nationalists believe that they ought to rule themselves and share their own destinies, and that they should therefore be in control of their social, economic, and political institu-

tions" (E. U. Essien-Udom, *Black Nationalism: A Search for Identity in America* [Chicago: University of Chicago Press, 1962], 6). However, he immediately noted that "it must be admitted at the outset that neither the Nation of Islam nor any other black nationalist organization wholly conforms to this definition" (Essien-Udom, *Black Nationalism,* 7). As a result, Edward E. Curtis IV has adopted the term "black particularism" in order to more accurately describe trends in the conceptualization of Black identity typically referred to as "Black nationalist" (Edward E. Curtis IV, *Islam in Black America: Identity, Liberation, and Difference in African-American Islamic Thought* [Albany: State University of New York Press, 2002], 14). For the sake of clarity and as a result of the specific focus of multiple figures in this book on the building of a "Black nation," this book will generally use the term "Black nationalism" in order to refer to these movements, while attempting to acknowledge difference in what the concept of "the nation" meant for different figures and groups throughout.

29. Elijah Muhammad, *Message to the Blackman in America* (Phoenix, AZ: Secretarius MEMPS Publications, 1973), 273.

30. Elijah Muhammad, *The Fall of America* (Phoenix, AZ: Secretarius MEMPS Ministries, 1973), 138-43.

31. "A Partial Transcript of a Sermon by Malcolm X at Elder Lightfoot Michaux's New York Church of God, June 16, 1961," included in Louis A. DeCaro Jr., *Malcolm and the Cross: The Nation of Islam, Malcolm X, and Christianity* (New York: New York University Press, 1998), 231.

32. Joseph, *Stokely,* 162.

33. This term derives from an influential chapter, "Religious Diversification during the Era of Advanced Industrial Capitalism" (1992), by social scientists Hans A. Baer and Merrill Singer, which provided a broad outline of the diverse religious movements that emerged within Black communities in northern urban centers as a result of the Great Migration. Baer and Singer categorized Black religion as largely fitting into four types: mainstream denominations, messianic-nationalist sects, conversionist sects, and thaumaturgic sects. Baer and Singer were primarily concerned with erasure of religious difference in scholarship on Black religion: "we concluded that there was a need for a typology that systematically recognizes the diversity of Black religious groups while placing them in a shared

context" (Hans A. Baer and Merrill Singer, "Religious Diversification during the Era of Advanced Industrial Capitalism," in *African American Religious Thought: An Anthology*, ed. Cornel West and Eddie S. Glaude Jr. [Louisville, KY: Westminster John Knox Press, 2003], 522).

34. Baer and Singer, "Religious Diversification," 524-26.

35. Baer and Singer, "Religious Diversification," 525.

36. E.g., see Muhammad, *Message to the Blackman*, 97: "The New Testament and Holy Quran's teaching of a resurrection ... [means] a mental resurrection of us, the black nation, who are mentally dead to the knowledge of truth; the truth of self, God and the arch-enemy of God and His people."

37. Malcolm X, *The End of White World Supremacy: Four Speeches*, ed. Imam Benjamin Karim (New York: Arcade Publishing, 1971), 192-93.

38. Malcolm X, *Malcolm X Speaks: Selected Speeches and Statements*, ed. George Breitman (New York: Grove Weidenfeld, 1965), 216.

39. Willa Boesak, *God's Wrathful Children: Political Oppression & Christian Ethics* (Grand Rapids, MI: William B. Eerdmans, 1995), 173-74.

40. Boesak, *God's Wrathful Children*, 217.

41. Kerry Pimblott, "Beyond De-Christianization: Rethinking the Religious Landscapes and Legacies of Black Power in the Age of #BlackLivesMatter," in *Race, Religion, and Black Lives Matter: Essays on a Moment and a Movement*, ed. Christopher Cameron and Philip Luke Sinitiere (Nashville, TN: Vanderbilt University Press, 2021), 39-66.

42. Jeffrey O. G. Ogbar, *Black Power: Radical Politics and African American Identity* (Baltimore, MD: Johns Hopkins University Press, 2004), 12.

43. Louis A. DeCaro Jr., *On the Side of My People: A Religious Life of Malcolm X* (New York: New York University Press, 1996), 1-2. In part, this derives, as DeCaro notes, from contemporary media sources' portrayal of Malcolm, as these sources were concerned almost exclusively with his challenge to the integrationist orientation of the broader civil rights movement, as well as to the version of Malcolm X promoted by his "white revolutionary supporters." The latter interpreters have maintained a durable imprint on the public perception of Malcolm X due to the fact that white socialists, particularly the

Trotskyite activist George Breitman, were responsible for many of the earliest and most popular compilations of Malcolm X's speeches and statements, through Breitman's leadership of the Socialist Worker Party's Pathfinder Press.

44. See, e.g., DeCaro Jr., *On the Side of My People*; Louis A. DeCaro Jr., *Malcolm and the Cross: The Nation of Islam, Malcolm X, and Christianity* (New York: New York University Press, 1998); James H. Cone, *Martin & Malcolm & America: A Dream or a Nightmare* (Maryknoll, NY: Orbis Books, 1991); Aminah Beverly McCloud, *African American Islam* (New York: Routledge, 1995); Richard Brent Turner, *Islam in the African American Experience* (Bloomington, IN: Indiana University Press, 1997); Edward E. Curtis IV, *Islam in Black America: Identity, Liberation, and Difference in African-American Islamic Thought* (Albany: State University of New York Press, 2002); Edward E. Curtis IV, *Black Muslim Religion in the Nation of Islam, 1960–1975* (Chapel Hill: University of North Carolina Press, 2006); Dawn-Marie Gibson, *A History of the Nation of Islam: Race, Islam, and the Quest for Freedom* (Santa Barbara, CA: Praeger, 2012); Sherman Jackson, *Islam and the Blackamerican: Looking toward the Third Resurrection* (New York: Oxford University Press, 2005); Herbert Berg, *Elijah Muhammad*, Makers of the Muslim World Series (London: Oneworld Publications, 2013); Herbert Berg, *Elijah Muhammad and Islam* (New York: New York University Press, 2009). Different scholars have provided varying lenses for interpreting the relationship between Malcolm X's religious convictions and his political contributions. Edward E. Curtis IV has described Malcolm X's expression of Islam in the context of the tension between conceptions of "Islamic universalism" and Muslim-identified "black particularism" (Curtis, *Islam in Black America*, 85-105, and Curtis, "Islamism and Its African American Muslim Critics: Black Muslims in the Era of the Arab Cold War," in *Black Routes to Islam*, ed. Manning Marable and Hishaam D. Aidi [New York: Palgrave Macmillan, 2009], 49-68), while Zain Abdullah has focused on Malcolm's attempts to bridge racial and religious discourses into "a kind of Islamic liberation theology" (Zain Abdullah, "Malcolm X, Islam, and the Black Self," in *Malcolm X's Michigan Worldview: An Exemplar for Contemporary Black Studies*, ed. Rita Kiki Edozie and Curtis Stokes [East Lansing: Michigan State University Press, 2015], 214), while Adil Ahmed, drawing upon Sherman

Jackson's conception of a "third resurrection" of Black Muslims in America, has interpreted Malcolm X's religious "conversion" as less of a conversion and more an "adaptation and appropriation of Islamic knowledge and praxis, in service to his life, his self-interpretation, and his mission to his kin" (Adil Ahmed, "Islam and Black America: the Religious Life of Malcolm X," *Journal of African American Studies* 24 [2020]: 456-81).

1. The Final Disaster

1. Letter from Malcolm X to Philbert Little, August 9, 1949, Malcolm X Collection, Schomburg Center for Research in Black Culture, Box 3, Folder 1.

2. Letter from Malcolm X to Philbert Little, August 9, 1949.

3. Letter from Malcolm X to Philbert Little, n.d., 1948, Malcolm X Collection, Schomburg Center for Research in Black Culture, Box 3, Folder 1.

4. Malcolm X and Alex Haley, *The Autobiography of Malcolm X* (New York: Ballantine Books, 1965), 152, 155.

5. Letter from Malcolm X to Philbert Little, November 28, 1948, Malcolm X Collection, Schomburg Center for Research in Black Culture, Box 3, Folder 1.

6. Letter from Malcolm X to Philbert Little, December 11, 1950, Malcolm X Collection, Schomburg Center for Research in Black Culture, Box 3, Folder 1.

7. Letter from Malcolm X to Henrietta Little, March 25, 1951, Malcolm X Collection, Schomburg Center for Research in Black Culture, Box 3, Folder 1.

8. E.g., Elijah Muhammad, *Message to the Blackman in America* (Phoenix, AZ: Secretarius MEMPS Publications, 1973), 231.

9. Letter from Malcolm X to Philbert Little, January 29, 1950, from the Malcolm X Collection at the Schomburg Center for Research in Black Culture, Box 3, Folder 1.

10. Letter from Malcolm X to Philbert Little, November 28, 1948.

11. Letter from Malcolm X to Henrietta Little, October 16, 1950, Malcolm X Collection, Schomburg Center, Box 3, Folder 1.

12. Malcolm X and Haley, *The Autobiography of Malcolm X*, 177.

13. "Lost-Found Muslim Lesson No. 2," n.d., answer 39.

14. Malcolm X and Haley, *The Autobiography of Malcolm X*, 159.

15. Malcolm X and Haley, *The Autobiography of Malcolm X*, 183.

16. Malcolm X and Haley, *The Autobiography of Malcolm X*, 3.

17. Malcolm X and Haley, *The Autobiography of Malcolm X*, 9-10.

18. Malcolm X and Haley, *The Autobiography of Malcolm X*, 17-21.

19. Manning Marable, *Malcolm X: A Life of Reinvention* (New York: Viking, 2011), 39-69; Malcolm X and Haley, *The Autobiography of Malcolm X*, 23-150.

20. Malcolm X and Haley, *The Autobiography of Malcolm X*, 149-50.

21. Malcolm X and Haley, *The Autobiography of Malcolm X*, 163.

22. Malcolm X and Haley, *The Autobiography of Malcolm X*, 169.

23. Malcolm X and Haley, *The Autobiography of Malcolm X*, 186-87.

24. Malcolm X and Haley, *The Autobiography of Malcolm X*, 189.

25. Louis A. DeCaro Jr., *On the Side of My People: A Religious Life of Malcolm X* (New York: New York University Press, 1996), 88-89.

26. Marable, *Malcolm X*, 334.

27. DeCaro, *On the Side of My People*, 36.

28. Letter from Malcolm X to Philbert Little, November 28, 1948.

29. Letter from Malcolm X to Philbert Little, December 18, 1949, Malcolm X Collection, Schomburg Center for Research in Black Culture, Box 3, Folder 1.

30. Letter to Brother Raymond, March 18, 1950, reproduced in Charles Ezra Ferrell, "Malcolm X's Pre-Nation of Islam (NOI) Discourses," in Rita Kiki Edozie and Curtis Stokes, *Malcolm X's Michigan Worldview: An Exemplar for Contemporary Black Studies* (East Lansing: Michigan State University, 2015), 132.

31. James Baldwin, *The Fire Next Time* (New York: Vintage Books, 1993), 50.

32. "The Muslim Program," n.d.

33. Herbert Berg, *Elijah Muhammad*, Makers of the Muslim World Series (London: Oneworld Publications, 2013), 26-27.

34. Berg, *Elijah Muhammad*, 27-29.

35. Berg, *Elijah Muhammad*, 27-29.

36. Hatim A. Sahib, "The Nation of Islam," *Contributions in Black Studies* 13 , Article 3 (1995), 67. https://scholarworks.umass.edu/cibs/vol13/iss1/3 .

37. Sahib, "The Nation of Islam," 68; Berg, *Elijah Muhammad*, 30.

38. Sahib, "The Nation of Islam," 68.

39. Hans A. Baer and Merrill Singer, "Religious Diversification during the Era of Advanced Industrial Capitalism," in *African American Religious Thought: An Anthology*, ed. Cornel West and Eddie S. Glaude Jr. (Louisville, KY: Westminster John Knox Press, 2003), 495.

40. Baer and Singer, "Religious Diversification," 517-19. For more on how earlier Muslim-identified sects may have influenced the Nation of Islam's theology of divine judgment, see the second chapter of Marjorie Corbman, "Divine Discontent: The Influence of Messianic-Nationalist Movements on Early Black Theology's Portrayal of God's Judgment" (PhD diss., Fordham University, 2020).

41. Jackson, *Islam and the Blackamerican*, 44-45. Edward Curtis has similarly noted that Islam was associated with "political protest and black resistance to colonialism and racism" in the writings of nineteenth- and twentieth-century Black writers, in Edward E. Curtis IV, "Debating the Origins of the Moorish Science Temple: Toward a New Cultural History," in *The New Black Gods: Arthur Huff Fauset and the Study of African American Religions*, ed. Edward E. Curtis IV and Danielle Brune Sigler (Bloomington: Indiana University Press, 2009), 82. See also Curtis's in-depth discussion of Edward Wilmot Blyden's "black particularist" interpretation of Islam in *Islam in Black America: Identity, Liberation, and Difference in African-American Islamic Thought* (Albany: State University of New York Press, 2002), 21-43.

42. These were the words emblazoned on the Nation of Islam's flag. See, e.g., E. U. Essien-Udom's description of the juxtaposition of the American and Nation of Islam flags at Chicago's Temple No. 2: "An American flag appears in the upper left corner of the blackboard and directly below it, painted against a white background, a tree with a black man hanging from a branch. Opposite the tree is the cross, another symbol of oppression, shame, suffering, and death. Below the cross appears the word 'Christianity.' In the upper right corner the flag of the Nation of Islam is painted—the moon and stars in white against a red background which represented the sun. The letters, I., F., J., and E. are inscribed on the flag, one on each corner. These stand for Islam (Peace), Freedom, Justice, and Equality. Below the flag and directly opposite the word 'Christianity,' is inscribed 'Islam.' Between the two flags and the names of the two religions is a large question

mark with the question: Which One Will Survive the War of Armageddon?" See Essien-Udom, *Black Nationalism*, 217. See also Imam Benjamin Karim's description of this display in New York's Temple No. 7 (Malcolm X, *The End of White World Supremacy*, 18-19), and Sonsyrea Tate's detailing of the same at Washington, DC's Temple No. 4 (Sonsyrea Tate, *Little X: Growing Up in the Nation of Islam* [New York: HarperCollins Publishers, 1997], 52-53).

43. Sahib, "The Nation of Islam," 68.

44. Erdmann Doane Benyon, "The Voodoo Cult among Negro Migrants in Detroit," *American Journal of Sociology* 43, no. 6 (May 1938): 896.

45. Berg, *Elijah Muhammad*, 19-20.

46. Berg, *Elijah Muhammad*, 19.

47. Elijah Muhammad, *The True History of Master Fard Muhammad (Allah in Person)*, ed. Nasir Makr Hakim (Phoenix, AZ: Secretarius MEMPS Ministries, 1996), 91-92.

48. Benyon, "Voodoo Cult," 895.

49. Sahib, "The Nation of Islam," 70.

50. Benyon, "Voodoo Cult," 896.

51. Benyon, "Voodoo Cult," 897.

52. Berg, *Elijah Muhammad*, 22-23.

53. Gibson, *A History of the Nation of Islam*, 19-20.

54. Sahib, "The Nation of Islam," 61.

55. Sahib, "The Nation of Islam," 62.

56. Sahib, "The Nation of Islam," 62-63.

57. Gibson, *A History of the Nation of Islam*, 27.

58. Gibson, *A History of the Nation of Islam*, 36.

59. "Lost-Found Muslim Lesson No. 1," n.d., answer 1.

60. "Lost-Found Muslim Lesson No. 1," answer 2. The Nation of Islam's central teachings were transmitted in the form of lessons that were normatively expected to be memorized by members, including passages from the Qur'an and, more regularly, from a handful of documents passed down from W. D. Fard himself. At the heart of these materials are the "Lost-Found Muslim Lessons No. 1 and 2," which consist of questions asked by Fard and answers provided by Elijah Muhammad. These lessons contain the seeds of most of Elijah Muhammad's later teachings in some form (Essien-Udom, *Black Nationalism*, 202; Curtis IV, *Black Muslim Religion*, 157-58).

61. "Lost-Found Muslim Lesson No. 2," answer 33.

62. "Lost-Found Muslim Lesson No. 2," answer 24.

63. "Lost-Found Muslim Lesson No. 2," answer 32.

64. "Lost-Found Muslim Lesson No. 2," answer 28.

65. Malcolm X, *The End of White World Supremacy*, 83-84.

66. "Lost-Found Muslim Lesson No. 2," answer 34.

67. "Lost-Found Muslim Lesson No. 1," answer 9.

68. "Lost-Found Muslim Lesson No. 1," answer 10.

69. E.g., see Elijah Muhammad, *Message to the Blackman*, 158: "[The Prophet] must overcome [the enemy] with nothing but the Truth and the power and guidance of Allah as Moses did with Pharaoh and his well-armed army, because he is not in a position to arm himself and his followers with carnal weapons. The enemy controls the manufacture of arms." "We are forbidden by Allah to carry weapons. It is well-known that this is our rule. No armed person is to sit in our meetings, and because of this rule we have been successful in enjoying a peaceful assemblage wherever we have gone" (p. 215). "I have said many times that the solution to our problem is divine ... Please do not think that they can be conquered by brickbats, shotguns, a few arms or homemade bombs. It takes the forces of nature and the confusion of minds and thoughts, which are controlled by the power of Allah. Be wise and submit to Allah, who has the power to defend you and destroy your enemies who are too powerful for you" (pp. 224-25).

70. Tate, *Little X*, 42.

71. "Lost-Found Muslim Lesson No. 2," answer 15.

72. "Lost-Found Muslim Lesson No. 2," answer 16. Like Noble Drew Ali, the Nation of Islam described Black identity as ultimately rooted in West Asia, the home of biblical and Qur'anic narrative, and only secondarily in Africa.

73. "Lost-Found Muslim Lesson No. 1," answer 1.

74. Elijah Muhammad, *Message to the Blackman*, 7.

75. Elijah Muhammad, *Message to the Blackman*, 14.

76. Elijah Muhammad, "Exclusive Text of: Muhammad's Historic Message," *Muhammad Speaks* 5, no. 51 (September 9, 1966): 4.

77. Elijah Muhammad, *Message to the Blackman*, 96-97.

78. Elijah Muhammad, *The Theology of Time: The Secret of the Time*, ed. Nasir Makr Hakim (Phoenix, AZ: Secretarius MEMPS Publications, 2002), 204.

79. Elijah Muhammad, *The Theology of Time*, 14-16.

80. "Lost-Found Muslim Lesson No. 1," answer 1.

81. Tate, *Little X*, 32.

82. Berg, *Elijah Muhammad and Islam*, 89; Gibson, *A History of the Nation of Islam*, 17.

83. Elijah Muhammad, *The Fall of America* (Phoenix, AZ: Secretarius MEMPS Publications, 1973), 57.

84. Malcolm X, *The End of White World Supremacy*, 183.

85. DeCaro, *Malcolm and the Cross*, 87.

86. Letter from Malcolm X to Philbert Little, November 28, 1948, Malcolm X Collection, Schomburg Center for Research in Black Culture, Box 3, Folder 1.

87. Letter from Malcolm X to Philbert Little, June 29, 1949, Malcolm X Collection, Schomburg Center for Research in Black Culture, Box 3, Folder 1.

88. Letter from Malcolm X to Philbert Little, June 29, 1949.

89. Letter from Malcolm X to Philbert Little, June 29, 1949.

90. Letter from Malcolm X to Philbert Little, December 11, 1950, Malcolm X Collection, Schomburg Center, Box 3, Folder 1.

91. Letter from Malcolm X to Philbert Little, March 26, 1950, Malcolm X Collection, Schomburg Center, Box 3, Folder 1.

92. Letter from Malcolm X to Philbert Little, December 18, 1949, Malcolm X Collection, Schomburg Center, Box 3, Folder 1.

93. Curtis IV, *Black Muslim Religion*, 67-93.

94. See Marable, *Malcolm X*, 15-38.

95. Marable, *Malcolm X*, 15-38.

96. Radio script, Harlem, Malcolm X Collection, Schomburg Center, Box 6, Folder 1, Section V.

97. Claude Andrew Clegg, *An Original Man: The Life and Times of Elijah Muhammad* (New York: St. Martin's Griffin, 1997), 163.

98. Clegg, *An Original Man*, 39, 98, 163; Essien-Udom, *Black Nationalism*, 63-68.

99. Clegg, *An Original Man*, 98.

100. Malcolm X, "Harlem Freedom Rally, 1960," in Malcolm X Collection, Schomburg Center, Box 5, Folder 1.

101. Malcolm X, "Harlem Freedom Rally, 1960."

102. Malcolm X, "Harlem Freedom Rally, 1960."

103. Malcolm X, "Harlem Freedom Rally, 1960."

104. Malcolm X, "Harlem Freedom Rally, 1960."

105. "Where Is the American Negro Headed?," *The Open Mind* (Sunday, October 15, 1961), NBC Television, in Malcolm X Collection, Schomburg Center, Box 5, Folder 11.

106. Peniel E. Joseph, *The Sword and the Shield: The Revolutionary Lives of Malcolm X and Martin Luther King, Jr.* (New York: Basic Books, 2020), 172.

107. Joseph, *The Sword and the Shield,* 175.

2. God's Judgment of White America

1. Benjamin Karim, *Remembering Malcolm* (New York: Ballantine Books, 1992), 61.

2. Karim, *Remembering Malcolm,* 63.

3. Karim, *Remembering Malcolm,* 61.

4. Karim, *Remembering Malcolm,* 66-67.

5. Karim, *Remembering Malcolm,* 9.

6. Malcolm X and Alex Haley, *The Autobiography of Malcolm X* (New York: Ballantine Books, 1965), 13.

7. Malcolm X and Haley, *The Autobiography of Malcolm X,* 5-6.

8. Malcolm X and Haley, *The Autobiography of Malcolm X,* 8.

9. Malcolm X and Haley, *The Autobiography of Malcolm X,* 8.

10. Malcolm X and Haley, *The Autobiography of Malcolm X,* 12.

11. Malcolm X and Haley, *The Autobiography of Malcolm X,* 5.

12. Karim, *Remembering Malcolm,* 122-23.

13. Karim, *Remembering Malcolm,* 123-24.

14. Karim, *Remembering Malcolm,* 124.

15. Benjamin Karim, interview conducted by Blackside, Inc. for *Malcolm X: Make It Plain,* June 27, 1992, transcript, Washington University in St. Louis Film & Media Archive, St. Louis, MO.

16. Karim, interview for *Malcolm X: Make It Plain.*

17. In the Nation of Islam, receiving one's "X," which stood in for one's ancestral name lost during the period of slavery, signified one's entrance into the Nation. If another individual of the same first name was already a member of the Nation, then the newly joining individual would be called "[Name] 2X." If additional members of the same first name joined, the number would increase.

18. Karim, *Remembering Malcolm,* 142-43.

19. Karim, interview for *Malcolm X: Make It Plain*.

20. Karim, *Remembering Malcolm*, 65.

21. Louis Lomax, *When the Word Is Given: A Report on Elijah Muhammad, Malcolm X, and the Black Muslim World* (Westport, CT: Greenwood Press, 1963), 17.

22. See Curtis, *Black Muslim Religion*, 95-130; Mary Potorti, "Eat to Live: Culinary Nationalism and Black Capitalism in Elijah Muhammad's Nation of Islam," in *New Perspectives on the Nation of Islam*, ed. Dawn-Marie Gibson and Herbert Berg (New York: Routledge, 2017), 68-94.

23. Karim, interview for *Malcolm X: Make It Plain*.

24. Karim, *Remembering Malcolm*, 142.

25. Karim, *Remembering Malcolm*, 141.

26. Karim, interview for *Malcolm X: Make It Plain*.

27. Karim, *Remembering Malcolm*, 29.

28. Karim, *Remembering Malcolm*, 31.

29. Karim, *Remembering Malcolm*, 14, 29.

30. Karim, *Remembering Malcolm*, 10.

31. Karim, *Remembering Malcolm*, 29-31.

32. Karim, *Remembering Malcolm*, 33.

33. Karim, *Remembering Malcolm*, 40.

34. James L. Hicks, "Riot Threat as Cops Beat Muslim: 'God's Angry Men' Tangle with Police," *Amsterdam News*, May 4, 1957, included in Manning Marable and Garrett Felber, eds., *The Portable Malcolm X Reader* (New York: Penguin, 2013), 85.

35. Hicks, "Riot Threat as Cops Beat Muslim," 88.

36. Peter Goldman, *The Death and Life of Malcolm X*, 2nd ed. (Urbana, IL: University of Illinois Press, 1979), 56.

37. Hicks, "Riot Threat as Cops Beat Muslim," 87.

38. Hicks, "Riot Threat as Cops Beat Muslim," 87.

39. Benjamin Karim, "Introduction," in Malcolm X, *The End of White World Supremacy: Four Speeches*, ed. Benjamin Karim (New York: Arcade Publishing, 1971), 8.

40. Karim, "Introduction," 8.

41. Karim, "Introduction," 15.

42. Karim, "Introduction," 10; "Malcolm X FBI File, Summary Report, New York Office, April 30, 1958, 18-31," in Marable and Felber, eds., *The Portable Malcolm X Reader*, 106-107.

43. Malcolm X, "God's Angry Men," *Los Angeles Herald-Dispatch*, August 22, 1957.

44. Marable and Felber, eds., *The Portable Malcolm X Reader*, 97-98.

45. "Malcolm X FBI File, Summary Report," 107.

46. Goldman, *The Death and Life of Malcolm X*, 60.

47. Karim, *Remembering Malcolm*, 200.

48. Karim, *Remembering Malcolm*, 200.

49. Karim, "Introduction," *The End of White World Supremacy*, 14-15.

50. Karim, *Remembering Malcolm*, 55.

51. Karim, *Remembering Malcolm*, 97, 99.

52. Karim, *Remembering Malcolm*, 98.

53. Karim, *Remembering Malcolm*, 97.

54. Karim, *Remembering Malcolm*, 97.

55. Karim, *Remembering Malcolm*, 95.

56. Karim, *Remembering Malcolm*, 95.

57. Karim, *Remembering Malcolm*, 157.

58. Malcolm X and Haley, *The Autobiography of Malcolm X*, 295-99.

59. Malcolm X and Haley, *The Autobiography of Malcolm X*, 297.

60. Gibson, *A History of the Nation of Islam*, 71.

61. Zafar Ishaq Ansari, "W. D. Muhammad: The Making of a 'Black Muslim' Leader (1933–1961)," *American Journal of Islamic Social Sciences* 2, no. 2 (1985): 255-256.

62. Ansari, "W. D. Muhammad," 256.

63. Ansari, "W. D. Muhammad," 256.

64. Karim, *Remembering Malcolm*, 157-58.

65. Edward E. Curtis IV, "Islamism and Its African American Muslim Critics: Black Muslims in the Era of the Arab Cold War," in *Black Routes to Islam*, ed. Manning Marable and Hishaam D. Aidi; Critical Black Studies Series (New York: Palgrave Macmillan, 2009), 56.

66. "Malcolm X Attends March on Washington," in Marable and Felber, eds., *The Portable Malcolm X Reader*, 238-41.

67. Curtis, "Islamism and Its African American Muslim Critics," 49-68.

68. Malcolm X, "The Last Interview," *Al-Muslimoon Magazine*, February, 1965, on malcolm-x.org, http://www.malcolm-x.org/docs/

int_almus.htm. See also Curtis, "Islamism and Its African American Muslim Critics," 58.

69. Malcolm X, "The Last Interview."

70. Malcolm X, "The Last Interview."

71. Letter from Malcolm X to Beatrice Clomax X, June 11, 1952, Malcolm X Collection, Schomburg Center for Research in Black Culture, Box 3, Folder 3.

72. Letter from Malcolm X to Elijah Muhammad, March 21, 1964, Malcolm X Collection, Schomburg Center for Research in Black Culture, Box 3, Folder 3.

73. See Marable, *Malcolm X: A Life of Reinvention*, 269-96; Malcolm X and Haley, *The Autobiography of Malcolm X*, 300-303.

74. Elijah Muhammad, "We Seek Truth and Justice," *Muhammad Speaks* 2, no. 10 (February 4, 1963): 1.

75. Elijah Muhammad, "Truth Is the Best Guidance," *Muhammad Speaks* 2, no. 15 (April 15, 1963): 9.

76. Marable, *Malcolm X: A Life of Reinvention*, 269.

77. Elijah Muhammad, "Muhammad on President Kennedy: Nation Still Mourns Death," *Muhammad Speaks* 3, no. 7 (December 20, 1963): 1.

78. "Raymond Sharrieff FBI File, Summary Report, Chicago Office, February 19, 1964, 12-13," in *The Portable Malcolm X Reader*, 279. Malcolm also related Elijah Muhammad's explanation in similar terms: "The country loved this man ... [Malcolm's comments after Kennedy's death were] very ill-timed. A statement like that can make it hard on Muslims in general" (Malcolm X and Haley, *The Autobiography of Malcolm X*, 301).

79. Elijah Muhammad, *The Fall of America* (Phoenix: Secretarius MEMPS Ministries, 1973), 44.

80. Elijah Muhammad, *The Fall of America*, 45.

81. Malcolm X, *The End of White World Supremacy*, 179-80.

82. Malcolm X, *The End of White World Supremacy*, 185.

83. Malcolm X, *The End of White World Supremacy*, 185.

84. Malcolm X, *The End of White World Supremacy*, 218.

85. Malcolm X, *The End of White World Supremacy*, 180.

86. Malcolm X, *The End of White World Supremacy*, 195-96.

87. Malcolm X, *The End of White World Supremacy*, 197-98.

88. Malcolm X, *The End of White World Supremacy*, 211.

89. Malcolm X, *The End of White World Supremacy*, 215-16.

90. Malcolm X, *The End of White World Supremacy*, 203.

91. Malcolm X, *The End of White World Supremacy*, 203.

92. Elijah Muhammad, *Message to the Blackman*, 164.

93. Elijah Muhammad, *Message to the Blackman*, 281, 284.

94. Malcolm X, *The End of White World Supremacy*, 216.

95. Malcolm X, *The End of White World Supremacy*, 216.

96. Malcolm X, *The End of White World Supremacy*, 218-19.

97. Malcolm X, *The End of White World Supremacy*, 211.

98. Karim, *Remembering Malcolm*, 159.

99. Malcolm X and Haley, *The Autobiography of Malcolm X*, 300.

100. Marable, *Malcolm X: A Life of Reinvention*, 272.

101. "Malcolm X Scores U.S. and Kennedy," *The New York Times*, December 2, 1963, 21; Malcolm X and Haley, *The Autobiography of Malcolm X*, 301; "Malcolm X FBI File, Memo from FBI Director J. Edgar Hoover to Secret Service Chief, December 6, 1963," in *The Portable Malcolm X Reader*, 280.

102. "Malcolm X Scores U.S. and Kennedy," 21.

103. "Malcolm X Scores U.S. and Kennedy," 21.

104. "Malcolm X Scores U.S. and Kennedy," 21.

105. Karim, *Remembering Malcolm*, 161.

106. Karim, *Remembering Malcolm*, 164-65.

107. Malcolm X, "A Declaration of Independence," in *Malcolm X Speaks: Selected Speeches and Statements*, ed. George Breitman (New York: Grove Press, 1965), 20.

108. Malcolm X, "A Declaration of Independence," 20.

109. Malcolm X, "A Declaration of Independence," 21.

110. Malcolm X, "A Declaration of Independence," 21.

111. Malcolm X, "A Declaration of Independence," 22.

112. Malcolm X, "A Declaration of Independence," 21.

113. Malcolm X, "A Declaration of Independence," 21-22.

114. Malcolm X, "The Founding Rally of the OAAU," in Malcolm X, *By Any Means Necessary* (New York: Pathfinder Press, 1970), 59-60.

115. Malcolm X, "The Founding Rally of the OAAU," 61.

116. Malcolm X, "The Founding Rally of the OAAU," 93.

117. Malcolm X, "The Founding Rally of the OAAU," 66.

118. Malcolm X, "The Founding Rally of the OAAU," 65-84.

119. Malcolm X, "The Founding Rally of the OAAU," 84.

120. Malcolm X and Haley, *The Autobiography of Malcolm X*, 340.

121. Malcolm X, "The Founding Rally of the OAAU," 85.

122. Malcolm X, "Not Just an American Problem, but a World Problem," in *Malcolm X: The Last Speeches*, ed. Bruce Perry (New York: Pathfinder Press, 1989), 159.

123. Malcolm X, "Last Answers and Interviews," *Malcolm X Speaks*, 225.

124. Malcolm X, "The Ballot or the Bullet," in *Malcolm X Speaks*, 38.

125. Malcolm X, *The End of White World Supremacy*, 203.

126. Malcolm X, "Our People Identify with Africa," in *Malcolm X: The Last Speeches*, 109.

127. Malcolm X, *Malcolm X Speaks*, 216.

128. Malcolm X, "At a Meeting in Paris," in Malcolm X, *By Any Means Necessary*, 144-45.

129. Huey P. Newton, with J. Herman Blake, *Revolutionary Suicide* (New York: Penguin Books, 2009), 71-72.

130. Angela Davis, *Angela Davis: An Autobiography* (New York: International Publishers, 1988), 127.

131. Elaine Brown, *A Taste of Power: A Black Woman's Story* (New York: Pantheon Books, 1992), 288.

132. Brown, *A Taste of Power*, 288.

133. Karim, *Remembering Malcolm*, 187.

134. Karim, *Remembering Malcolm*, 187.

135. Karim, *Remembering Malcolm*, 187.

136. Karim, *Remembering Malcolm*, 197.

137. Khury Petersen-Smith, interview with Emory Douglas, "We Always Had Solidarity," *SocialistWorker.org*, May 13, 2015, https://socialistworker.org/2015/05/13/we-always-had-solidarity.

138. Newton, *Revolutionary Suicide*, 118.

139. Julius Lester, "The Angry Children of Malcolm X," in *Black Protest Thought in the Twentieth Century*, ed. August Meier, Elliott Rudwick, and Francis L. Broderick (Indianapolis: Bobbs-Merrill, 1971), 469-84.

3. The Religion of Black Power

1. Elaine Brown, *A Taste of Power: A Black Woman's Story* (New York: Pantheon Books, 1992), 249.

2. Brown, *A Taste of Power*, 300.

3. Brown, *A Taste of Power*, 20.

4. Brown, *A Taste of Power*, 300.

5. Brown, *A Taste of Power*, 252-53.

6. Brown, *A Taste of Power*, 321.

7. Brown, *A Taste of Power*, 321.

8. Brown, *A Taste of Power*, 440.

9. Brown, *A Taste of Power*, 448-49.

10. Brown, *A Taste of Power*, 447.

11. Brown, *A Taste of Power*, 49.

12. Brown, *A Taste of Power*, 252-53.

13. Huey P. Newton, with J. Herman Blake, *Revolutionary Suicide* (New York: Penguin Books, 2009), 197.

14. Newton, *Revolutionary Suicide*, 197.

15. Eldridge Cleaver, *Soul on Ice* (New York: Dell, 1968), 34.

16. Cleaver, *Soul on Ice*, 95.

17. Assata Shakur, *Assata: An Autobiography* (London: Zed Books, 1987), 92.

18. Shakur, *Assata*, 92.

19. Shakur, *Assata*, 92.

20. Imam Jamil Al-Amin, *Revolution by the Book: The Rap Is Live* (Beltsville, MD: Writers' Inc. International, 1994), xvi.

21. Julius Lester, "The Angry Children of Malcolm X," in *Black Protest Thought in the Twentieth Century*, ed. August Meier, Elliott Rudwick, and Francis L. Broderick (Indianapolis: Bobbs-Merrill, 1971), 479.

22. Julius Lester, "A Dead Man Alive in His Speeches, a Live Man Dead in His Speeches," *The New York Times*, May 16, 1971, 4.

23. Vincent Harding, "The Religion of Black Power," in *Black Theology: A Documentary History, Volume One: 1966–1979*, ed. James H. Cone and Gayraud S. Wilmore, 2nd ed. (Maryknoll, NY: Orbis Books, 1993), 48.

24. Vincent Harding, *There Is a River: The Black Struggle for Freedom in America* (San Diego: Harcourt, Brace & Company, 1981), xiii.

25. Harding, *There Is a River*, xiv.

26. Harding, *There Is a River*, xv.

27. Harding, *There Is a River*, xv.

28. Martin Luther King Jr., "Remaining Awake through a Great

Revolution (31 March 1968)," in *A Testament of Hope: The Essential Writings and Speeches of Martin Luther King, Jr.*, ed. James M. Washington (New York: HarperCollins Publishers, 1986), 276.

29. King, "The Drum Major Instinct (4 February 1968)," in *A Testament of Hope*, 265.

30. James H. Cone, *Martin & Malcolm & America: A Dream or a Nightmare* (Maryknoll, NY: Orbis Books, 1991), 237.

31. Cone, *Martin & Malcolm & America*, 221-22.

32. Gerald Horne, *Fire This Time: The Watts Uprising and the 1960s* (Charlottesville: University of Virginia Press, 1995), 54-55.

33. Horne, *Fire This Time*, 207.

34. King, from *The Trumpet of Conscience* (1968), in *A Testament of Hope*, 646.

35. Harding, *There Is a River*, xv.

36. Vincent Harding, "Black Power and the American Christ," *The Christian Century* 84, no. 1 (January 4, 1967): 13.

37. Harding, "The Religion of Black Power," 41.

38. Harding, "The Religion of Black Power," 44.

39. Harding, "The Religion of Black Power," 46-47.

40. Harding, "The Religion of Black Power," 47.

41. Harding, "The Religion of Black Power," 48-49.

42. Harding, "The Religion of Black Power," 48.

43. Harding, "The Religion of Black Power," 49.

44. Harding, "The Religion of Black Power," 57.

45. Harding, "The Religion of Black Power," 49.

46. Harding, "The Religion of Black Power," 64.

47. Harding, "The Religion of Black Power," 62.

48. Harding, "The Religion of Black Power," 64.

49. Harding, "The Religion of Black Power," 60.

50. James Baldwin, *No Name in the Street*, in James Baldwin, *Collected Essays*, ed. Toni Morrison (New York: Library of America, 1998), 410.

51. Baldwin, *The Fire Next Time*, in *Collected Essays*, 294.

52. Baldwin, *The Fire Next Time*, 346.

53. Baldwin, *No Name in the Street*, 408-409.

54. Baldwin, *The Fire Next Time*, in 346-47.

55. James Baldwin, *James Baldwin: The Last Interview and Other Conversations* (Brooklyn: Melville House Publishing, 2014), 73.

56. Baldwin, *No Name in the Street*, 408.

57. Baldwin, *No Name in the Street*, 406.

58. Baldwin, *No Name in the Street*, 406.

59. Baldwin, *No Name in the Street*, 407.

60. Baldwin, *No Name in the Street*, 474.

61. Baldwin, *No Name in the Street*, 475.

62. Baldwin, *No Name in the Street*, 474.

63. The title of the chapter itself is a reference to a passage in one of the biblical books Baldwin refers to most frequently, Revelation 14:17-20. More directly, the title is a reference to the opening lines of "The Battle Hymn of the Republic," whose lyrics were written by Julia Ward Howe during the American Civil War in order to connect the biblical depiction of God's judgment with the downfall of the slave-holding South.

64. Baldwin, *The Devil Finds Work*, in *Collected Essays*, 572. In addition to the obvious reference to Revelation, this passage also contains a second allusion to a vision of divine judgment in the book of the prophet Joel (2:28-32). Baldwin was almost certainly aware that the imagery of the wine press of God's wrath in Revelation was itself a reference to Joel 3:12-13, among other similar texts in the Hebrew Bible, such as Isaiah 63:1-6 and Lamentations 1:15.

65. Baldwin, *The Fire Next Time*, 325.

66. Baldwin, *The Fire Next Time*, 314.

67. Baldwin, *The Fire Next Time*, 315.

68. Sonia Sanchez, interview conducted by Blackside, Inc. for *Eyes on the Prize: America at the Racial Crossroads, 1965–1985 [Eyes on the Prize II]*, March 7, 1989, transcript, Washington University in St. Louis Film & Media Archive, St. Louis, MO.

69. Sanchez, interview for *Eyes on the Prize II*.

70. Sanchez, interview for *Eyes on the Prize II*.

71. "Sonia Sanchez: My First Visit to the Schomburg Library," YouTube video, posted by visionaryproject, March 22, 2010, https://www.youtube.com/watch?v=-8gbAh2bNWg.

72. Sanchez, interview for *Eyes on the Prize II*.

73. Sanchez, interview for *Eyes on the Prize II*.

74. Sanchez, interview for *Eyes on the Prize II*.

75. Sanchez, interview for *Eyes on the Prize II*.

76. Sanchez, interview for *Eyes on the Prize II*.

77. Sonia Sanchez, *A Blues Book for Blue Black Magical Women* (Detroit: Broadside Press, 1974), 12, 19.

78. Sanchez, *A Blues Book,* 55.

79. Sanchez, interview for *Eyes on the Prize II.*

80. Sanchez, interview for *Eyes on the Prize II.*

81. Sonia Sanchez, "The Poetry of the BAM: Meditation, Critique, Praise," in *SOS—Calling All Black People: A Black Arts Movement Reader,* ed. John H. Bracey Jr., Sonia Sanchez, and James Smethurst (Amherst: University of Massachusetts Press, 2014), 248.

82. Sanchez, "The Poetry of the BAM," 248.

83. Lisa Gail Collins and Margo Natalie Crawford, "Introduction: Power to the People! The Art of Black Power," in *New Thoughts on the Black Arts Movement,* ed. Lisa Gail Collins and Margo Natalie Crawford (New Brunswick, NJ: Rutgers University Press, 2006), 1-19.

84. Larry Neal, "The Black Arts Movement," in *SOS—Calling All Black People: A Black Arts Movement Reader,* 55.

85. Sanchez, interview for *Eyes on the Prize II.*

86. Ammar Abduh Aqeeli, *The Nation of Islam and Black Consciousness: The Works of Amiri Baraka, Sonia Sanchez, and Other Writers* (New York: Peter Lang, 2019).

87. Sanchez, "The Poetry of the BAM," 251.

88. Sanchez, "The Poetry of the BAM," 251.

89. Scholarly treatments of "Black religion" as a phenomenon distinct from the broader religious traditions in which Black people participate dates back to Joseph R. Washington Jr.'s controversial but seminal work, *Black Religion: The Negro and Christianity in the United States* (Boston: Beacon Press, 1964). While Washington in *Black Religion* depicted the "folk" religion of Black people in America as a deviation from Protestant Christianity that needed to be integrated into the broader (white-led) church, a number of later theologians and scholars have built on the aspect of Washington's argument that stresses the distinction between Black religion and Christianity more broadly defined. Hart is not the only scholar to discuss "Black religion" as a discrete concept in terms that transcend Christianity; see, e.g., Jackson, *Islam and the Blackamerican,* 29-45. For a brief overview of the scholarship on "Black religion," see Frederick L. Ware, *African American Theology: An Introduction* (Louisville, KY: Westminster John Knox Press, 2016), 44-47.

90. William David Hart, *Black Religion: Malcolm X, Julius Lester, and Jan Willis* (New York: Palgrave Macmillan, 2008), 8.

91. Hart, *Black Religion*, 15.

92. Marvin X and Faruk, "Islam and Black Art: An Interview with LeRoi Jones," in *Conversations with Amiri Baraka*, ed. Charlie Reilly (Jackson, MS: University of Mississippi Press, 1994), 54-55.

93. Marvin X and Faruk, "Islam and Black Art," 51.

94. Marvin X and Faruk, "Islam and Black Art," 51.

95. Neal, "The Black Arts Movement," 56.

96. Neal, "The Black Arts Movement," 63.

97. Neal, "The Black Arts Movement," 65.

98. Carolyn M. Rodgers, "Black Poetry—Where It's At," in *SOS—Calling All Black People*, 188-97.

99. Marvin X and Faruk, "Islam and Black Art," 52.

100. For the Nation of Islam's use of these terms in connection with Christianity, see, e.g., Mattias Gardell, *In the Name of Elijah Muhammad: Louis Farrakhan and the Nation of Islam* (Durham, NC: Duke University Press, 1996), 237.

101. Gardell, *In the Name of Elijah Muhammad*, 55.

4. The Rage of the Powerless

1. Alta Harrison (Fundi Difie), "A History of the Shrine of the Black Madonna with a Focus on the Development of Printed, Audio, and Visual Media," Albert B. Cleage Jr. Papers, Bentley Historical Library, University of Michigan, Box 4, Folder: "History."

2. "The Black Madonna," Albert B. Cleage Jr. Papers, Bentley Historical Library, University of Michigan, Box 6, Folder: "Miscellaneous."

3. Melanee Harvey, "Black Power and Black Madonna: Charting the Aesthetic Influence of Rev. Albert Cleage, Glanton Dowdell & the Shrine of the Black Madonna, #1," in *Albert Cleage Jr. and the Black Madonna and Child*, ed. Jawanza Eric Clark (New York: Palgrave Macmillan, 2016), 140.

4. Hiley H. Ward, *Prophet of the Black Nation* (Philadelphia: Pilgrim Press, 1969), 8.

5. Ward, *Prophet of the Black Nation*, 8.

6. In 1972, Albert Cleage took on a new name, Jaramogi Abebe

Agyeman, the name by which he is most frequently known by members of the religious movement he founded today. ("Jaramogi Abebe Agyeman," Pan African Orthodox Christian Church, *Shrines of the Black Madonna*, https://www.theyearofrestoration.org/Jaramogi-Abebe-Agyeman.html). In order to avoid confusion in the relation of this historical narrative, this book follows the examples of previous scholars such as Angela D. Dillard in *Faith in the City: Preaching Radical Social Change in Detroit* (Ann Arbor: University of Michigan Press, 2007), and the majority of the contributors to Jawanza Eric Clark (ed.), *Albert Cleage Jr. and the Black Madonna and Child* (New York: Palgrave Macmillan, 2016), in referring to Cleage/Jaramogi throughout as Cleage, even when discussing events that occurred subsequent to 1972. As Dillard wrote, "No disrespect [by this] is intended to the current members of the individual Shrines of the Black Madonna in Detroit, Houston, or Atlanta or the PAOCC overall" (*Faith in the City*, 10).

7. Edward Vaughn, "Heritage Committee Report 1967," Albert B. Cleage Jr. Papers, Bentley Historical Library, University of Michigan, Box 4, Folder: "Annual Report, 1967."

8. Albert B. Cleage Jr., *The Black Messiah* (New York: Sheed and Ward, 1968), 85.

9. Cleage, "The Black Madonna."

10. Cleage, "The Black Madonna."

11. Albert B. Cleage Jr., *Black Christian Nationalism: New Directions for the Black Church* (New York: William Morrow & Company, 1972), 105-108.

12. Joe T. Darden and Richard W. Thomas, *Detroit: Race Riots, Racial Conflicts, and Efforts to Bridge the Racial Divide* (East Lansing: Michigan State University Press, 2013), 40.

13. Darden and Thomas, *Detroit*, 2-3.

14. Darden and Thomas, *Detroit*, 1.

15. Darden and Thomas, *Detroit*, 2.

16. Darden and Thomas, *Detroit*, 40.

17. Harrison, "A History of the Shrine of the Black Madonna."

18. Harrison, "A History of the Shrine of the Black Madonna."

19. Peniel Joseph, *Waiting 'Til the Midnight Hour: A Narrative History of Black Power in America* (New York: Henry Holt and Company, 2006), 54-55.

20. Ward, *Prophet of the Black Nation*, 146, 220.

21. Dillard, *Faith in the City*, 272-75.

22. Malcolm X, "Message to the Grass Roots," in *Malcolm X Speaks: Selected Speeches and Statements*, ed. George Breitman (New York: Grove Press, 1965), 12. Malcolm X went on, grounding his own position in his Muslim identity: "There is nothing in our book, the Koran, that teaches us to suffer peacefully. Our religion teaches us to be intelligent. Be peaceful, be courteous, obey the law, respect everyone; but if someone puts his hand on you, send him to the cemetery. That's a good religion. In fact, that's that old-time religion."

23. Edward Vaughn, "Welcome to the Black Nation! A Guide for Members of Central United Church of Christ, 'The Shrine of the Black Madonna,'" Albert B. Cleage Jr. Papers, Bentley Historical Library, University of Michigan, Box 6, Folder: "History, Draft 1968."

24. Vaughn, "Welcome to the Black Nation!"

25. Vincent Harding, "The Religion of Black Power," in *Black Theology: A Documentary History, Volume One: 1966–1979*, ed. James H. Cone and Gayraud S. Wilmore, 2nd edition (Maryknoll, NY: Orbis Books, 1993), 59.

26. Harding, "The Religion of Black Power," 58.

27. Ward, *Prophet of the Black Nation*, 22.

28. Ward, *Prophet of the Black Nation*, xiv.

29. Ward, *Prophet of the Black Nation*, 38-41.

30. Ward, *Prophet of the Black Nation*, 42; Dillard, *Faith in the City*, 241-42.

31. Ward, *Prophet of the Black Nation*, 42.

32. Ward, *Prophet of the Black Nation*, 55.

33. Ward, *Prophet of the Black Nation*.

34. Ward, *Prophet of the Black Nation*, 55-57.

35. See Dillard, *Faith in the City*, 251-63.

36. Joseph, *Waiting 'Til the Midnight Hour*, 55.

37. Dillard, *Faith in the City*, 237-85.

38. Aswad Walker, "Politics Is Sacred: The Activism of Albert B. Cleage Jr.," in *Albert Cleage Jr. and the Black Madonna and Child*, 106.

39. Walker, "Politics Is Sacred," 101; and Velma Maia Thomas, "The Black Madonna and the Role of Women," in *Albert Cleage Jr. and the Black Madonna and Child*, 134.

40. See Dillard, *Faith in the City*, 197.

41. Ward, *Prophet of the Black Nation*, 207.

42. "First Public Rally for a Freedom Now Party" flyer, Albert B. Cleage Jr. Papers, Bentley Historical Library, University of Michigan, Box 6, Folder: "Freedom Now Party 1964."

43. Ward, *Prophet of the Black Nation*, 204.

44. Sonia Sanchez, "don't wanna be," in liner notes, *a sun lady for all seasons reads her poetry*, Folkways Records FL 9793, 1971, vinyl record, 4.

45. *The Black Leaders Summit of 1972 and the 1998 Follow Up: Part II.* Produced by Tony Brown Productions, 1998. https://search.alexanderstreet.com/view/work/bibliographic_entity%7Cvideo_work%7C2090096

46. *The Black Leaders Summit of 1972*, 16.

47. Nikki Giovanni, "The Great Pax Whitie," in *The Collected Poetry of Nikki Giovanni* (New York: HarperCollins, 2003), 54.

48. Giovanni, "Reflections on April 4, 1968," in *The Collected Poetry of Nikki Giovanni*, 49-50.

49. *Shrine of the Black Madonna.* Produced by Tony Brown Productions, 2013, https://video.alexanderstreet.com/watch/shrine-of-the-black-madonna

50. Sonia Sanchez, interview conducted by Blackside, Inc. for *Eyes on the Prize: America at the Racial Crossroads, 1965-1985 [Eyes on the Prize II]*, March 7, 1989, transcript, Washington University in St. Louis Film & Media Archive, St. Louis, MO.

51. Ward, *Prophet of the Black Nation*, x.

52. Charles Lattimore Howard, *Black Theology as a Mass Movement* (New York: Palgrave Macmillan, 2014), 18.

53. Howard, *Black Theology as a Mass Movement*, 13.

54. See Dillard, *Faith in the City*, 361.

55. Albert B. Cleage Jr., *Black Christian Nationalism*, xvii, n.

56. Howard, *Black Theology as a Mass Movement*, 12-13.

57. See Clark (ed.), *Albert Cleage Jr. and the Black Madonna and Child*, a collection of essays on Cleage's theological and historical legacy, and Jawanza Eric Clark, *Indigenous Black Theology: Toward an African-Centered Theology of the African-American Religious Experience* (New York: Palgrave Macmillan, 2012), in which Clark expanded upon Cleage's Afrocentric framework in order to develop a Christian theology grounded in a "psychic conversion" from Eurocentric

Protestant Christianity to "a lost African heritage" (ix-x), in particular through the construction of "a doctrine of the ancestors that can serve as the beginning of a new Black theology" (15). See also Earle J. Fisher, *The Reverend Albert Cleage Jr. and the Black Prophetic Tradition: A Reintroduction of* The Black Messiah (Lanham, MD: Lexington Books, 2021), especially the fourth chapter, in which Fisher discusses Cleage's theology in the broader context of Black theology and the Black Power movement. See also Angela Dillard, *Faith in the City*.

58. Albert B. Cleage Jr., "The Death of Fear," *Negro Digest* 17, no. 1 (November 1967): 30.

59. Albert B. Cleage Jr., *The Black Messiah* (New York: Sheed & Ward, 1968), 11.

60. Cleage, *The Black Messiah,* 193.

61. Cleage, *The Black Messiah,* 197-98.

62. Cleage, *Black Christian Nationalism*, 104.

63. Cleage, *Black Christian Nationalism*, 119.

64. Cleage, *The Black Messiah*, 6.

65. Cleage, *Black Christian Nationalism*, 251.

66. Cleage, *Black Christian Nationalism*, 111.

67. Cleage, *Black Christian Nationalism*, 133.

68. Cleage, *Black Christian Nationalism*, 172.

69. Cleage, *The Black Messiah*, 16.

70. Malcolm X, *The End of White World Supremacy: Four Speeches*, ed. Imam Benjamin Karim (New York: Arcade Publishing, 1971), 192.

71. "A Chronology of the PAOCC: Building a Black Nation Fifty Years in the Making and Still Counting ... 1953–Present," Albert B. Cleage Jr. Papers, Bentley Historical Library, University of Michigan, Box 4, Folder: "History."

72. Cleage, *Black Christian Nationalism*, xiii.

73. Cleage, *The Black Messiah*, 86.

74. "Ritual of Confirmation," Albert B. Cleage Jr. Papers, Bentley Historical Library, University of Michigan, Box 5, Folder: "Rite of Passage."

75. Cleage, *Black Christian Nationalism,* xvii.

76. Clark, *Indigenous Black Theology,* 3.

77. "Articles of Association: Constitutions and By-Laws of the Pan African Orthodox Christian Church," July 3, 1978, Albert B. Cleage

Jr. Papers, Bentley Historical Library, University of Michigan, Box 4, Folder: "Articles of Association: Pan African Orthodox Christian Church 1978."

78. "Theology of the Group Experience," September 24, 1978, Albert B. Cleage Jr. Papers, Bentley Historical Library, University of Michigan, Box 1, Folder: "Theology of the Group Experience, September 24, 1978."

79. "Theology of the Group Experience."

80. "End of an Era: We Are the Messianic Hope of the Twentieth Century," December 25, 1977, Albert B. Cleage Jr. Papers, Bentley Historical Library, University of Michigan, Box 1, Folder: "End of an Era: We Are the Messianic Hope of the Twentieth Century, December 25, 1977."

81. Cleage, *The Black Messiah*, 53-54.

82. Cleage, *The Black Messiah*, 54.

83. Cleage, *The Black Messiah*, 7.

84. See, e.g., Alex Poinsett, "The Quest for a Black Christ: Radical Clerics Reject 'Honky Christ' Created by American Culture-Religion," *Ebony* 25, no. 5 (March 1969): 170-78.

85. "Beyond Rational Consciousness: Spiritual Encounters—You Need to Study KUA," June 17, 1979, Albert B. Cleage Jr. Papers, Bentley Historical Library, University of Michigan, Box 2, Folder: "Beyond Rational Consciousness: Spiritual Encounters—You Need to Study KUA, June 17, 1979."

86. "New Church for a New Era," January 15, 1978, Albert B. Cleage Jr. Papers, Bentley Historical Library, University of Michigan, Box 1, Folder: "New Church for a New Era, January 15, 1978."

87. "New Church for a New Era."

88. Cleage, *Black Christian Nationalism*, 249.

89. Cleage, *The Black Messiah*, 3.

90. Cleage, *Black Christian Nationalism*, xxii.

91. Cleage, *Black Christian Nationalism*, xxxiv.

92. Cleage, *Black Christian Nationalism*, 37.

93. Cleage, *Black Christian Nationalism*, 3.

94. Maccabee Training Materials, Albert B. Cleage Jr. Papers, Bentley Historical Library, University of Michigan, Box 6, Folder: "Maccabee Training Materials, undated."

95. "In Loving Memory of Our Beloved Juan Bell (Lt. Olabesi

Kariuki), Clifford Franklin McAfee, Jr. (Sgt. Nosakhere Akil Maongozi), and John Albert Scaife (Cpl. Kangwana Jomo)," Thursday, December 3, 1981; "A Celebration of Life: General Masai Balogun (James Robert Dismuke)," September 27, 1993, Albert B. Cleage Jr. Papers, Bentley Historical Library, University of Michigan, Box 6, Folder: "Funeral Obsequies."

96. "Rite of Passage," March 1983, Albert B. Cleage Jr. Papers, Bentley Historical Library, University of Michigan, Box 5, Folder: "Rite of Passage."

97. "Exodus through Deuteronomy," Book # 2, Alkebu-lan Academy Bible Study Series, March 1995, Albert B. Cleage Jr. Papers, Bentley Historical Library, University of Michigan, Box 7, Folder: "Youth Miscellaneous."

98. See also Velma Maia Thomas, "The Black Madonna and the Role of Women," in Clark (ed.), *Albert Cleage Jr. and the Black Madonna and Child*, 117-34, for a nuanced discussion of the history of Mtoto House and the project of communal child-rearing in the Black Christian Nationalist movement.

99. These Swahili terms are explained in another devotional, written by Cleage: "KUTAFUTA means that we have entered the sacred circle and we seek the experience of God … KUTAMUNGU means that we can come upon God, here where we are … When we are open, our inner divinity can be touched by the cosmic power of God and KUGASANA will come like a mystical explosion … In our surrender to God, KUJITOA, we have new strength for our earthly battles." See Shelley McIntosh, *Mtoto House: Vision to Victory, Raising African American Children Communally* (Lanham, MD: Hamilton Books, 2005), 143.

100. McIntosh, *Mtoto House*, 39.

101. Cleage, *Black Christian Nationalism*, 117-18.

102. "The Revolutionary Mysticism of Jesus," October 1, 1978, Albert B. Cleage Jr. Papers, Bentley Historical Library, University of Michigan, Box 1, Folder: "The Revolutionary Mysticism of Jesus, October 1, 1978."

103. Cleage, *Black Christian Nationalism*, 94-103.

104. Cleage, *Black Christian Nationalism*, 104-19.

105. "An Introduction to BCN Theology: Personal Change: The Key to Black Liberation," August 5, 1984, Albert B. Cleage Jr. Papers,

Bentley Historical Library, University of Michigan, Box 2, Folder: "An Introduction to BCN Theology: Personal Change: The Key to Black Liberation, August 5, 1984."

106. "Holy Crusade 1984: Words of Inspiration (Poems of Jaramogi)," Albert B. Cleage Jr. Papers, Bentley Historical Library, University of Michigan, Box 3, Folder: "Poetry: Holy Crusade Words of Inspiration: Poems of Jaramogi, 1984."

107. "Lesson 1—Introduction to the New Testament Notes, Appocalyptic [*sic*] Nationalism," BCN Bible Study, 1976, Albert B. Cleage Jr. Papers, Bentley Historical Library, University of Michigan, Box 4, Folder: "Bible Study, 1976." Underscore in the original.

108. James H. Cone, *Said I Wasn't Gonna Tell Nobody* (Maryknoll, NY: Orbis Books, 2018), 1.

109. James H. Cone, *Black Theology & Black Power* (Maryknoll, NY: Orbis Books, 1997), 114.

110. Cone, *Black Theology & Black Power*, 116.

111. Cone, *Black Theology & Black Power*, 117.

112. Cone, *Black Theology & Black Power*, 117.

5. Christ Means Black Power!

1. James H. Cone, *Black Theology & Black Power* (Maryknoll, NY: Orbis Books, 1997), 115.

2. Cone, *Black Theology & Black Power*, 103.

3. Cone, *Black Theology & Black Power*, 92.

4. Cone, *Black Theology & Black Power*, 115.

5. James H. Cone, *God of the Oppressed* (Maryknoll, NY: Orbis Books, 1997), 1.

6. James H. Cone, *My Soul Looks Back* (Nashville, TN: Abingdon, 1982), 18-19.

7. Cone, *My Soul Looks Back*, 19.

8. James H. Cone, *The Cross and the Lynching Tree* (Maryknoll, NY: Orbis Books, 2011), xvi.

9. James H. Cone, *Said I Wasn't Gonna Tell Nobody* (Maryknoll, NY: Orbis Books, 2018), 4.

10. Cone, *Said I Wasn't Gonna Tell Nobody*, 22.

11. Cone, *My Soul Looks Back*, 20.

12. Cone, *My Soul Looks Back*, 21-22.

13. Cone, *My Soul Looks Back*, 19-20.

14. Cone, *My Soul Looks Back*, 22.

15. Cone, *The Cross and the Lynching Tree*, 22.

16. Cone, *My Soul Looks Back*, 22.

17. Cone, *God of the Oppressed*, 1.

18. Cone, *My Soul Looks Back*, 23.

19. Cone, *My Soul Looks Back*, 24.

20. Cone, *My Soul Looks Back*, 80.

21. Cone, *Black Theology & Black Power*, 112.

22. Cone, *Said I Wasn't Gonna Tell Nobody*, 6.

23. Cone, *Said I Wasn't Gonna Tell Nobody*, 6.

24. Cone, *Said I Wasn't Gonna Tell Nobody*, 6.

25. James H. Cone, "The Cry of Black Blood: The Rise of Black Liberation Theology," YouTube video, posted by Union Theological Seminary, February 25, 2016, https://www.youtube.com/watch?v=P_Q768HvabU

26. Cone, *Said I Wasn't Gonna Tell Nobody*, 8.

27. Cone, *Said I Wasn't Gonna Tell Nobody*, 8.

28. Cone, *Said I Wasn't Gonna Tell Nobody*, 8, 62.

29. Cone, *My Soul Looks Back*, 44.

30. Cone, *Said I Wasn't Gonna Tell Nobody*, 13.

31. Cone, *Said I Wasn't Gonna Tell Nobody*, 14.

32. Cone, *Said I Wasn't Gonna Tell Nobody*.

33. Cone, *Said I Wasn't Gonna Tell Nobody*, 14-15.

34. Cone, *Black Theology & Black Power*, 116-17.

35. Albert B. Cleage Jr., *Black Christian Nationalism: New Directions for the Black Church* (New York: William Morrow & Company, 1972), xvii.

36. Letter from James Cone to John Webster and the Shrine of the Black Madonna, June 4, 1969, Albert B. Cleage Jr. Papers, Bentley Historical Library, University of Michigan, Box 7, Folder: "John Webster Forum Committee 1969."

37. Myran Elizabeth Lewis, "Cleage: A Rhetorical Study of Black Religious Nationalism" (PhD diss., Ohio State University, 1974), vii.

38. Cone, *My Soul Looks Back*, 64-92.

39. Cone, *My Soul Looks Back*, 17: "When people ask me about the decisive influences on my theological and political perspectives, my response always includes something about my mother and father, and

what it meant for a black person to grow up in Bearden, Arkansas, during the 1940s and 1950s. I have written briefly about Bearden and the Macedonia A.M.E. Church in other places. The more I reflect on who I am, and what is important to me, the more the Bearden experience looms large in my consciousness … The importance of Bearden is the way it enters my thinking … It is as if the people of Bearden are present, around my desk as I think and write. Their voices are clear and insistent: 'All right, James Hal, speak for your people.'"

40. Cone, *Said I Wasn't Gonna Tell Nobody*, 35.

41. Cone, *Said I Wasn't Gonna Tell Nobody*, 35.

42. Cone, *Black Theology & Black Power*, 3.

43. Cone, *Said I Wasn't Gonna Tell Nobody*, 9.

44. See Amos Jones Jr., "In Defense of the Apostle Paul: A Discussion with Albert Cleage and James Cone" (DMin diss., Vanderbilt University Divinity School, 1975).

45. "The Black Paper," included in C. Eric Lincoln, *The Black Church since Frazier* (New York: Schocken Books, 1974), 195-96.

46. "Black Power: Statement by the National Committee of Negro Churchmen, July 31, 1966," *Black Theology: A Documentary History, Volume One: 1966–1979*, ed. James H. Cone and Gayraud S. Wilmore, 2nd edition (Maryknoll, NY: Orbis Books, 1993), 20.

47. Cone, *Said I Wasn't Gonna Tell Nobody*, 19.

48. Cone, *My Soul Looks Back*, 80.

49. To give one example, Maurice Pugh, in his 2006 dissertation, "Black Theology: Cone, King, and Malcolm X," sorts through King's and Malcolm X's respective influences on Cone, examining carefully Cone's own statements on the topic. Pugh concludes that Malcolm X's thought provided Cone with (1) Black consciousness, (2) a searing critique of white Christianity, and (3) a revolutionary commitment for theology to Cone's project (Maurice Pugh, "Black Theology: Cone, King, and Malcolm X" [PhD diss., Dallas Theological Seminary, 2006], 89-113). Pugh incisively argues that without Malcolm X's Black nationalist influence, Cone's development of a theology of God's and Jesus' Blackness would not have been possible. "The 'blackness of God' argument," asserted Pugh, "integrated King's revelation of God as God's self-disclosure to the oppressed community (illustrated by his Old Testament involvement in the liberation of Israel from Egypt) with Malcolm's black nationalism" (147). Pugh notes in

a footnote that the "blackness of God" was not original to Cone, but had its origins in the earlier Black religious tradition, including in Marcus Garvey's thought, the Nation of Islam, and in Malcolm X's own theology, but this is not emphasized (148 n. 112).

50. James H. Cone, *Risks of Faith: The Emergence of a Black Theology of Liberation, 1968–1998* (Boston: Beacon Press, 1999), xviii.

51. Mark L. Chapman, *Christianity on Trial: African-American Religious Thought before and after Black Power* (Maryknoll, NY: Orbis Books, 1996). Per Chapman, "the Nation of Islam's critique of Christianity prompted the articulation of black liberation theology as much, if not more, than the emergence of Black Power in the summer of 1966" (9). Chapman places Cleage alongside the National Conference of Black Clergymen, whose 1966 statement on Black Power is often cited as a starting point for Black theology, as two examples of Black Christians acting "as apologists for Christianity at a time when *Christian* and *Black* appeared to be a contradiction in terms," largely as a result of Elijah Muhammad's and Malcolm X's searing critiques of Christianity as a religion of white supremacy (70). Chapman argues that it is important both to recognize the shared concerns of the NCBC clergy, Cleage, and Cone in the formation of Black theology, but also the difference that Cleage represents, as one who "crossed 'the boundary'" to a full and unequivocal identification with Black nationalism (91-92).

52. See, e.g., Delores Williams's incisive critique of Black theology's overreliance on this theme in Delores S. Williams, *Sisters in the Wilderness: The Challenge of Womanist God-Talk* (Maryknoll, NY: Orbis Books, 1996), 143-77.

53. Cone, *Black Theology & Black Power*, 33.

54. Cone, *Black Theology & Black Power*, 34.

55. Cone, *Black Theology & Black Power*, 35. See, e.g., Karl Barth, *Church Dogmatics* III/2, ed. G. W. Bromiley and T. F. Torrance; trans. H. Knight, G. W. Bromiley, J. K. S. Reid, and R. H. Fuller (Edinburgh: T. & T. Clark, 1960), 274. "[Jesus'] being *for* others ... must correspond as at least a minimum on our side the fact that our human being is at root a free being *with* others."

56. Cone, *Black Theology & Black Power*, 35. See, e.g., Barth, *Church Dogmatics* IV/2, ed. G. W. Bromiley and T. F. Torrance; trans. G. W. Bromiley (Edinburgh: T. & T. Clark, 1958), 231-32: "He is Him-

self a victim of the slavery from which He dares to try to free others ... The activity of Jesus, and revealed in it God Himself and His Kingdom, are a defiance of the power of destruction which enslaves man ... They are not a neutral force or omnipotence, but the omnipotence of mercy—not quiet and passive mercy, but a mercy which is active, and therefore hostile to that power on behalf of poor man."

57. Cone, *Black Theology & Black Power*, 40.

58. Karl Barth, *Church Dogmatics* IV/2, 232. For the full section (§64.3), see 154-263.

59. Cone, *Black Theology & Black Power*, 17.

60. Cone, *Black Theology & Black Power*, 40.

61. Cone, *Black Theology & Black Power*, 40-41.

62. Cone, *Black Theology & Black Power*, 150.

63. Cone, *Black Theology & Black Power*, 150.

64. Cone, *Black Theology & Black Power*, 39.

65. James H. Cone, *A Black Theology of Liberation* (Maryknoll, NY: Orbis Books, 2010), 69.

66. Cone, *A Black Theology of Liberation*, 73-74.

67. Cone, *Black Theology & Black Power*, 46.

68. Cone, *Black Theology & Black Power*, 55.

69. Cone, *Black Theology & Black Power*, 40.

70. Cone, *A Black Theology of Liberation*, 26.

71. Cone, *God of the Oppressed*, 63.

72. Cone, *God of the Oppressed*, 67-68.

73. Cone, *Said I Wasn't Gonna Tell Nobody*, 19.

74. Father Andrew M. Greeley, "Sees Resurgence of Nazi Mentality in America," syndicated column, in *The Anchor* 15, no. 48 (December 2, 1971): 18.

75. Greeley, "Sees Resurgence of Nazi Mentality," 18.

76. Cone, *A Black Theology of Liberation*, xvii.

77. James H. Cone, *Martin & Malcolm & America: A Dream or a Nightmare* (Maryknoll, NY: Orbis Books, 1991), 125-26.

78. Cone, *Risks of Faith*, 64-69, 91.

79. James H. Cone, "God and Black Suffering: Calling the Oppressors to Account," *Anglican Theological Review* 90, no. 4 (2008): 702-703.

80. Cone, *Martin & Malcolm & America*, 158-59.

81. Cone, *Martin & Malcolm & America*, 179.

82. Cone, *Martin & Malcolm & America*, 160.

83. Cone, *Martin & Malcolm & America*, 160.

84. Cone, *Martin & Malcolm & America*, 168.

85. Cone, *Martin & Malcolm & America*, 182.

86. James H. Cone, *The Spirituals and the Blues: An Interpretation* (New York: Seabury Press, 1972), 99-100.

87. Cone, *The Spirituals and the Blues,* 100.

88. Cone, *The Spirituals and the Blues,* 105.

89. Cone, *Said I Wasn't Gonna Tell Nobody,* 85-107.

90. Cone, *Said I Wasn't Gonna Tell Nobody,* 68.

91. Cone, *The Spirituals and the Blues,* 5.

92. Cone, *The Spirituals and the Blues,* 73.

93. Cone, *The Spirituals and the Blues,* 66.

94. Cone, *The Spirituals and the Blues,* 79.

95. James H. Cone, *Speaking the Truth: Ecumenicism, Liberation, and Black Theology* (Grand Rapids, MI: William B. Eerdmans, 1986), 84.

96. Marvin E. Jackmon (Marvin X), "That Old-Time Religion," in *SOS—Calling All Black People: A Black Arts Movement Reader,* ed. John H. Bracey Jr., Sonia Sanchez, and James Smethurst (Amherst: University of Massachusetts Press, 2014), 314.

97. Malcolm X, *Malcolm X Speaks,* 216.

98. Joshua Bloom and Waldo E. Martin Jr., *Black against Empire: The History and Politics of the Black Panther Party* (Oakland: University of California Press, 2016), 395-97.

99. Cleage, *Black Christian Nationalism,* 166.

100. Cleage, *Black Christian Nationalism,* 249-60.

101. Cleage, *Black Christian Nationalism,* 258.

102. "Prelude to a New Era: The New Fantasy," June 25, 1978, Albert B. Cleage Jr. Papers, Bentley Historical Library, University of Michigan, Box 1, Folder: "Prelude to a New Era: The New Fantasy, June 25, 1978."

6. The Twilight of Black Power

1. John Hearsey, *The Algiers Motel Incident* (Baltimore, MD: Johns Hopkins University Press, 1998), 345, 348.

2. Hearsey, *The Algiers Motel Incident,* 344.

3. Hearsey, *The Algiers Motel Incident*, 348.

4. Albert B. Cleage Jr., "The Death of Fear," *Negro Digest* 17, no. 1 (November 1967): 30.

5. Cleage, "The Death of Fear," 30.

6. Hearsey, *The Algiers Motel Incident*, 349.

7. Cleage, "The Death of Fear," 30.

8. Cleage, "The Death of Fear," 30.

9. Cleage, "The Death of Fear," 31.

10. Cleage, "The Death of Fear," 31.

11. Cleage, "The Death of Fear," 31.

12. Albert B. Cleage Jr., *The Black Messiah* (New York: Sheed & Ward, 1968), 15-16.

13. Cleage, *The Black Messiah*, 11.

14. Cleage, *The Black Messiah*, 131.

15. See John Stauffer and Benjamin Soskis, "Julia Ward Howe and the Making of the 'Battle Hymn of the Republic,'" in Stauffer and Soskis, *The Battle Hymn of the Republic: A Biography of the Song That Marches On* (New York: Oxford University Press, 2013), 73-105.

16. David Walker, "Walker's Appeal, in Four Articles; Together with a Preamble, to the Coloured Citizens of the World, but in Particular, and Very Expressly, to Those of the United States of America, Written in Boston, State of Massachusetts, September 28, 1829," electronic edition, *Documenting the American South*, 11, https://docsouth.unc.edu/nc/walker/walker.html.

17. Walker, "Walker's Appeal," 84.

18. Sarah Grimké, "An Epistle to the Clergy of the Southern States," in Sarah Grimké and Angelina Grimké, *On Slavery and Abolitionism: Essays and Letters* (New York: Penguin Books, 2014), 17.

19. Grimké, "An Epistle to the Clergy of the Southern States," 17.

20. Cone, *The Spirituals and the Blues*, 45.

21. Lucy A. Delaney, *From the Darkness Cometh the Light, or, Struggles for Freedom*, electronic edition, *Documenting the American South*, 14-15, https://docsouth.unc.edu/neh/delaney/delaney.html.

22. William Lloyd Garrison, Letter No. 48, "To Charles Reed," Boston, February 1, 1870, in *The Letters of William Lloyd Garrison, Volume VI, 1868–1879*, ed. Walter M. Merrill and Louis Ruchames (Cambridge, MA: Harvard University Press, 1981), 157.

23. Garrison, Letter No. 48, "To Charles Reed," 157.

24. Cleage, *The Black Messiah*, 131.

25. Cleage, *The Black Messiah*, 131.

26. Cleage, *The Black Messiah*, 131-32.

27. Hubert G. Locke, "Riot Aftermath: New Dimensions of the Racial Struggle," Albert B. Cleage Jr. Papers, Bentley Historical Library, University of Michigan, Box 6, Folder: "Locke—The Detroit Riots of 1967."

28. "End of an Era: We Are the Messianic Hope of the Twentieth Century," December 25, 1977, Albert B. Cleage Jr. Papers, Bentley Historical Library, University of Michigan, Box 1, Folder: "End of an Era: We Are the Messianic Hope of the Twentieth Century, December 25, 1977."

29. "End of an Era."

30. Peniel Joseph, *Waiting 'Til the Midnight Hour: A Narrative History of Black Power in America* (New York: Henry Holt and Company, 2006), 297.

31. Aswad Walker, "Politics Is Sacred: The Activism of Albert B. Cleage Jr.," in *Albert Cleage Jr. and the Black Madonna and Child*, ed. Jawanza Eric Clark (New York: Palgrave Macmillan, 2016), 103-104.

32. "The Community of Jesus ... Today's Messianic Hope," January 29, 1978, Albert B. Cleage Jr. Papers, Bentley Historical Library, University of Michigan, Box 1, Folder: "The Community of Jesus ... Today's Messianic Hope, January 29, 1978."

33. "The Community of Jesus."

34. James H. Cone, *The Cross and the Lynching Tree* (Maryknoll, NY: Orbis Books, 2011), 165-66.

35. James H. Cone, *A Black Theology of Liberation* (Maryknoll, NY: Orbis Books, 2010), 21.

36. James H. Cone, *God of the Oppressed* (Maryknoll, NY: Orbis Books, 1997), 132.

37. Cone, *God of the Oppressed,* 132.

38. Cone, *God of the Oppressed,* 132.

39. James H. Cone, *Black Theology & Black Power* (Maryknoll, NY: Orbis Books, 1997), 125.

40. Cone, *Black Theology & Black Power,* 33.

41. "The Community of Jesus."

42. D. Kimathi Nelson, "The Theological Journey of Albert B. Cleage Jr.: Reflections from Jaramogi's Protégé and Successor," in

Clark (ed.), *Albert B. Cleage, Jr. and the Black Madonna and Child*, 34.

43. "BCN 10 Year Projection," 1973, Albert B. Cleage Jr. Papers, Bentley Historical Library, University of Michigan, Box 4, Folder: "Annual Meeting, 1973."

44. "Understanding My Faith," Edition #1, May 1993, Albert B. Cleage Jr. Papers, Bentley Historical Library, University of Michigan, Box 7, Folder: "Youth Miscellaneous."

45. "End of an Era."

46. "End of an Era."

47. Nelson, "The Theological Journey of Albert B. Cleage Jr.," 27. The word "KUA" is sometimes capitalized and sometimes not capitalized in speeches and documents written by Cleage or PAOCC members.

48. Nelson, "The Theological Journey of Albert B. Cleage Jr.," 28.

49. Nelson, "The Theological Journey of Albert B. Cleage Jr.," 36.

50. Nelson, "The Theological Journey of Albert B. Cleage Jr.," 34.

51. In the late 1960s immediately following the Detroit riots, Hiley H. Ward described Cleage's church as essentially following the "traditional order of worship" of a Congregationalist church, including the celebration of two sacraments, the Lord's Supper and baptism (Hiley H. Ward, *Prophet of the Black Nation* [Philadelphia, PA: United Church Press, 1969], 1-3). However, in the mid-1970s, Cleage and the PAOCC radically reimagined the meaning of the term "sacrament" and what sacramental worship entailed. A 1992 pamphlet defines sacraments as "serious, religious ceremonies used and practiced by Jesus and observed by his followers, which renewed and confirmed their relationship with him. Through participation in the Sacraments, God's holy spirit can be experienced and people can be prepared to realize that God is in them—that they have an Inner Divinity." This document lists eleven sacraments, each associated with rituals practiced by the PAOCC: invocation, confirmation, confession and absolution, baptism and purification, renewal and rebirth, commitment, kingdom, Holy Orders, incarnation, Holy Matrimony, and Holy Unction. ("The Eleven Holy Sacraments," Albert B. Cleage Jr. Papers, Bentley Historical Library, University of Michigan, Box 4, Folder: "History.")

52. "BCN Ideology," February 12, 1981, Albert B. Cleage Jr. Papers,

Bentley Historical Library, University of Michigan, Box 5, Folder: "Communalism Rituals 1982."

53. "An Introduction to BCN Theology: Personal Change: The Key to Black Liberation," August 5, 1984, Albert B. Cleage Jr. Papers, Bentley Historical Library, University of Michigan, Box 2, Folder: "An Introduction to BCN Theology: Personal Change: The Key to Black Liberation, August 5, 1984."

54. Albert B. Cleage Jr., *Black Christian Nationalism: New Directions for the Black Church* (New York: William Morrow & Company, 1972), 4-5.

55. "God Is Power," November 13, 1983, Albert B. Cleage Jr. Papers, Bentley Historical Library, University of Michigan, Box 2, Folder: "God Is Power, November 13, 1983."

56. "God Is Power."

57. "An Introduction to BCN Theology."

58. "The Revolutionary Mysticism of Jesus," October 1, 1978, Albert B. Cleage Jr. Papers, Bentley Historical Library, University of Michigan, Box 1, Folder: "The Revolutionary Mysticism of Jesus, October 1, 1978."

59. "The Revolutionary Mysticism of Jesus."

60. "Christianity and the Consciousness Revolution," November 19, 1978, Albert B. Cleage Jr. Papers, Bentley Historical Library, University of Michigan, Box 1, Folder: "Christianity and the Consciousness Revolution, November 19, 1978."

61. "Christianity and the Consciousness Revolution."

62. "Christianity and the Consciousness Revolution."

63. "Christianity and the Consciousness Revolution."

64. "THE SEVEN KUA AFFIRMATIONS: 'The Laying On of Hands'—Basic KUA Ritual of Healing," Albert B. Cleage Jr. Papers, Bentley Historical Library, University of Michigan, Box 4, Folder: "History."

65. "THE SEVEN KUA AFFIRMATIONS."

66. Shelley McIntosh, *Mtoto House: Vision to Victory, Raising African American Children Communally* (Lanham, MD: Hamilton Books, 2005), 31.

67. McIntosh, *Mtoto House*, 31, 51, 39.

68. "Prelude to a New Era: KUA: Fifth in Series," July 16, 1978, Albert B. Cleage Jr. Papers, Bentley Historical Library, University of

Michigan, Box 1, Folder: "Prelude to a New Era: KUA: Fifth in Series, July 16, 1978."

69. "Transforming Community: Struggle for Change #2," Albert B. Cleage Jr. Papers, Bentley Historical Library, University of Michigan, Box 2, Folder: "Transforming Community: Struggle for Change #2, March 1, 1984."

70. "Holy Crusade 1984."

71. James H. Cone, *Said I Wasn't Gonna Tell Nobody* (Maryknoll, NY: Orbis Books, 2018), 36.

72. Cone, *Said I Wasn't Gonna Tell Nobody*, 35.

73. Cone, *Said I Wasn't Gonna Tell Nobody*, 85-107. See also James H. Cone, "Epilogue: An Interpretation of the Debate among Black Theologians," in James H. Cone and Gayraud S. Wilmore (eds.), *Black Theology: A Documentary History, Volume One: 1966–1979* (Maryknoll, NY: Orbis Books, 1993), 430-34.

74. Cone, *Said I Wasn't Gonna Tell Nobody*, 92.

75. Cone, *Said I Wasn't Gonna Tell Nobody*, 85.

76. Cone, *Said I Wasn't Gonna Tell Nobody*, 94.

77. James H. Cone, *My Soul Looks Back* (Nashville, TN: Abingdon, 1982), 97.

78. Victor Anderson critiqued Cone's and other Black theologians' tendency to erase the "social and cultural elements of differentiation" that exist among Black Americans in favor of a constructed, ideologically totalized "Black community" monolithically espousing "Black faith." See Victor Anderson, *Beyond Ontological Blackness: An Essay on African American Religious and Cultural Criticism* (London and New York: Bloomsbury, 2016), 103, also 86-104. A related critique was made by the philosopher William R. Jones in his assessment of Black theology; per Jones, Cone's and other theologians' exclusive commitment to the Black Christian tradition ignored a long and vital tradition of Black humanism, which provided an alternative framework for liberation. See William R. Jones, *Is God a White Racist? A Preamble to Black Theology* (Boston: Beacon Press, 1998), 24-39. However, Cone's continued engagement with Malcolm X as a primary influence as well as the increasing importance of the thought of James Baldwin for his theology in his final years counteracted this general tendency. On Baldwin's influence on the later Cone, see Cone, *Said I Wasn't Gonna Tell Nobody*, 144-69.

79. Mark L. Chapman, *Christianity on Trial: African-American Religious Thought Before and After Black Power* (Maryknoll, NY: Orbis Books, 1996), 130-33.

80. Cone, *God of the Oppressed*, vi.

81. Cone, *A Black Theology of Liberation*, 27.

82. James H. Cone, *The Spirituals and the Blues: An Interpretation* (New York: Seabury Press, 1972), 2.

83. See, e.g., Cone, *The Spirituals and the Blues*, 101-107.

84. Cone, *The Spirituals and the Blues*, 116.

85. Cone, *Said I Wasn't Gonna Tell Nobody*, 160.

86. James H. Cone, *Martin & Malcolm & America: A Dream or a Nightmare* (Maryknoll, NY: Orbis Books, 1991), 122.

87. Cone, *God of the Oppressed*, 4.

88. Cone, *God of the Oppressed*, 187-88.

7. Of Malcolm and Merton

1. Thomas Merton, *Conjectures of a Guilty Bystander* (New York: Doubleday Religion, 1966), 153.

2. Merton, *Conjectures of a Guilty Bystander,* 153-54.

3. James T. Fisher, *The Catholic Counterculture in America, 1933–1962* (Chapel Hill: University of North Carolina Press, 1989), 206.

4. Fisher, *The Catholic Counterculture,* 230.

5. Mary Gordon, *On Thomas Merton* (Boulder, CO: Shambhala, 2018), 5.

6. Thomas Merton, *The Seven Storey Mountain* (Orlando, FL: Harcourt, Inc., 1998), 449.

7. Albert Raboteau, "A Hidden Wholeness: Thomas Merton and Martin Luther King, Jr.," *Spirituality Today* 40 (Winter 1988 supplement): 80.

8. Eldridge Cleaver, *Soul on Ice* (New York: Dell Publishing, 1968), 31-32.

9. Cleaver, *Soul on Ice*, 32.

10. Cleaver, *Soul on Ice*, 32.

11. Cleaver, *Soul on Ice*, 32.

12. Cleaver, *Soul on Ice*, 35.

13. Merton, *The Seven Storey Mountain*, 380.

14. Thomas Merton, *Run to the Mountain, The Story of a Vocation,*

*Volume One, 1939–1941, The Journals of Thomas Merto*n, ed. Patrick Hart, O.C.S.O. (New York: HarperCollins, 1996), 445.

15. Cleaver, *Soul on Ice*, 35.

16. Cleaver, *Soul on Ice*, 35.

17. Cleaver, *Soul on Ice*, 34.

18. Julius Lester, *All Is Well* (New York: William Morrow and Company, 1976), 75-76.

19. Merton, *The Seven Storey Mountain*, 151.

20. Merton, *The Seven Storey Mountain*, 346.

21. Merton, *The Seven Storey Mountain*, 407.

22. Wade Hall, *The Rest of the Dream: The Black Odyssey of Lyman Johnson* (Lexington: University Press of Kentucky, 1988), 127.

23. Thomas Merton, *A Search for Solitude, Pursuing the Monk's Life, Volume Three, 1952–1960, The Journals of Thomas Merton*, ed. Lawrence S. Cunningham (New York: HarperCollins, 1996), 391.

24. Thomas Merton, *Faith and Violence: Christian Teaching and Christian Practice* (Notre Dame, IN: University of Notre Dame Press, 1968), 144.

25. Merton, *Faith and Violence*, 144.

26. Merton, *Faith and Violence*, 121-24.

27. Merton, *Faith and Violence*, 6.

28. Merton, *Faith and Violence*, 187.

29. Merton, *Faith and Violence*, 20.

30. Merton, *Faith and Violence*, 142-43.

31. Merton, *Faith and Violence*, 142.

32. Thomas Merton, *Learning to Love: Exploring Solitude and Freedom, Volume Six, 1966–1967, The Journals of Thomas Merton*, ed. Christine M. Bochen (New York: HarperCollins, 1998), 233.

33. Merton, *Learning to Love*, 233.

34. Merton, *Learning to Love*, 160.

35. Merton, *Learning to Love*, 224.

36. Merton, *Learning to Love*, 224.

37. Merton, *Learning to Love*, 283.

38. Lester, *All Is Well*, 284.

39. Julius Lester, *Lovesong: Becoming a Jew* (New York: Henry Holt, 1988), 13, 23.

40. Lester, *All Is Well*, 284-85.

41. Lester, *All Is Well*, 285.

42. Lester, *Lovesong*, 25.

43. Lester, *All Is Well*, 290.

44. Lester, *All Is Well*, 290.

45. Lester, *All Is Well*, 290.

46. Truman Nelson, "Guerilla of the Mind," *New York Times*, October 13, 1968, 16.

47. Nelson, "Guerilla of the Mind," 16.

48. Lester, *All Is Well*, 108, 110.

49. James Forman, SDS, "United States 1967: High Tide of Black Resistance," pamphlet, *Roz Payne Sixties Archive*, 2022, https://roz sixties.unl.edu/items/show/517.

50. Lester, *All Is Well*, 148.

51. Lester, *All Is Well*, 136.

52. Lester, *All Is Well*, 27.

53. Lester, *All Is Well*, 318-19.

54. Lester, *Lovesong*, 10-11.

55. Lester, *Lovesong*, 39.

56. Lester, *Lovesong*, 39.

57. Lester, *All Is Well*, 108.

58. Lester, *All Is Well*, 111.

59. Lester, *Lovesong*, 40.

60. Lester, *All Is Well*, 145.

61. Lester, *All Is Well*, 145.

62. Lester, *All Is Well*, 139.

63. Lester, *All Is Well*, 139.

64. Lester, *All Is Well*, 232.

65. Lester, *All Is Well*, 233.

66. Lester, *All Is Well*, 234.

67. Lester, *All Is Well*, 234-35.

68. Lester, *All Is Well*, 235.

69. Lester, *All Is Well*, 236.

70. Lester, *All Is Well*, 225.

71. Lester, *All Is Well*, 105.

72. Julius Lester, "The Angry Children of Malcolm X," in *Black Protest Thought in the Twentieth Century*, ed. August Meier, Elliott Rudwick, and Francis L. Broderick (Indianapolis, IN: Bobbs-Merrill Company, 1971), 479.

73. Lester, "The Angry Children of Malcolm X," 483.

74. Lester, *Lovesong*, 41.

75. Lester, *Lovesong*, 41.

76. Julius Lester, "At Merton's Grave," *The Catholic Worker* 41, no. 9 (December 1975): 4.

77. Transcript, Gwendolyn Zoharah Simmons, Oral History Interview with Justin Dunnavant, October 25, 2012, 10, Samuel Proctor Oral History Program Collection, P. K. Yonge Library of Florida History, University of Florida.

78. Simmons, Oral History Interview with Justin Dunnavant.

79. Gwendolyn Zoharah Simmons, "From Little Memphis Girl to Mississippi Amazon," in *Hands on the Freedom Plow: Personal Accounts by Women in SNCC*, ed. Faith S. Holsaert, Martha Prescod Norman Noonan, Judy Richardson, Betty Garman Robinson, Jean Smith Young, and Dorothy M. Zellner (Champaign: University of Illinois Press, 2010), 15.

80. Simmons, "From Little Memphis Girl to Mississippi Amazon," 10.

81. Simmons, Oral History Interview with Justin Dunnavant, 2.

82. Simmons, Oral History Interview with Justin Dunnavant, 2.

83. Simmons, Oral History Interview with Justin Dunnavant, 1.

84. Gwendolyn Zoharah Simmons, "Martin Luther King Jr. Revisited: A Black Power Feminist Pays Homage to the King," *Journal of Feminist Studies in Religion* 24, no. 2 (2008): 193.

85. Simmons, "From Little Memphis Girl to Mississippi Amazon," 10.

86. Simmons, "From Little Memphis Girl to Mississippi Amazon," 10.

87. Simmons, "From Little Memphis Girl to Mississippi Amazon," 9.

88. Simmons, Oral History Interview with Justin Dunnavant, 5-6.

89. Simmons, "From Little Memphis Girl to Mississippi Amazon," 9.

90. Simmons, "From Little Memphis Girl to Mississippi Amazon," 10.

91. Joseph Mosnier interview of Gwendolyn Zoharah Simmons. U.S. Civil Rights History Project, Oral History Interview in Gainesville, Florida, 2011, transcript, 6. https://www.loc.gov/item/2015669148.

92. Simmons, "Martin Luther King Jr. Revisited," 190; Simmons, Oral History Interview with Justin Dunnavant, 11.

93. Simmons, "Martin Luther King Jr. Revisited," 190-91.

94. Simmons, Oral History Interview with Justin Dunnavant, 11.

95. Simmons, Oral History Interview with Justin Dunnavant, 10.

96. Simmons, Oral History Interview with Justin Dunnavant, 10.

97. Simmons, "Martin Luther King Jr. Revisited," 191.

98. Simmons, "From Little Memphis Girl to Mississippi Amazon," 16-17; "Gwendolyn Zoharah Simmons and Lucas Johnson: The Movement, Remembered Forward," *On Being with Krista Tippett*, January 16, 2014, https://onbeing.org/programs/gwendolyn-zoharah-simmons-and-lucas-johnson-the-movement-remembered-forward.

99. Simmons, Oral History Interview with Justin Dunnavant, 13.

100. Simmons, Oral History Interview with Justin Dunnavant, 14, 16.

101. Simmons, Oral History Interview with Justin Dunnavant, 20.

102. Simmons, Oral History Interview with Justin Dunnavant, 17-18.

103. Mosnier interview of Gwendolyn Zoharah Simmons, U.S. Civil Rights History Project, 8.

104. Mosnier interview of Gwendolyn Zoharah Simmons, U.S. Civil Rights History Project, 8.

105. Mosnier interview of Gwendolyn Zoharah Simmons, U.S. Civil Rights History Project, 8, 12.

106. Mosnier interview of Gwendolyn Zoharah Simmons, U.S. Civil Rights History Project, 9.

107. Mosnier interview of Gwendolyn Zoharah Simmons, U.S. Civil Rights History Project.

108. Mosnier interview of Gwendolyn Zoharah Simmons, U.S. Civil Rights History Project, 12-13.

109. Mosnier interview of Gwendolyn Zoharah Simmons, U.S. Civil Rights History Project, 16.

110. Simmons, Oral History Interview with Justin Dunnavant, 26-28.

111. Simmons, "From Little Memphis Girl to Mississippi Amazon," 28.

112. Mosnier interview of Gwendolyn Zoharah Simmons, U.S. Civil Rights History Project, 17.

113. Mosnier interview of Gwendolyn Zoharah Simmons, U.S. Civil Rights History Project, 22-23.

114. Mosnier interview of Gwendolyn Zoharah Simmons, U.S. Civil Rights History Project, 24.

115. Simmons, "From Little Memphis Girl to Mississippi Amazon," 30.

116. Simmons, Oral History Interview with Justin Dunnavant, 31.

117. "March 17, 65: Hello Freedom Fighting Friend," Freedom Summer Digital Collection, Wisconsin Historical Society, Alicia Kaplow papers, 1964–1968; Archives Main Stacks, Mss 507, Box 1, Folder 3, page 1.

118. Simmons, Oral History Interview with Justin Dunnavant, 29; Mosnier interview of Gwendolyn Zoharah Simmons, U.S. Civil Rights History Project, 25.

119. Simmons, Oral History Interview with Justin Dunnavant, 29.

120. Mosnier interview of Gwendolyn Zoharah Simmons, U.S. Civil Rights History Project, 26.

121. Simmons, Oral History Interview with Justin Dunnavant, 29-30.

122. Mosnier interview of Gwendolyn Zoharah Simmons, U.S. Civil Rights History Project, 26-27.

123. Mosnier interview of Gwendolyn Zoharah Simmons, U.S. Civil Rights History Project, 27.

124. "Gwendolyn Zoharah Simmons and Lucas Johnson: The Movement, Remembered Forward," *On Being with Krista Tippett.*

125. Mosnier interview of Gwendolyn Zoharah Simmons, U.S. Civil Rights History Project, 27.

126. Ula Yvette Taylor, *The Promise of Patriarchy: Women and the Nation of Islam* (Chapel Hill: University of North Carolina Press, 2017), 143.

127. Taylor, *The Promise of Patriarchy,* 143.

128. Taylor, *The Promise of Patriarchy,* 28.

129. Simmons, "Martin Luther King Jr. Revisited," 192.

130. Clayborne Carson, "Student Nonviolent Coordinating Committee," in *Organizing Black America: An Encyclopedia of African American Associations,* ed. Nina Mjagkij (New York: Routledge, 2001), 649-50.

131. SNCC Vine City Project, *Black Power: A Reprint of a Position*

Paper for the SNCC Vine City Project, United States National Student Association, pamphlet, Summer 1966.

132. SNCC Vine City Project, *Black Power,* 5.

133. SNCC Vine City Project, *Black Power,* 4.

134. Mosnier interview of Gwendolyn Zoharah Simmons, U.S. Civil Rights History Project, 30.

135. Debra L. Schultz, *Going South: Jewish Women in the Civil Rights Movement* (New York: New York University Press, 2001), 194.

136. Mosnier interview of Gwendolyn Zoharah Simmons, U.S. Civil Rights History Project, 32.

137. Emilye Crosby, John Melville Bishop, and U.S. Civil Rights History Project, interview of Dorothy Zellner, conducted by Emilye Crosby in Baltimore, Maryland, 2015, transcript, 71. https://www.loc.gov/item/2016655416/.

138. Emilye Crosby, John Melville Bishop, and U.S. Civil Rights History Project, interview of Dorothy Zellner, 73.

139. Lester, *All Is Well*, 135.

140. Hettie Jones, *How I Became Hettie Jones* (New York: E. P. Dutton, 1990), 223.

141. Simmons, "Martin Luther King Jr. Revisited," 191.

142. Gwendolyn Zoharah Simmons, "Are We Up to the Challenge? The Need for a Radical Re-ordering of the Islamic Discourse on Women," in *Progressive Muslims: On Justice, Gender and Pluralism,* ed. Omid Safi (London: Oneworld, 2003), 236.

143. Gwendolyn Zoharah Simmons, "African American Islam as an Expression of Converts' Religious Faith and Nationalist Dreams and Ambitions," in *Women Embracing Islam: Gender and Conversion in the West,* ed. Karin van Nieuwkerk (Austin: University of Texas Press, 2006), 180.

144. Simmons, Oral History Interview with Justin Dunnavant, 32.

145. Simmons, Oral History Interview with Justin Dunnavant, 32-33, 35.

146. "Gwendolyn Zoharah Simmons and Lucas Johnson: The Movement, Remembered Forward," *On Being with Krista Tippett.*

147. "Gwendolyn Zoharah Simmons and Lucas Johnson: The Movement, Remembered Forward," *On Being with Krista Tippett.*

148. Simmons, "Are We Up to the Challenge?," 238.

149. "WisdomTalk 8 with Gwendolyn Zoharah Simmons, Ph.D.,"

YouTube video, posted by Sunseed, May 23, 2021, https://www.you tube.com/watch?v=mQTDq4EutqM.

150. "Gwendolyn Zoharah Simmons and Lucas Johnson: The Movement, Remembered Forward," *On Being with Krista Tippett*.

151. M. R. Baawa Muhaiyaddeen, *To Die before Death: The Sufi Way of Life* (Philadelphia: Fellowship Press, 1997), 12.

152. Muhaiyaddeen, *To Die before Death*, 224.

153. Mosnier interview of Gwendolyn Zoharah Simmons, U.S. Civil Rights History Project, 40.

154. Mosnier interview of Gwendolyn Zoharah Simmons, U.S. Civil Rights History Project, 41.

155. Simmons, "Martin Luther King Jr. Revisited," 208.

156. "WisdomTalk 8 with Gwendolyn Zoharah Simmons, Ph.D."

8. People's Churches

1. Cha-Cha Jiménez Defense Committee, *"Que Viva El Pueblo"*: *A Biographical History of Jose Cha-Cha Jimenez, General Secretary of the Young Lords Organization,* pamphlet, n.d., 5.

2. Jiménez Defense Committee, *"Que Viva El Pueblo,"* 4; Johanna Fernández, *The Young Lords: A Radical History* (Chapel Hill: University of North Carolina Press, 2020), 17.

3. Jiménez Defense Committee, *"Que Viva El Pueblo,"* 5-6; Michael Robert Gonzales, "Ruffians and Revolutionaries: The Development of the Young Lords Organization in Chicago" (MA thesis, University of Wisconsin-Milwaukee, 2015), 48.

4. Jiménez Defense Committee, *"Que Viva El Pueblo,"* 6-7; Gonzales, "Ruffians and Revolutionaries," 49; Johanna Fernández, *The Young Lords: A Radical History*, 18.

5. Jiménez Defense Committee, *"Que Viva El Pueblo,"* 6.

6. Jiménez Defense Committee, *"Que Viva El Pueblo,"* 6.

7. Jiménez Defense Committee, *"Que Viva El Pueblo,"* 6.

8. Jiménez Defense Committee, *"Que Viva El Pueblo,"* 7.

9. Jiménez Defense Committee, *"Que Viva El Pueblo,"* 7-8.

10. Jiménez Defense Committee, *"Que Viva El Pueblo,"* 8, 9.

11. Jiménez Defense Committee, *"Que Viva El Pueblo,"* 8, 9.

12. Jiménez Defense Committee, *"Que Viva El Pueblo,"* 8.

13. Jiménez Defense Committee, *"Que Viva El Pueblo,"* 9-14; Johanna Fernández, *The Young Lords: A Radical History*, 26-35.

14. Jiménez Defense Committee, *"Que Viva El Pueblo,"* 10.

15. Jiménez Defense Committee, *"Que Viva El Pueblo,"* 14.

16. Jiménez Defense Committee, *"Que Viva El Pueblo,"* 15.

17. Jiménez Defense Committee, *"Que Viva El Pueblo,"* 15-16; Fernández, *The Young Lords*, 36; "Jose Jimenez Interview: Young Lords Part I," YouTube video, posted by Jeff Smith, March 30, 2016, https://www.youtube.com/watch?v=iUPit9t74Ao

18. "Jose Jimenez Interview: Young Lords Part I."

19. "Jose Jimenez Interview: Young Lords Part I."

20. See, e.g., Leonard Crow Dog, *Crow Dog: Four Generations of Sioux Medicine Men* (New York: HarperCollins, 1995); Dennis Banks with Richard Erdoes, "Crow Dog," *Ojibwa Warrior: Dennis Banks and the Rise of the American Indian Movement* (Norman: University of Oklahoma Press, 2004), 95-104; Mary Brave Bird with Richard Erdoes, *Ohitika Woman* (New York: Grove Press, 1993); Mary Crow Dog with Richard Erdoes, *Lakota Woman* (New York: HarperCollins, 1990).

21. Mary Brave Bird with Richard Erdoes, *Ohitika Woman*, 73.

22. Mary Brave Bird with Richard Erdoes, *Ohitika Woman*, 75.

23. Martha Shelley, "The Young Lords Go to Church," *Come Out!*, 1, no. 3 (April/May 1970): 10; Editorial Board, "The Queer History of the Women's House of Detention," *The Activist History Review* (May 31, 2019), https://activisthistory.com/2019/05/31/the-queer-history-of-the-womens-house-of-detention/

24. Fernández, *The Young Lords*, 155-91.

25. Fernández, *The Young Lords*, 163-90.

26. Shelley, "The Young Lords Go to Church."

27. Mickey Melendez, *We Took the Streets: Fighting for Latino Rights with the Young Lords* (New York: St. Martin's Press, 2003), 123.

28. Melendez, *We Took the Streets*, 123-24.

29. Fernández, *The Young Lords,* 161.

30. Shelley, "The Young Lords Go to Church."

31. Fernández, *The Young Lords,* 163.

32. Fernández, *The Young Lords,* 174.

33. Melendez, *We Took the Streets*, 10, 90, 116-17.

34. Melendez, *We Took the Streets*, 117.

35. Melendez, *We Took the Streets*, 117.

36. Fernández, *The Young Lords,* 47-48.

37. Fernández, *The Young Lords,* 48.

38. "You Can't Kill a Revolution," *Y.L.O.* 1, no. 4 (October 1969): 3.

39. "You Can't Kill a Revolution," 3.

40. "You Can't Kill a Revolution," 3.

41. "You Can't Kill a Revolution," 3.

42. "Chicago Blacks Honor Malcolm," *Y.L.O.* 1, no. 1 (March 19, 1969): 2.

43. Umar Muntu Bakr, "Malcolm X," *Palante* 2, no. 3 (May 22, 1970), 7.

44. Bakr, "Malcolm X," 7.

45. Bakr, "Malcolm X," 7.

46. Bakr, "Malcolm X," 7.

47. Fernández, *The Young Lords,* 341, 352.

48. Fernández, *The Young Lords,* 364-72.

49. Shelley, "The Young Lords Go to Church."

50. Sylvia Rivera, in *Stonewall Romances: A Tenth Anniversary Celebration* (New York: "Flower Beneath the Foot" Press, 1979), 29; Marsha P. Johnson, from interview with Allen Young, in *The Stonewall Reader,* ed. New York Public Library (New York: Penguin Books, 2019), 228; Steve Watson, "Stonewall 1979: The Drag of Politics," *The Village Voice,* June 15, 1979, https://www.villagevoice.com/2019/06/04/stonewall-1979-the-drag-of-politics.

51. Rivera, *Stonewall Romances,* 29.

52. Sylvia Rivera, "Queens in Exile: The Forgotten Ones," in *Street Transvestite Action Revolutionaries: Survival, Revolt, and Queer Antagonist Struggle* (New York: Untorelli Press, 2013), 40-42.

53. Rivera, "Queens in Exile," 28, 30.

54. Rivera, "Queens in Exile," 29.

55. Marsha P. Johnson, from interview with Eric Marcus, in *The Stonewall Reader,* 138.

56. Sylvia Rivera, from interview with Eric Marcus, in *The Stonewall Reader,* 141.

57. Sylvia Rivera, "'I'm Glad I Was in the Stonewall Riot': An Interview with Sylvia Rivera," in *Street Transvestite Action Revolutionaries,* 13.

58. Rivera, "'I'm Glad I Was in the Stonewall Riot,'" 13.

59. Rivera, from interview with Eric Marcus, in *The Stonewall Reader,* 146.

60. Rivera, "Queens in Exile," 52.

61. Rivera, from interview with Eric Marcus, in *The Stonewall Reader*, 146.

62. Rivera, from interview with Eric Marcus, in *The Stonewall Reader*, 146.

63. Pat Maxwell, "Homosexuals in the Movement," *Come Out!*, 1, no. 3 (April/May 1970): 8.

64. Bob Kohler, "Where Have All the Flowers Gone," *Come Out!* 1, no. 2 (January 10, 1970): 14.

65. Sylvia Rivera, "Bitch on Wheels: A Speech by Sylvia Rivera, 2001," in *Street Transvestite Action Revolutionaries*, 32.

66. Johnson, from interview with Allen Young, in *The Stonewall Reader*, 227.

67. "Drags & T.V.s Join the March," *Digital Reporter* 3, no. 11 (1973): 5-11, 44; Rivera, "Queens in Exile," 53.

68. "Sylvia Rivera Reflects on the Spirit of Marsha P. Johnson," *Radical Access Mapping Project*, posted on Amara, April 11, 2013, https://amara.org/en/videos/dg9xAQZLHBU2/info/sylvia-rivera-reflects-on-the-spirit-of-marsha-p-johnson.

69. Rivera, from interview with Eric Marcus, in *The Stonewall Reader*, 146.

70. Rivera, *Stonewall Romances*, 29-30.

71. Joy Ellison and Nicholas Hoffman, "The Afterward: Sylvia Rivera and Marsha P. Johnson in the Medieval Imaginary," *Medieval Feminist Forum: A Journal of Gender and Sexuality* 55, no. 1 (2019): 280-83.

72. Lázaro Lima, "Locas al Rescate: The Transnational Hauntings of Queer *Cubanidad*," *Journal of Transnational American Studies* 3, no. 2 (2011): 88-93.

73. Marsha P. Johnson, interview in *Pay It No Mind: Marsha P. Johnson*, directed by Michael Kasino (Redux Pictures, 2012).

74. Johnson, interview in *Pay It No Mind*.

75. Rivera, "Queens in Exile," 44-45.

76. Rivera, "Queens in Exile," 44.

77. Johnson, interview in *Pay It No Mind*.

78. David Carter, *Stonewall: The Riots That Sparked the Gay Revolution* (New York: St. Martin's Press, 2004), 65.

79. Johnson, interview in *Pay It No Mind*.

80. Carter, *Stonewall*, 65.

81. Johnson, interview in *Pay It No Mind*.

82. Rivera, "Queens in Exile," 44.

83. See, e.g., Justin Sayre, *From Gay to Z: A Queer Compendium* (San Francisco: Chronicle Books, 2022), 143.

84. Jeanette Spicer, "Meet the Pastor of Manhattan's LGBTQ+ Church," *NYC: The Official Guide*, June 22, 2021, https://www.nycgo.com/articles/meet-the-pastor-of-manhattans-lgbtq-church/

85. Martin Duberman, *Stonewall: The Definitive Story of the LGBTQ Rights Uprising That Changed America* (New York: Penguin Books, 2019), 312.

86. Anole Harper, in *Trans Bodies, Trans Selves*, ed. Laura Erickson-Schroth (New York: Oxford University Press, 2022), 599.

87. Leo Louis Martello, "A Positive Image for the Homosexual," *Come Out!* 1, no. 1 (November 14, 1969): 15.

88. See, e.g., Leo Louis Martello, "The Gay Witch," *Gay* 1, no. 3 (December 31, 1969): 6.

89. Sandy DeWine, "For Diego Viñales, for Ourselves," *Come Out!* 1, no. 4 (June/July 1970): 11.

90. Roy Birchard, "In Dialogue with the Bible," *MCC—New York!* 1, no. 1 (March 1972), 6-7.

91. Birchard, "In Dialogue with the Bible," 6.

92. Birchard, "In Dialogue with the Bible," 6.

93. Sylvia Rivera, "'I'm Glad I Was in the Stonewall Riot,'" 13-14.

94. Johnson, from interview with Allen Young, in *The Stonewall Reader*, 225.

95. Johnson, interview in *Pay It No Mind*.

96. Allan Warshawsky and Ellen Bedoz, "G.L.F. and the Movement," *Come Out!* 1, no. 2 (January 10, 1970): 4-5.

97. "Black Elk Speaks," *Come Out!* 1, no. 2 (January 10, 1970): 8.

Coda: "They Don't Know That Their Hearts Are Breaking"

1. Erik Tormoen, "At a Crossroads: The Evolution of George Floyd Square," *Minnesota Monthly*, April 14, 2021, https://www.minnesotamonthly.com/lifestyle/business-politics/at-a-crossroads-the-evolution-of-george-floyd-square.

2. Jacob Turcotte and Mark Trumbull, "How Support for Black Lives Matter Has Surged, in One Chart," *Christian Science Monitor*,

June 12, 2020, https://www.csmonitor.com/USA/Justice/2020/0612/How-support-for-Black-Lives-Matter-has-surged-in-one-chart.

3. Wesley Lowery, *They Can't Kill Us All* (New York: Little, Brown, 2016), 86.

4. Lowery, *They Can't Kill Us All*, 87.

5. Lowery, *They Can't Kill Us All*, 87.

6. Lowery, *They Can't Kill Us All*, 88-89.

7. Keeanga Yamahtta-Taylor, *From #BlackLivesMatter to Black Liberation* (Chicago: Haymarket Books, 2016), 153-54.

8. Yamahtta-Taylor, *From #BlackLivesMatter to Black Liberation*, 3-4.

9. Yamahtta-Taylor, *From #BlackLivesMatter to Black Liberation*, 4-5.

10. Yamahtta-Taylor, *From #BlackLivesMatter to Black Liberation*, 5-6.

11. "[LIVE] Minneapolis: George Floyd Square Celebrates Malcolm X," YouTube video, posted by Unicorn Riot, February 21, 2021, https://www.youtube.com/watch?v=HcFI8TxD4tQ

12. "[LIVE] Minneapolis: George Floyd Square."

13. "[LIVE] Minneapolis: George Floyd Square."

14. "[LIVE] Minneapolis: George Floyd Square."

15. "[LIVE] Minneapolis: George Floyd Square."

Index

Wallace, Mike, on Nation of
Islam, 41
Ward, Hiley, on Christianity
and Black revolutionary
spirituality, 84
Warren, Robert Penn, on segregation in the South, 149
Washington, Joseph R., Jr.,
critique of nonviolence, 6
Watts Riot/Rebellion, 64, 65, 81
White, Reverend Horace A., 84,
85
white devil, 17, 46, 77, 91, 113
whites, expulsion from SNCC,
167–69
Wilfred X, 86
Wilmore, Gayraud, 117, 140

"X," meaning of, in names,
215n17

Yacub, Nation of Islam story of,
24, 25, 46, 77
Young Lords, 147, 173, 175–77
and Black Power movement,
177
and Christianity, 177, 180–82
fracturing of, 183
influence of Malcolm X, 182
and Jesus as radical icon, 180,
181
occupation of First Spanish
United Methodist Church,
179, 180
Young, Coleman A., 85

Zellner, Dorothy, 5
Zellner, Dorothy and Bob,
expulsion from SNCC, 168
Zimmerman, George, 196